# HUNGRY HEARTS
A Food Odyssey across Britain and Spain
1968 - 69

Ann McColl Lindsay

Photographs by David Lindsay

Copyright © 2011 by Ann McColl Lindsay

All rights reserved. No part of this work covered by the copyrights hereon may be reproduced or used in any form or by any means – graphic, electronic or mechanical, including photocopying, recording, taping or information
storage and retrieval systems –
without the prior written permission of the author.

Library and Archives Canada Cataloguing in Publication

CIP data on file with the National Library and Archives

ISBN 978-1-55483-895-0

To Hestia

Greek Goddess of Hearth and Home

*For without you mortals hold no banquet*
Homeric Hymn number 29

and

to David

who lights the fire

# HUNGRY HEARTS

*"...for always travelling with a hungry heart"*   Tennyson's Ulysses

A Food Odyssey
Volume One: Britain and Spain, 1968 - 69

| | | |
|---|---|---|
| Prologue | | 7 |
| 1. | Hungry Hearts Meet - Windsor, Ontario, 1960 | 9 |
| 2. | Sea Voyage - On Board the Empress | 21 |
| 3. | The City of Reality | 33 |
| 4. | Glasgow Revisited | 57 |
| 5. | Taking the High Road - from Dunfermline to Braemar | 77 |
| 6. | Road to the Isles - From Braemar to the Trossachs | 101 |
| 7. | A Nation of Shopkeepers - Northern England | 137 |
| 8. | Along the South Coast | 151 |
| 9. | Inland | 183 |
| 10. | Towns and Gowns | 197 |
| 11. | Heading North | 219 |
| 12. | Swinging London | 231 |
| 13. | London's Markets | 249 |
| 14. | Christmas in London | 261 |
| 15. | Kitchen Aesthetics | 283 |
| 16. | A Brave New Year | 295 |
| 17. | Sol y Sombra | 309 |
| 18. | Camping on Spanish Beaches | 347 |
| Recipe Index | | 387 |

# PROLOGUE

This book is an account of what my former professor of Victorian literature, Dr. Eugene LeMire, termed, *a miraculous year.* It covers only the first half of that year, August 1968 to February 1969, when we met him on sabbatical in the British Museum during December. He was working on the unpublished manuscripts of the poet/craftsman/artist, William Morris. We were travelling across Britain and Europe to satisfy a hunger for a similar three dimensional life.

Forty years later, in March of 2007, I read a book review of a new bibliography of William Morris' work, compiled by Dr. Eugene LeMire. I tracked him down to a University in Australia, sent him my congratulations with memories of the year that was so special to us. This was his reply.

Dear Mrs. Lindsay,

Your letter warmed my heart. After such an interval - it's now forty years since you attended my Morris seminar - to hear about a life, perhaps even two, that William Morris and I might have influenced towards such obviously productive and happy ends, seems little short of miraculous. London in 1968 was clearly a historic time for our little circle, considering what we did and thought then. I can't remember much of the detail, but I recall the Christmas Eve at the little flat in Goodenough House, and the excitement Margaret and I felt when we discovered Elizabeth David in her shop. She was so welcoming and ready to talk, and we so happily intent on exploring the whole business of devising a proper home for a family for a lifetime, that the meeting for me typifies the year. Now I look back on it, our time in London seems a time that has the special glow of life well lived. Unfortunately, in 1968 I had not yet started my later practice of keeping a fairly detailed diary of long trips, so I am without a ready reference to events and people.

I am delighted to know your story. You do me a great kindness in making contact. It makes me more aware of how much there is in my life to be happy about. I write this on my seventy-eighth birthday, in the hour or two before our three children with their spouses and their children come here for dinner and a small celebration. There will be nine grandchildren (there is a tenth on the way) and they all live here in Adelaide within easy reach. Tonight will be a lively time.

My best regards to you and your husband David. If you were here, you could join us for a drink and some of our lasagna.

If you travel to London anytime soon, you could probably see a copy of the Bibliography in the British Library bookshop.

Again, my thanks for a delightful letter.

Yours,
Eugene LeMire

His letter includes the essential ingredients that satisfied our hungry hearts - creative occupations, the daily celebration of food, the value of connecting the tapestry of lives lived with the thread of current life. All skills discovered on the road. Unlike Dr. LeMire, I did keep a detailed diary, in five old ledger books. Recipes inspired by the adventures of that year add flesh to the bones of the journal.

# Chapter One

# HUNGRY HEARTS MEET

*When I told my mother that I was going to be married in June,
she asked, "Who's the groom?"
Journal entry, May, 1961*

Few first year teachers could have been greener. A nineteen year old in charge of a room full of eleven year olds, I survived from one recess to the next. The coffee urn was the focal point of the staff room, a comfort zone. As I filled my mug with shaky hand, a tall, handsome blond man pressed in beside me. "I'm a first year teacher here too, how about going out for dinner?"

"Sorry, I'm engaged to marry a plumber." That was the truth, but David took it personally.

"So is everyone else around here."

Hard to believe he'd had such a run of bad luck. He seemed so dejected I immediately became unengaged.

"Sure, I'll go out with you." In a life directed by spontaneous decisions, that one takes the prize.

For several months, our students carried unsealed notes for assignations between his science room and my grade six classroom. I fell into marriage with the good fortune that surfaces when most needed. If I had been silly enough to reject the man who wooed me with bits from opera, read poetry and painted me a red rose, I would not have deserved my future. The parent-teacher association was relieved when we married as soon as the closing bell rang on the last day of school, June 1961.

I was determined to make our wedding cake, even though my baking repertoire consisted of inedible muffins thrown out by the home economics instructor. The kindergarten teacher gave me her mother's recipe for a rich dark fruit cake. Luckily, the three graduated layers slid out of their tins looking edible. A neighbour with experience in cake decoration iced it with cascades of yellow roses. A grease fire in my family's kitchen on the morning of our wedding threatened to ruin this confection. I dashed downstairs in pre-nuptial baby doll pyjamas, whisked the three-tiered white iced wedding cake from the smoke-filled kitchen, raced out the back door, carrying it through the oscillating lawn sprinkler. At our reception, everyone enjoyed the slices David and I handed around my parents' livingroom.

Cutting the Good Luck Wedding Cake in my mother's living room.

# GOOD LUCK WHITE FRUIT CAKE

*Those who do not like the traditional holiday dark, spice-laden fruit cakes, may enjoy a slice of this one, packed with pecans and fruit, held together with very little batter. As my awareness of food values grew over the years, I started to substitute dried local fruits for the glazed cherries.*

### INGREDIENTS
1/2 pound of unsalted butter
1 cup of fine granulated sugar (honey works if you prefer)
5 large eggs
1 tablespoon vanilla extract
1 tablespoon lemon or almond extract depending on your taste
1-3/4 cups unsifted cake and pastry flour
1/2 teaspoon baking powder
1/2 teaspoon salt
4 pineapple rings finely chopped - these can be fresh, glazed, or dried
2 cups light raisins
1 cup seeded dark muscat raisins (Lexia)
1/2 pound of mixed whole green and red glazed cherries were called for in the kindergarten teacher's original recipe. I usually substitute an equal amount of dried fruits as follows:
1/4 cup chopped dried papaya
1/4 cup dried cherries
1/4 cup dried cranberries

1/2 cup dried chopped apricots
1/4 cup dried mango
1 pound of pecans, left whole - do not skimp on this ingredient
1 cup of fresh, sweet cider.

### Method

1. The night before you intend to bake this cake, cut the dried fruits into 1/4 inch pieces. Toss all of the fruits and raisins in a large non-reactive bowl. Pour 1 cup of cider over them, stir and let sit loosely covered overnight in a cool spot to moisten the fruits and plump the raisins.
2. Preheat the oven to 275F. On a low rack, set a large rectangular baker of water to keep the oven moist during the baking time.
3. If you are lucky, someone will offer to prepare the baking tins while you make the cake. For our wedding, I used three square tins in graduated sizes. Now I use four 6 inch by 4 inch heavy bread tins. They should be lined with two layers of heavy brown paper cut to size. The layer next to the batter should be parchment paper. The triple thickness is to prevent the fruit from scorching.
4. Cream the butter until it is light and blend in the sugar gradually until very smooth. Beat in the eggs one at a time, amalgamating thoroughly. It helps if you have eggs and butter at room temperature. Originally, I spent an hour labouring over a large gripstand bowl with a heavy wooden spatula to produce a smooth, creamy batter. Now you can whirl each step in the processor.
5. Beat in the vanilla and almond extract.
6. Sift the flour, baking powder and salt into another bowl.
7. Add the pecans to the bowl of soaked fruit. Coat the nuts and fruits with one third of the dry mixture.
8. Add the creamed mixture about one cup at a time, alternating with some of the flour mixture, blending everything until you cannot detect any flour particles.

9. Fill the pans 2/3 of the way. Spatula the tops to even the batter. It will be very thick.
10. Place the pans on a rack above the dish of hot water in the oven.
11. Bake from 2-1/2 to 3 hours depending on the thickness and size of your pans and temperature control in the oven. I find close to 3 hours does it for me. Take a look after 2 hours to see how advanced they are. The darkening of the exposed fruit can be used as a gauge.
12. Set on a rack to cool in the pans then turn out to cool completely. Wrap in fresh greaseproof paper and foil for storage. Aging is not necessary with this cake.

*I call it Lucky Cake because we are still making it.*

The honeymoon had to be a two-day dash to Southampton because our extra-mural English literature classes at the University of Windsor started that week. The plan was to pile up benefits in the Teachers' Federation retirement fund while attending night and summer classes to inch up our pitiful $3,000 per annum salary. For the first seven years we dutifully climbed this tower of chalk until David became an English teacher at Canada's first vocational college and I was offered a Robarts' Fellowship while working toward a masters degree in English literature. Meanwhile, cracks appeared in the tower. By the time David had finished his master's thesis on Percy Bysshe Shelley, we owned a rug brick bungalow and sat on an accumulation of pension payments in the Teachers' Federation. Our plates were full but we were still hungry. The years stretched ahead of us with a disturbing sameness.

Most things in that house were pseudo, including my menus, taken from the women's magazines piled at the super market check-out. As a young sixties' bride with no experience in meal preparation, I was relying on the magic of popular homemakers' guides to transform a rump roast with a package of onion soup mix. The can opener was our utensil of choice - to open tins of water chestnuts and pineapple bits for 'theme' Hawaiian dinners. Guests came in hula skirts. A wide range of cake mixes solved the dessert problem. I added elegance to our dining room by trimming red drapes, made from an old bedspread, with yards of yellow ball fringe. Someone needed to take me in hand. Alfred Lord Tennyson came to the rescue.

On May 6, 1968, as I scooped a tin of mushroom soup over chicken bits at our electric stove, Tennyson whispered a line from his *Lady of Shalott*, 'I am half sick of shadows'. I related to the imprisoned maid's predicament. The least I could do was draft a more adventurous shopping list for tomorrow. Only one recipe, clipped from a Sunday supplement, is worth saving from these first years as homemaker. It has evolved into a company dish.

# CITRUS CORNISH HENS

*This dish can be made successfully with chicken breasts instead of the Cornish hens. It bakes well in an enamelled cast iron or ovenproof porcelain au gratin dish.*

### INGREDIENTS
2 Cornish hens, split in half or 4 chicken breasts
2 tablespoons lemon juice
1 teaspoon salt
1 teaspoon finely chopped fresh sage or half this amount crumbled dry sage
1 minced clove of garlic
1/2 teaspoon of freshly grated nutmeg
1/2 cup unsalted butter
2 tablespoons zested rinds of orange and lemon mixed
1/2 cup orange juice
slices of lemon and orange for garnish
chopped parsley

### METHOD
1. Preheat oven to 350F.
2. In a small bowl, combine lemon juice, sage, garlic, nutmeg and salt.
3. Rub the poultry with this mixture.
4. Melt the butter in the au gratin dish in the oven.

5. Place the birds or breasts skin side down in the butter.
6. Bake 15 minutes for hens, 10 minutes for breasts, then turn over. Repeat for the same time period.
7. Pour orange juice combined with citrus zests over the birds before the final 15 minutes baking.
8. Ring a platter with cooked wild rice and basmati rice mixed.
9. Place the cooked breasts or beasts in the centre.
10. Spoon citrus sauce over the chicken.
11. Garnish with alternating half slices of lemons and oranges. Sprinkle any dull bits with parsley.

Ten minutes later, David pulled up on his Honda bike. His announcement threw a dash of cayenne into the pot, "I have just resigned from the teaching staff of St.Clair College." I didn't need to ask which poet he'd been consulting. For the past couple of years, he had been trying to untie the Gordian knot of Shelley's theory of evil and had adopted as gospel this poet's faith in the powers of the imaginative leap. We are to leap, without a parachute, from the security of careers and health insurance benefits, into the creative chaos of a year's camping in Europe. I stopped making the marshmallow salad long enough to say, "Let's go." The dust was gathering on a row of red plastic geraniums in continual bloom on the window ledge and the artificial fireplace was cold. Tennyson's *Ulysses* told me what happened when wives got left behind to tend a barren hearth.

David went to collect his severance pay and pension fund from the purser at St. Clair College who puzzled, "Why would a young man throw away a promising future in vocational training, one of Canada's prime growth industries?"

"Do you have the cheque ready?" murmured David through a weak smile.

All assets were liquidated. The Honda motor bike, then the colonial furniture. After I withdrew my pension fund, we had enough to purchase our escape mobile - the icon of the times, a Volkswagen camper. David made all the arrangements through the dealership in Windsor. He brought home pamphlets that depicted happy couples boiling coffee by the side of the van in a forest glade on a gas camping stove. We decided to forego the luxury of a pop-up roof, an omission we would later regret, but were insistent on the inclusion of cocoa mats, which I assumed were for holding hot milky drinks.

David returned from the dealer with the good news. We had enough money ($2,800) to pay for a new van to be picked up near Cologne, Germany in August. And the bad news, cocoa mats were a floor covering option, not a convenient drinks tray.

To finance the rest of the trip, we had to sell the house. We decided to call an appraiser and then list it ourselves. He did not seem impressed by the built-in vanity in the bedroom, the breakfast nook, the artificial fireplace and our mature wisteria arbour. It had been planted ten years before we bought the house to commemorate the birth of the previous owner's daughter, and it was now one of the finest in the city. He pegged our nooks, arbours and fake fire at $8,000 for the lot. We listed the house ourselves at $13,000 and sold it within a few weeks. The first thing the new owners did was cut down the wisteria arbour. "Too messy", they decreed. I was becoming increasingly anxious to travel to places where wisteria arbours flourished.

The parting wrench came when we deposited our slightly pampered beagle, Tippy, with a family of five children who all promised to walk the dog.

We sold lock, stock but stashed a few barrels in friends' basements. Some practical streak urged me to hold onto the only things that would turn out to be useful in the next phase of our lives. These reserved treasures were mainly finds from the Goodwill and Salvation Army stores located near the school where I had taught. Every noon hour I'd rush down to unearth silver soup tureens, eighteenth century carved wedding chests and brass beds. Instead of shopping for sensible shoes, I was culling charity store bins for heavy, white ironstone platters. Canadians were upgrading to Danish modern in the sixties. With very little capital expenditure, I had accumulated a small horde which an investment advisor would term "futures".

One large blue metal trunk was packed with what we thought we would need for a year abroad. Absolutely nothing practical was included. The journey was inspired by writers long dead. They accompanied us, lifetime companions whose stories influenced my wardrobe. In went fur-trimmed coats and patent leather pumps rather than the more suitable anoraks and hiking boots. Little velvet pouches held my favourite pieces of old jewellery, but I did not pack so much as a spoon or a can opener in the way of food prep equipment. This was a serious omission. *The Oxford Book of English Verse* was included, but sadly, *The Joy of Cooking* was not. There may have been a VW camper waiting for us, but I saw it as a Victorian coach and four, complete with gas stove and portable sink, as one would expect on a Jamesian expedition. The matching set of ivory luggage had the solidity and weight of Vuittons, without the flair. We subsequently used them as chairs and tables in the campsites. Up to this point, I had never prepared for any trip beyond Toronto.

As it turned out, what we put in that blue trunk was immaterial. Like a magician's box, its contents would change continually over the next year, reflecting our growing compulsion to collect the tools of a new trade. We set out as empty vessels - no ties left at home, no aims, no ambitions. As Tennyson would have it, *You are roaming with a hungry heart.* We were not on a mission, but we did have a fire in the belly for new experiences as well as for new tastes. If anything, we thought that we might come back with enough bags of notes to start a doctoral thesis in literature. Instead, the return luggage would contain five old ledgers filled, single spaced, with recipes, concepts, notes, and details on kitchen design. This journey satisfied both hungers.

Our ambitious itinerary proposed reading Burns amidst the Scottish heather in September. Tour the homes of English literary giants in October. Splurge on a flat in London November and December to experience a Dickensian Christmas. Set sail to find the sun January and February in Spain. Follow spring and the Romantic poets through France and Italy before heading over to Austria for April and Easter. May would bring us up the Rhine into Holland for the tulip festival. A quick sail over to Denmark before returning to Germany to send the van home. We would sail home from Greenock on the Empress of England in the summer of 1969.

David tracked down caravan campsite guides for every country. Since we were travelling out of season, we usually had them to ourselves.

Most of the time we were in farmyards with the ducks or on windswept heather moors. On a series of road maps, we marked the route followed with a black magic marker. They stand as proof that we covered the whole proposed itinerary.

This book stops after the first seven months, at the border between Spain and France. Spain marks a fundamental personal and professional change. France and Italy deserve a separate book.

Chapter Two

# SEA VOYAGE

The stevedores cried *Mon Dieu* as they hoisted our blue trunk on board the Empress of Canada. Journal entry Montreal docks, August 15, 1968.

The custom of linking ship to shore by a network of pastel paper streamers dramatizes the departure. Those waving *bon voyage* from the pier remained linked to friends and relatives on board, until two tugs took the Empress of Canada out far enough to break this last fragile connection with land. Somehow I managed to hold onto the last linking streamer. It would have been more meaningful if a friend had held the other end. Eighteen years earlier our family had been waved off from Scotland by parents and relatives we might never see again. David and I floated away from Canada unnoticed. White farmhouses on the shores of the St. Lawrence River replaced the islands of Montreal as our canvas chairs were set on deck.

At ten p.m. we held onto each other against a warm funnel on the breezy top deck as the liner passed the Citadel and Chateau of Quebec City, sparkling with lights against the black sky. The exhilaration of that moment marked the beginning of our new life. To the throbbing of the Empress' engines below us, The Avons in the Cabaret Lounge

Holding on to the last streamer as the Empress of Canada
leaves the dock at Montreal.

were providing appropriate background music:

*And we'll live all alone*
*In a world of our own*

The ship responded to our feelings. Sea voyages are associated with glamour, but reality hits with the swell of the ocean. There was no mistaking the moment its prow entered the Gulf, threshold to the Atlantic Ocean. The Empress changed from being a firm, confident craft cutting through friendly water, to a tin toy bobbing at the whim of a greater force.

Early the next morning, the captain steered towards a large iceberg sighted off the starboard bow a few miles beyond the straits of Belle Island so that we could take pictures. Hadn't he seen *A Night to Remember*? In terms of experiences, icebergs stand literally in a field of their own. This sparkling floating mountain of pristine ice loomed haughtily above a steely sea, commanding respect, as unapproachable as a monarch. It was the part that I couldn't see that intrigued me; the pyramid of frozen ocean that could rip the sides off ships. The sighting of whales blowing off steam posed less of a threat and we photographed them without angst.

We felt the first serious swell of the Atlantic at seven p.m. in the cinema while watching James Bond in *You Only Live Twice*. At that point, living once was a concern. The captain announced that we were entering a force ten gale (two points off a hurricane). We tried to follow the advice of more seasoned sea-salts. Walk the open decks in the fresh air going with the motion of the ship. Blasts of icy wind and a perpendicular deck put paid to that tip. David said we were obviously rocking the boat, and it would be better to sit quite still at the bar. The angry waves were well above the railings, obliterating the horizon and sending us indoors to try another piece of helpful advice - a glass of cognac.

This Atlantic crossing was following the same disturbing pattern as the one made at age nine. When my family immigrated in 1950, our first morning at sea my father trotted me down to the *Franconia's* main dining room to have breakfast. Awed by the choices on a printed menu, I blurted out, "Tomato juice and kippers please." This is the breakfast choice to be avoided if any of you are planning a cruise. The combination of salt, grease and acid were lethal. Within minutes I was flying down aisles of white tablecloths, hands clamped firmly over my mouth. Many years would pass before tomato juice became palatable again. Safely back in the cabin, whiffs from the galley, which crept insidiously under our doors, kept mother and I flat for the five-day crossing.

I was roused from my second class bunk by the Captain's invitation to all of the children on board. There was to be a proper tea in the First Class dining room, a temptation no curious nine-year old from the slums of Glasgow could resist. The menu is still in the blue steamer trunk in our attic. On October 26, 1950 at 4:00 p.m. white linen tables were set with:

*Snow White Pastries*
*Jack and Jill Fruit*
*Boy Blue Biscuits*
*Little Jack Horner Cake*

Drinks were also imaginatively titled:
*Bells of St. Clements Orange Juice*
*Sleeping Beauty Tea*
*Mother Hubbard Milk*

It was a literary event.

# JACK HORNER'S PLUM CAKE

*To a child raised on the docks in Glasgow, these names indicated a cultural shift into a world beyond mince and tatties where food could be playful or resonate with Bow Bells and all that they historically implied. After a series of attempts, over the next 40 years, I devised a version of plum cake. Jack doesn't have to stick his thumb in too far to pull out one of these plums; they end up in a circle on top of the batter. Once back in Canada, the invention of the food processor arrived in time to boost my baking skills.*

INGREDIENTS
For the base:
12 small black plums
1/4 cup butter
1/4 cup of honey
6 teaspoons of ground almonds
1/4 teaspoon of ground allspice

For the batter:
1-1/3 cup cake and pastry flour
2 teaspoons baking powder
1/4 teaspoon salt
3/4 cup fruit powdered sugar
1/4 cup butter at room temperature
1 egg (also at room temperature)

1/2 cup milk (ditto)

1 teaspoon almond extract

**METHOD**

For the base:

1. Preheat oven to 350F.
2. Cut the plums in half over a bowl to save any juice. Remove the stones. Peeling gives a sweeter cake but is not obligatory.
3. Coat the sides of an 8-9 inch wide, deep round cake pan with butter.
4. Melt the 1/4 cup butter in the base of the dish. Stir in the honey and allspice. Warm the mixture gently for a few minutes in the oven.
5. Place the halved plums in circles, skin side down, cavity up, to cover the base of the pan.
6. Sprinkle a 1/4 teaspoon of ground almond into each cavity.

**METHOD**

For the batter:

1. Sift the flour, salt and baking powder together several times.
2. Cut the butter into small cubes, drop it into the processor fitted with the steel blade, and whirl until fluffy as down. You can achieve this by hand with a stout wooden spoon and a bowl.
3. Cream 1/4 cup of the sugar into the butter. Scrape away from the sides.
4. Whirl in another 1/4 cup of the sugar. Scrape again.
5. Blend in the egg and the remaining sugar until smooth as cream.
6. Whisk extract into the milk.
7. Spoon some of the dry ingredients into the bowl of the processor, then some of the milk.
8. Continue alternating dry with wet, scraping down after each addition, until all ingredients are mixed into a smooth, light batter.
9. Turn batter on to the prepared base using a spatula to spread evenly.
10. Bake in the centre of a 350F oven for between 50 to 60 minutes.

Top should be level and lightly browned.
11. Allow the cake to sit on a rack in the pan until cool enough to turn it over. Place a large flat plate on top and reverse the cake. If any pieces stick, pick them off as Jack would have done.

*Dribble any reserved plum juice over the fruit.*
*Whip a tablespoon of Amaretto liqueur into a cup of whipping cream to serve on top of each slice.*

Captain's invitation to the children on board the Franconia, October, 1950.

The printed menus from our 1968 crossing indicate yet another cultural gap to be crossed:

*Sauté of Veal Marengo*
*Veloute Pierre le Grande*
*Pressed Ox Tongue*
*Brizola Steak Andalouse*
*Oxford Brawn*
*Croûte-au-Pot*

This might as well have been written in Sanskrit. I don't recall tasting any of these dishes. The sea limited our intake to toast and tea. One of the blessings of the coming year was our gradual change from two innocents raised on white bread, tinned soup and cherry cokes, to adventurous eaters, appreciative of baby eels and bouillabaisse. Menus encountered that year became landmark recipes to conquer.

When the ship's steward knocked on the cabin door to ask how we were faring, I asked if *Croûte-au-Pot* was suitable for weak stomachs. He gave me an impromptu cooking lesson:

"Pot au Feu has simmered on farmhouse stoves since the days of Asterix. A joint of beef, a chicken, a piece of pork, a sausage, vegetables and herbs are covered with water in your largest stock pot. While it simmers, the chef makes toasted *croûtes* or bread cases from slices of baguette. After several hours, he scoops out the best bits, stuffs them into the crusts and ladles on some mustard cream sauce."

I had visions of a giant stock pot, lashed to the stove in the ship's galley, with a pork leg sloshing around inside. Many years later, I watched a chef at La Varenne Cooking School in Paris sing with joy as he filled a 20 gallon pot by attaching a hose to the kitchen sink then throwing in everything but the sink.

"We'll have some unbuttered toast and weak tea please."

# SAUTÉ OF VEAL MARENGO

*There are many variations of Veal Marengo and all of them start with a history lesson. Legend attributes this dish to Napoleon's chef, who created it after the victory in 1800 at the Battle of Marengo in Northern Italy. It contains all the Italian classic staples - olives, wine, garlic, tomatoes. If veal is difficult to get, this delicious sauce can transform chicken or beef alla Marengo.*

### INGREDIENTS

For four servings with pasta:

- 1-1/2 pound shoulder of veal or thick shoulder chops
- flour, salt and pepper for dredging
- 3 tablespoons olive oil
- 1 onion finely chopped
- 1 clove of garlic, finely chopped
- 1 cup of veal stock (vegetable, chicken or beef stock depending on the protein being used)
- a bouquet garni composed of 3 stems of parsley, 2 branches of thyme, 1 bay leaf, a strip of orange rind, tied together with string or in a piece of cheesecloth for easy removal
- 1/2 cup of tomato purée ( sauce not paste)
- 1/4 cup of white wine
- 8 black kalamata olives, pitted and sliced
- 6 firm, medium mushrooms
- 1 tablespoon flour
- 1 tablespoon butter
- salt and pepper to taste

**INGREDIENTS FOR VEAL STOCK:**
veal bones from the chops
1/2 an onion, sliced
6 whole black peppercorns
1 stalk of celery with leafy top, cut in slices
1 carrot, scrubbed and cut in chunks
a stem of parsley, include the stalk

**METHOD**
1. Cut the meat off the bone. Reserve bones for stock. Cube meat into 1 inch chunks.
2. Start simmering the veal bones with the other ingredients listed above under stock-making. Use enough water to cover. Skim and strain after a half hour, while preparing rest of dish.
3. Shake the cubes in a bag with some flour, salt and pepper.
4. Brown meat in the olive oil in a large skillet or sauté pan.
5. Remove meat to a platter while you deglaze the pan with the wine. A spoon of brandy (a nod to Napoleon) is optional.
6. Simmer the chopped onion and garlic in the wine to soften.
7. Add the meat.
8. In a saucepan, combine 1 cup of broth, tomato purée, wine and include the bouquet garni. Heat. Pour over the browned meat.
9. Cover and simmer gently for at least one hour. Test a cube to see if tender.
10. Meanwhile, wipe and slice the mushrooms. Toss them in a skillet with butter. Add to the sauce along with the olives which have been pitted and sliced.
11. Thicken the sauce if necessary by stirring in a beurre manié of 1 tablespoon flour kneaded in a small bowl with 1 tablespoon butter.
12. Serve with pasta and garnish with chopped parsley.

We rushed to the upper deck of the Empress to celebrate the sighting of the north coast of Ireland. Standing beside us at the railing was a South African veteran who had participated in the defense of Malta. To record the moment, he presented David with three bun pennies. These large British coppers are stamped with the profile of a young Queen Victoria, hair tied in a bun at the back. They are dated 1874, 76, 78 and they lie beside me now on my inkstand as I write. On the reverse side, Britannia sits on a chariot, trident aloft. Regarded primarily as a memento of an odd shipboard acquaintance, these coins in retrospect could be considered portents of our involvement in all things Victorian. They echo the ancient token payment made on mythological journeys when a traveller passes to the other side. Then again, this gift could also be construed as an indication that our future lay in the exchange of coin.

As we sailed down the Clyde David asked me, "Who lives in those impressive stone mansions high on the hills?'

"Those belong to the owners of the shipyards."

"So, do the workers live in those small stone cottages?"

"No, not quite so lucky. They were housed in miles of tenement buildings that we'll see as soon as we reach Glasgow."

*August 21, 1968*

As the Empress weighed anchor out in the middle of the Clyde, I pulled on a tartan wool dress for our arrival in Scotland. Small buildings of grey stone formed the main street behind the Greenock dock, our first indication of the intimate scale of the country. Two pipers, in full Highland dress, piped us aboard a tender for the trip into shore, a significantly more dramatic landing than stumbling down an airport ramp with several hundred dazed fellow passengers. Travellers now hurtle sightless through clouds in a steel tube. Then we felt as though we had made a crossing and had landed on a different continent. Newsboys on

the dock were selling papers with the headlines:
*"Russian Tanks Invade Czechoslovakia"*
Our travels in the coming year, would bring us close to that border.

Being piped ashore in a tartan dress at Greenock.

## Chapter Three

## CITY OF REALITY

*Nihil Sine Labore*
*Nothing Without Labour*
Motto for the District of Govan, Glasgow, August 21, 1968

Now that we were in Glasgow, the word *sentimental* took on a hollow ring. A cold splash of River Clyde spume reminds me that this City of Reality makes anyone searching for tender memories swim upstream against a current of cold facts.

Our first pilgrimage was to 129 Govan Road, a blackened workers' tenement built in the nineteenth century across from the docks, where in March 1941, Margaret Grant, brought me into a world at war. The Clydebank was blitzed for days by incendiary bombs. We were lucky. Thousands of buildings around us were flattened. The Luftwaffe only managed to blow in our kitchen windows as mother wrapped herself around me in a bed-nook-in-the-wall between the kitchen table and the cast iron range. The kitchen was the main room in every flat. Like a physical heart, all the life blood of a family flowed through it. Many Scottish kitchens still had coal hearths like ours, a nineteenth century, black iron, rectangular cook stove set into the wall. Coals had to be kept glowing through the bars of the grate or the room would not have heat or hot water. The midwife put the kettle on to boil. The pink booties

Washing on the drying line often dripped over the kitchen table. Photo courtesy of the National Trust for Scotland from their booklet *The Tenement House.*

The coal cookstove found in most Glasgow tenement kitchens with the bed tucked into the wall beside it. Photo courtesy of the National Trust for Scotland from their booklet *The Tenement House.*

Grandma Annie had knitted were hung on the rail of the stove to warm. I like to believe that good fortune has followed me through life because the blue booties were sacrificed to Hestia, the fireplace diety.

Solid blocks of these five story buildings snaked around the city, built to house the dock-workers, which included all of the men in our family, except those who were fighting for Britain. Ten chimneys on each roof had been belching coal smoke for a century. The tenements lined the four sides of each city block forming an interior cube of space, dark and dirty, where garbage was kept in middens and where children played. The thin sunlight sometimes tried to fight its way through steely clouds, but most of the time it gave in to the rain. David's comment, when he saw the dismal back court of middens hemmed in by tall soot-covered buildings, was "You actually *lived* here?"

But he was only seeing a ghost of the place without the relatives who had mitigated the gloom. I tried to draw word pictures that would capture their spirit for him before we visited their homes.

Because my father was battling his way across Europe, India and Africa for the first five years of my life, I was raised by my mother and her brothers and sister. All seven of us lived with grandma and grandpa McColl in that cold water tenement. Grandpa was a carpenter or *joiner* by trade. He kept planes, saws and screw drivers he had used to build the railings on the *Queen Mary* in a sturdy wooden chest. Food was either strictly rationed or unavailable. I have no memory of going hungry, but also, no memory of bountiful fresh food on the family table . The preparation of meals for six adults was haphazard due to adverse circumstances, such as air raids. Round the clock shift work - mother at the canteen on the docks, grandpa and uncles repairing warships - reduced meals to a survival level. There were no printed recipes. The ration book remained the bible. When we weren't huddled in bomb shelters, Grandma Annie cooked cauldrons of porridge, minced beef with onions, or spicy clootie dumpling for seven of us on the coal stove. An austere diet, scarcely changed for centuries in working folks' kitchens.

Scones were warmed on a round, cast iron griddle, forged by Uncle Joe at the shipyard where he worked. Relatives gathered around the big table to welcome the New Year, sing songs, play cards, put the kettle on the stove for the mid-wife, or even lay out their dead to rest.

Ann at the close (entrance) to her Govan Road birthplace in Glasgow.

# MINCE AND TATTIES

*A national dish, ladled out for the workers at the sound of the noon-hour whistle from the docks. This main meal at mid-day was dinner. My mother continued to make a pot of mince for her children and grandchildren after we immigrated to Canada. At her funeral, a grand daughter read a poem she had written to grandma's mince and tatties.*

*Every household has its variation, but ours was as basic as it gets. Because it is simply ground beef simmered in a little water, it bears a strong ressemblance to beef tea.*

### INGREDIENTS
1 pound of the finest quality steak or stewing beef you can afford, ground through a mincer
2 medium onions, diced
1/2 cup of water or beef broth
salt and pepper to taste
potatoes (tatties) peeled and boiled

### METHOD
1. Unlike other stews, my family did not brown the minced beef in any oil or fat. The meat was broken up and stirred around the heated pot until it released some moisture.
2. At this point, the diced onions are stirred in.
3. Add water or broth and seasonings.

4. Cover and braise slowly until all trace of pink has left the meat, about 30 minutes.
5. Place 3 or 4 halves of boiled tatties on the plate beside a generous serving of mince.
6. Mash the potatoes into the mince with each forkful.

*Optional side vegetables: green peas, diced carrots, diced turnips*

Every Friday night grannie would ask, "Do you want your egg Saturday night or Sunday morning?" Eggs were rationed to one a week and my uncles, who were building ships for Britain, agonized over the choice. Each person was limited to four ounces of cheese, four ounces of bacon or ham and four ounces of butter a week. This rationing continued after the war right up until 1954. My relatives put their best foot forward. Aunt Esther brightened the kitchen every birthday with an armful of daffodils and scarlet tulips. Mother would put a clootie dumpling to boil on the stove, filling the kitchen with the rich smell of spices and dough simmering in an old piece of towelling.

# GRANDMA ANNIE'S CLOOTIE DUMPLING

*Cloot refers to the clean cloth in which the pudding is wrapped. Sometimes spelled clout, the method has been used since College Pudding was served to the Cambridge dons in the first half of the seventeenth century. It should be pure white and of a heavy grade cotton or linen, at least 24 inches square.*

*Three penny bits and six pennies were wrapped in paper and hidden in the batter. Glee when we found one. Consternation when they were not all accounted for once the plate was empty.*

*A slice fried in dripping is even better the second day.*

### INGREDIENTS
2 cups self-raising flour
1 cup finely shredded beef suet
3/4 cup firmly packed brown sugar
1 teaspoon cinnamon
1 teaspoon allspice
1 teaspoon ginger
several gratings of nutmeg
1 cup each of currants, raisins and sultanas
1 tablespoon of golden syrup
2 beaten eggs
3/4 to 1 cup of milk - whatever it takes to bind the ingredients into a slightly sticky mass

## Method

1. Put a large stock pot of water, with a trivet or rack in the bottom, on to boil.
2. Rub the suet into the flour by hand.
3. Blend in the sugar and spices.
4. Stir in the fruits to incorporate thoroughly.
5. Whisk the syrup into the eggs with some of the milk.
6. Stir the liquids into the dry mixture adding milk as needed until it just holds together.
7. Soak the cloth in boiling water then wring out.
8. Drape it in a bowl about 7 to 8 inches across to form a support while filling.
9. Dredge the interior of the cloth with flour using a shaker or sifter.
10. Gather the edges of the cloth at the top and have someone tie firmly with stout white twine about 4 or 5 inches above the pudding mixture. It is important to include all of the cloth so that water does not get into the pudding while also leaving space for expansion.
11. Lift from the bowl and set the bundle directly in the hot water on a rack of some description so that it does not stick on the bottom.
12. The water should come about 3/4 of the way up the sides. If it is too near the top, water might leak in.
13. Drape any extra cloth ends over the edge of the pot so that they do not rest on the dumpling.
14. Keep the water at a steady simmer for 3 hours.
15. Near the end of the cooking time, set your oven at a low heat (200F).
16. Lift the pudding cloth out of the boiling pot onto a large plate. Carefully undo the cloth. The finish will be slippery. Reverse it on to another plate so that you can completely remove the cloth.
17. Set it in the warm oven for about 20 minutes to dry out and form a shiny skin.
18. Serve with a custard sauce.

Mrs. McGovern, neighbour and tablet maker.

The entrance and stairwell for each tenement is called the close. Each landing had a lavatory shared by those who lived on that floor. Tenants took their turn cleaning the stairs and toilets. Neighbours lived a close life. The widow across the hall would call me on the way home from school if she had made a batch of TABLET. It is like a white version of fudge, only sweeter and thinner, thus the name. The ingredients suggest everything you should not eat:

> sugar
> butter
> condensed milk
> cream

    I worked up a proper recipe, adding raisins soaked in David's single malt whisky, but decided not to include it here. Sorry, it is too fraught with negative possibilities.
    If you do not use a heavy enough or large enough pan, your stove will be covered in boiling sugar syrup, as was mine.
    If you do not reach the hard boil stage (250F) an entire sheet of tablet, containing a pound of sugar, will refuse to set.
    If you do not wear an apron, your front will be splattered by boiling sugar.
    If you do not hand-beat it for ten minutes after successfully passing these hurdles, it will be granular rather than creamy.
    I did eventually manage a fairly successful batch and distributed it to all of the kids in our neighbourhood because it would have rotted our aged teeth.
    The best part was the whisky soaked raisins that made this batch taste faintly of highland peat.
    Glaswegians all have a sweet tooth - it helps to cheer you up when it rains.

The large front bedroom where the uncles slept, looked out on the tram tracks that separated us from the Govan dockyards, a forest of cranes that would all but disappear in the next decades. Bicycles that hung from the bedroom ceiling all week, were taken down on Sundays when the uncles pedalled out into the Trossachs or the Campsie Fells. Lacking electronic forms of home entertainment, the aunts and uncles would sit around the kitchen fireplace taking turns singing Burns' *My Love is Like a Red, Red Rose* or *Annie Laurie*, until the sirens sounded and an uncle would carry me bundled up into an air raid shelter. One Hogmanay, as the relatives drank, danced and sang *Auld Lang Syne*, Uncle Robert joined the party around this table. He had discharged himself from the TB sanitorium to celebrate the New Year with the family. A few weeks later, mother led me up to a wooden coffin on the kitchen table to say goodbye to Uncle Robert, dressed in a white satin gown and clutching a bouquet of lilies.

Everything important happened in the kitchen because it was the only room that had water and heat. This heart of the home also held grandma and grandpa's bed in an alcove. I recall dozing in there once and watching mice scurry across the kitchen floor. The washing mangle was attached to the sink on laundry day; on other days potatoes and people got scrubbed under the cold water zinc tap. Drying lines were strung on pulleys over the table; dripping underwear enriched our bowls of broth.

Grandpa grasped my reluctant hand in his vise grip to steer me across the train tracks for a walk along the docks and into the canteens. In the 1940s this was a cauldron of activity with ships and seamen from every post of the Empire. Although we lived just across the street, no whiff of foreign food reached us. The most exotic meal I remember arrived by post. One morning when mother opened the door for the mailman, he handed her a dead rabbit, fur and all, with a label bearing our address fixed to its foot. Dad had caught it while training in the highlands and figured we'd appreciate a bit of game. "Could I have dreamt this scenario?" I asked my sister.

"No Ann, Mum told me that she would find rabbits tied to the door knob occasionally." At any rate, I do recall that grannie and mam braised the rabbit in a pot.

# RABBIT HOT POT

*Most all of our meals were one-pot affairs, as they had been since Scots sat around a cauldron over a peat fire. The French still cherish the pot au feu as an important part of their culinary legacy. In Scotland, the broth or brose was an oatmeal base with a few vegetables, such as cabbage. Mother's hot pot would have been based on simmering rabbit with vegetables. In my recipe, three different mustards give it heat and acknowledge the Auld Alliance, the Scots union with the French.*

INGREDIENTS
a rabbit between 1 and 2 pounds
For the marinade:
1 cup of cider or white wine
1 bay leaf
1 teaspoon rosemary
1 teaspoon sage
1 teaspoon coarse salt
1/2 teaspoon light mustard seeds
several grinds of black pepper
For the stewing:
2 thick slices of organic back end fat pork
2 thick slices of bacon
2 shallots
2 leeks

1/2 cup of chopped onion
2 large garlic cloves
1 tablespoon of flour
1 cup white wine
2 cups chicken stock
2 tablespoons grainy mustard
1 teaspoon thyme
2 teaspoons salt

For the sauce:
2 tablespoons of hot Dijon mustard mixed with 1 teaspoon fresh green peppercorns (this variety of mustard is available prepared)
1/2 cup of heavy cream

## Method

1. Cut the rabbit into about 8 large pieces - legs, tenderloins, back into quarters.
2. Mix marinade ingredients and pour over pieces. Refrigerate for 6 hours or overnight, turning several times.
3. Cut pork fat into 1/4 inch cubes and render slowly in a dutch oven large enough to accommodate all other ingredients.
4. When enough fat has been released to cover the bottom of the pan, dry the rabbit pieces and brown them in several batches so that they do not touch in the process. Keep browned pieces warm on a platter until browning is completed.
5. Cut the bacon into 1 inch pieces and cook slowly in the pan. Stir in the chopped onions, shallots and garlic. Stir until translucent, adding more oil if necessary to prevent sticking.
6. Slice the leeks and add them last. Sprinkle with the flour.
7. Pour on the wine, letting it bubble while you scrape up the brown bits with a flat-ended wooden spatula.
8. Stir in the chicken stock and grainy mustard.
9. Add the larger pieces of browned rabbit, keeping the tender bits and

any organs to add half way through the cooking.
10. Sprinkle on salt to taste and some dried thyme.
11. Preheat oven to 350F while bringing the rabbit and sauce to a near boil on the stove.
12. Simmer in the oven for 30 to 40 minutes.
13. The casserole can be prepared ahead to this point and finished just before serving.
14. Remove the rabbit pieces to a warm platter while finishing the sauce.
15. Bring the liquid in the casserole to a boil. Reduce if necessary.
16. Stir in the mustard and cream.
17. Serve with buttered noodles and green beans.

*We prefer a strong mustard flavour, but cut back at your discretion. Taste as you go.*

There were two regular high spots to the Glaswegian wartime diet. One was the soft, warm, yeasty morning rolls from the baker on the corner, Scotland's answer to croissants. The other treat was food parcels from grandpa Grant in Canada, with tins of salmon and nylon stockings, cause for celebration.

The Glasgow grandpa tightened his grip on my hand as we leaned over the edge of the dock to peer into the murky river where salmon once spawned. He tells me that just one hundred years earlier, before there was a great city here, a small village of fishermen had harvested schools of fresh salmon as they swam down the sparkling Clyde in front of our door.

"What's under the water now, grandpa?"

"Unexploded bombs, mines and submarines, lass."

To prevent U-boats from coming up the Clyde, a steel boom had been inserted to block passage at the mouth of the river immediately after war had been declared in 1939. So grandpa may have been mistaken. One thing was certain - no salmon lived there now.

Our tenement building was across from the dockyards of the Clyde River.

# SALMON IN ITS NATIVE WATERS

*This fish is so naturally rich, I like to treat it lightly, poaching it in flavourings from the highland streams.*

### INGREDIENTS
a half pound fillet of salmon serves two
1/2 cup of sparkling bottled spring water
2 tablespoons of single malt whisky (for the peat flavour)
1 teaspoon of heather honey (or alternative herbal honey)
1 cup of sliced white part of leek
salt
2 tablespoons fresh chives
2 tablespoons of butter
2 teaspoons lemon juice
a handful of watercress

### METHOD
1. Lay leek slices on the base of a skillet which is a few inches wider than the fillet and has a lid.
2. Place the fish, skin side down, on this natural rack.
3. Brush it gently with a little honey, then baptize it with the whisky by pouring directly over the flesh.
4. Sprinkle the spring water around the leeks. It should cover the base of the pan. If not, use a little more.

5. Sprinkle 1/2 teaspoon of salt over top.
6. Poach over a moderate heat, at a slow simmer, not a boil, for 10 minutes.
7. While it simmers, snip the chives into the softened butter. Blend with the lemon juice.
8. With a sharp knife, pierce down through the flesh to see if it is cooked.
9. Using a wide spatula, place the fish and the leeks on warmed plates while you make a light sauce.
10. Whisk the herbal butter into the liquid left in the poaching pan. Drizzle over the fish.
11. Garnish the plate with a handful of fresh watercress.

*Best served with parsley potatoes and steamed spinach.*

Uncle Joe, mother's younger brother, was special. A ships labourer by day, he would come home smeared with grease, stoke the range to bring a large kettle of water to a boil. He pulled out a galvanized wash tub, took off as many clothes as decency and the cold permitted, then scrubbed every inch until his skin shone. The only blond in the family, he dressed like a film star to go ballroom dancing at the Lucarno or other Glasgow venues.

I asked Uncle Joe how he learned to dance so well.

"Och pet, it's just rhythm, like the flow of waves washing up and back over the stones at Dunoon."

The family would board The Waverley pleasure steamer at the Broomielaw dock in the centre of Glasgow, listen to the piper's tunes and eat bags of salted crisps all the way doon the water to this seaside resort at the mouth of the river. Potato crisps came with little packets of salt in the bag that you would tear open to sprinkle on just the amount that satisfied you. Many chip lovers consider the removal of this little salt pack as a reversal of progress.

They would probably enjoy a recipe suggestion which came my way recently for preparing fish in crisps. Take a piece of whitefish - cod, halibut, or pollock. Smash a bag of your favourite potato chips to smithereens with a rolling pin. Put the fish in the bag and shake to cover it in chip crumbs. Fry as usual. It actually tastes better than bread crumbs and gives a whole new meaning to fish and chips.

A stroll along the windy promenade required Sunday finery - suit, white shirt and tie for the men; best coats and hats on the women. Casual clothing had no place at these seaside resorts. Uncle Joe introduced me to restaurant dining on these outings.

"Ann, dinna drown yer soup in pepper."

My first meal in a restaurant was a bowl of creamy tomato soup. I've tried unsuccessfully for years to capture the flavour. Finally, I found the magic ingredient.

Mother Margaret Langmuir McColl, Grandma Annie Bingham McColl, and Uncle Joe McColl walking along the Dunoon Promenade with wee Annie Bingham Langmuir McColl Grant. (family names as given on my birth certificate).

# DUNOON TOMATO SOUP

*This is the closest I've come to matching the memory of that first bowl of restaurant tomato soup, served to an excited five year-old 65 years ago. Best to try it when local field tomatoes are available, unless you have preserved your own. The tinned milk must be the secret ingredient that takes it back to the 1940s.*

### INGREDIENTS
4 tablespoons (1/4 cup) of unsalted butter
1/2 cup of finely chopped shallot or onion
3 tablespoons flour
1-1/2 teaspoons sugar
1-1/2 teaspoons salt
4 grinds of black pepper
4 cups of cooked and sieved fresh plum tomatoes
1 cup of Carnation evaporated milk

### METHOD
For preparing fresh tomatoes.
1. If you are using your own garden tomatoes, here is the easiest way to prepare them for soups or sauces. A cast iron enamelled dutch oven is the best to use. It must be coated or the acid in the tomatoes will draw out rust. An earthenware or porcelain casserole would also work, preferably large enough to hold about four quarts of tomatoes. A food mill fitted with a medium disc is essential.
2. Heat oven to 350F.

3. Wash the tomatoes and pack them into your pot. Do not peel, core or cut them unless you are removing a blemish. Plum tomatoes are best for reducing as they have more pulp.
4. Cover with a proper fitting lid and leave in the moderate oven for about an hour.
5. Remove when the tomatoes are a thoroughly softened mass.
6. Drain off any excess clear liquid and reserve if you wish for future use as a soup base.
7. Fit the food mill over a bowl large enough to receive the resulting sauce.
8. Ladle the stewed tomatoes into the mill. Turn until all are squeezed through. The skin and seeds are held back by the disc and you have a purée.
9. At this point, I put it into plastic containers of convenient size and freeze them to be doctored according to future use.
10. If you are making this soup recipe, reserve 4 cups of your tomato purée.
11. You can omit all of the above steps by puréeing a 28 ounce tin of San Maranzo plum tomatoes in a blender.

## Method

For the creamiest tomato soup without cream:
1. Melt the butter in a heavy-bottomed soup pot.
2. Cook the chopped onions/shallots in the butter until soft.
3. Whisk in the flour 1 tablespoon at a time to make a roux. Let it cook a few minutes on a low heat.
4. Blend in 1 cup of the tomato preparation, whisking until smooth.
5. Add the salt, pepper and sugar. Let it simmer for about 2 minutes over low heat.
6. Stir in 3 more cups of tomatoes.
7. Simmer for 5 minutes or until heated through.
8. Whisk in 1 cup of evaporated milk.

9. If you find the soup to be too thick, thin it with some of the reserved liquid or some tomato juice.
10. Add a fresh tomato finely diced if texture is desired.
11. Serve with a garnish of fresh baby leaf basil.

*You may want to substitute cream for the milk if you were not fortunate enough to taste your first soup in a seaside restaurant in postwar Scotland. Childhood tastes linger on, as Proust has proven.*

From left to right: Cousin James, Aunt Esther,
Uncle George, Aunt Peggy, Aunt Margaret, Uncle James.

## Chapter Four

## GLASGOW REVISITED

Glasgow's oldest house (1471) was a sweetie shop,
a butcher's and a green grocer's before the historical society
took the building over and restored it.
Journal entry, August 28, 1968

After an absence from Scotland of almost twenty years we are about to visit these aunts and uncles who had spoiled me during the war years. Several of them still lived in the old tenements. We were amazed that my relatives could transform dark, dank flats into warm, welcoming homes. These dour surroundings had always been in stark contrast with the fiesty warmth of the people. They killed the fatted sausage roll for us, then followed it with cabbage, gammon, buns, and whisky. Burns got it right when he wrote, "The man's the gowd for a' that."

Aunt Esther lived in Castlemilk, one of the massive housing schemes circling Glasgow that were built to get workingmen out of the tenement buildings. She missed the strong sense of community that had been erased with the bulldozers and felt that these urban renewal schemes were becoming as dreary as the slum buildings they were designed to replace. Her only source of heat was one small open fireplace in the sitting room, impotent against the gusts of wind that blew down from the hills of Carmunnock right under the gaps in the doors. Her husband, Uncle Ron, a navy man, died of TB. Miles of snaking terrace housing of a numbing banality killed most spirits. But not Aunt Esther's. She gave us a bed and a pot of tea, then invited all the other relatives over for a tot of Scotch with the Canadians.

Seven aunts and uncles, full of good cheer, had gathered around this tiny hearth to welcome us with boxes of pastries and bottles of Scotch. "Och, go on, Davie, ye can manage another eclair, surely, with a wee dram tae wash it doon." These two staples may well be the cornerstones of the Scottish strength and tenacity. Scots are lovers of baked goods. High tea, fortified with a piece of ham or a boiled egg, replaces the evening meal. The array of currant squares, ginger cakes, custard pies, scones, chocolate cups, sponge cakes on the table in front of us could have filled the window of a patisserie. Within days of our arrival we were willingly being tempted by the sugar sirens.

Scottish kitchens in the new housing estates had gotten smaller and duller since we left. Aunt Esther's kitchen was a cold, dim, drafty wee room, cut off from the heat in the front sitting room. You could smell the damp and the gas from a modern cooker. It stood on long, spindly legs and had a very efficient wall-of-flames grill at eye level. Sausages turned out a treat. Although auntie was thrilled to be free of shovelling coal and ashes for cooking, the cold and damp in these little box-like kitchens sent her scurrying to her chair beside a small coal fire in the sitting room. She kept holding her hand against the water tank next to the fireplace to see if it was hot enough for our baths. Within one generation, our family's kitchen had shrunk ninety percent. I am pleased to say that on more recent visits we have found our relatives enjoying beautiful bright new homes where the hospitality is extended by a new generation.

On that 1968 visit, our favourite haunt in the centre of the old town was Barrowland, "The Barras", a raucous, rambunctious workingman's flea market. Row upon row of wheelbarrows were piled mostly with cheap nylon blouses or plastic ornaments for the top of the telly. But the odd one concealed buried treasure. Since my nose had already been trained to sniff out the truffles in the underground of second hand goods, thanks to lunchtime forays to the Goodwill and Salvation Army stores in Windsor, we felt qualified to tackle this gutsy shopper's carnival. We began collecting objects that filled gaps in our spartan upbringings.

The hawkers were canny and could spot a visitor, but I slipped back into the Glaswegian patter to bargain for a walnut-framed mirror, brass candlesticks and an edition of Bunyan's works with steel engravings. Uncle Joe thought we'd been taken. "Och, pet, they saw ye comin'. Whit did ye gee them for that? Ten bob! (about one dollar). They'll be laughin' behind yer back."

Sensing that his niece had been bitten by the collectors' bug, Uncle Joe presented us with a cast iron pancake griddle he had forged in the shipyard's foundry. It had a hook in the centre of the hoop of black iron so that you could suspend it over an open fire. It was our first piece of hand made cookware. I assured him that we would work on getting a fireplace when we returned to Canada and I would perfect a potato pancake recipe.

News of the Canadians' interest in curios spread through Castlemilk. One evening, the chap who lived in the flat above Aunt Esther, brought down two oriental brass opium pipes to see if we wanted to buy them. Impossible for us to pass up this whiff of an eastern bazaar in suburban Glasgow. Apparently, goods from far ports still filtered through the Govan docks. We stashed them in the blue trunk that was filling fast.

# POTATO PANCAKES

*These bubble with little brown marks when fried on an iron stove plate or griddle. A ten inch cast iron fry pan will also do the job.*

### INGREDIENTS
8 ounces of potatoes (about 1 quite large or 2 medium)
2 tablespoons butter
1/4 teaspoon of salt
1/2 cup of all purpose flour

### METHOD
1. Get your pan or griddle preheated in an oven or stove top.
2. Boil the potatoes and mash with the butter and salt until fluffy.
3. Add the flour a few tablespoons at a time, incorporating well after each addition.
4. Sprinkle a board or countertop with flour. Spatula the potato mix onto the centre and hand-mould it into a smooth flat disc.
5. Dust a rolling pin with flour and roll the dough into a large very thin circle.
6. Lay a nine inch cake tin on the dough to help mark a circular cut.
7. Reserve the outside extra bits for another circle.
8. Cut the circle (a bannock) into half, quarters, and finally eighths (triangular farls).
9. Prick their entire surface with a fork.

10. Carefully lift them with a spatula onto the hot griddle or pan.
11. Cook on the stove top for about 4 minutes a side then move them to a basket, covered by a napkin as you repeat with a second batch of farls.
12. Butter them while warm. Reheat if they are to be eaten later.

*The Scots like them with jam or honey. I prefer serving them like a rosti potato, with smoked salmon, a bowl of sour cream and fresh dill.*

*August 30, 1968*

When David left to pick up our van in Cologne, Aunt Esther and I went shopping for ingredients to make a real Scotch Broth. She had a good laugh when I told her that Dr. Samuel Johnson had called it *divine brew*. Grocery shopping in Scotland was very different from our Canadian weekly routine of pushing a cart around the circuit of a supermarket. Everything was on an intimate scale, with the specialized stockists she patronized gathered in a little plaza. The greengrocer got right onto the spirit of our project.

"That'll be grand, makin' a broth wi' yer auntie. Noo ye'll need twa leeks an' this wee bunch a' carrots," which he wrapped in newspaper. As he trickled a few handfuls of barley into a brown paper poke he asked,

"An where's the bonny lass frae?"

I admitted to being a teacher from Canada but felt more like a wee yen back under the kitchen table playing store.

At the next shop, the butcher disappeared into a back room and came out with more blood on his apron and a scrag neck of mature mutton.

"Nae Scotch broth worth the name wud use anything in place of this." The neck was bundled up in brown paper and string. It had never occured to me back in Ontario, to enter into a meaningful dialogue with an obliging butcher. This friendly exchange of recipe nuances, ingredient choices and banter about our general welfare, was world's apart from rummaging through sealed plastic styrofoam packs in a super market refrigeration unit. Our conversion to a life of shopping in independent stores started here.

# SCOTCH BROTH

*Once all of the little packages from our expedition were unwrapped on a cutting board the size of a napkin, the cooking lesson began. A properly made Scotch broth has the same life-sustaining attributes of other revered ethnic soups. My aunt initiated me into the mysteries of soaking, boiling, dicing, and simmering – with the barest minimum of equipment and space. The tiny flat was soon warm and steamy from the heady mingled aromas of lamb and barley.*

### Ingredients

1 large, meaty lamb shank or 2 small (scrag neck of mutton if available - the stronger the better) or one pound of stewing lamb
1/2 cup of pot barley
2 cups of thinly sliced leeks, at least 1 inch in diameter
2 cups carrots diced
1 cup of cubed yellow turnip
2 cups of finely shredded then chopped green cabbage
salt and pepper to taste
1/2 cup minced flat leaf parsley
4 thin green onions finely sliced

### Method

1. Place lamb with 10 cups of water in a large soup pot. Bring to the boil. Skim then simmer for 1 hour, skimming as necesssary.

2. Meanwhile, rinse and soak the barley.
3. Add the barley to the lamb stock. Simmer for 1 hour while you prepare the vegetables as indicated above.
4. Remove the lamb bones. Separate the meat and return it to the pot.
5. Add the vegetables, salt and pepper and simmer for another hour.
6. Stir in the parsley once the veg are tender.
7. Serve in wide bowls with a garnish of green onions.

*August 30, 1968*

David needed a sustaining bowl of the divine brew when he arrived back from Germany with the van at midnight. He had a cold. A generous helping of broth near the coal fire soon put him right for our expedition the next day into the city's domestic history. When I had complimented Aunt Esther on managing so well in her cramped quarters she retorted, "I'll take ye doon tae the oldest hoose in Glasgie. Then ye'll see what they had to put up wi".

An elderly gentleman greeted us at the door of Provand's Lordship, Glasgow's oldest building (built about 1471) with the words, "Welcome. Yer in guid company. King James II and Mary Queen of Scots pulled the brass door bell afore ye. As I'm a tinsmith by trade, I'll take ye doon tae the kitchen." In this primitive kitchen with stone walls and cobbled floor he gave us a crash course in metallurgy, explaining the relative merits of various qualities of brass candlesticks, metal light fixtures and the bedwarmers that had kept Mary Queen of Scots cozy, perhaps while she was writing the incriminating letters to Darnley or implicating herself in an affair with Bothwell. The Silver Casket Letters (whether true or forged) were used in a court to change the course of Scottish history.

Massive heavy ceiling beams gave an oppressive air in this elemental fifteenth century kitchen. The impressive display of pewter in an open dresser that reached to the ceiling seemed incongruous with the starkness of this dim rustic space. In spite of the severity of the decor, I formed an immediate bond with the small hearth in the corner of bare stone walls that would have simmered the royal pot of porridge. I could feel my roots sprouting.

From now on, once through the door of a historic house, I would gravitate to the bolt hole that lead to the realm haunted by cooks and scullery maids. Cinderella in reverse, I was beginning to realize that the room of one's own that Virginia Woolf had been going on about, was, in my case, the kitchen. This single-room focus eliminated the standard tours of cathedrals, museums and stately drawing rooms. I carried a spiral-bound notepad with me into every historic kitchen visited on this trip, to record some design feature or useful implement. The set designer for *Upstairs,Downstairs* could have equipped Mrs. Bridges' kitchen from that book by the time the trip was over.

In the restored dining hall upstairs an amethyst wine jug reflected off the polished surface of a massive carved table. Jacobean chairs set under tapestries stood ready to receive a contemporary Queen should she wish to come on a visit.

*August 29, 1968*

The newspapers said that Princess Margaret would be stopping at Pollok House, an Adam's mansion bristling with paintings by Blake, El Greco, Goya and Murillo. Aunt Esther and I took the bus out to the estate. While she sat in the gardens, I disappeared in search of the twisting stone stairway that I now realized would lead me to the working heart of the estate. These definitely "unfitted" kitchens offered a more basic comment on the daily life of the house than the showcases of Limoges pill boxes in the elegant upstairs salon. Fully operational, turning out a continuous supply of substantial dishes, they were probably hell on earth to work in. Cleansed of the heat, stress, and constant bustle, they stand now chaste as chapels. The cool cream-coloured tiled walls were lined with twelve foot long walnut shelves housing a proud display of catering copper. An oak buffet of the same generous dimensions was laden with real cream cakes, tarts and scones, since this beautiful space now served as a tearoom. Penelope had discovered early in the voyage that Home is where the Hearth is. Kitchens were not six-foot square 1950's sterile boxes, but gracious flagstoned rooms with handsome furnishings and an aura that made them the true heart of the home. The waitress told us proudly, "It's a guid thing ye came today. We'll be closed the morrow. Princess Margaret is coming for a visit." I felt sorry for this royal who would probably have to stay upstairs with the gilded furniture.

In the late 1980s and 90s Glasgow pulled itself back from the brink of an economic sinkhole by staging a cultural revolution. An International Garden Festival blossomed on the grey dockyards. A key component was the building of a dramatic glass and wood home for their world famous Burrell Art Collection on the grounds of the historic Pollok Estate we had visited. Its great success has proven the city's wisdom in choosing to showcase its art to best advantage and ride the cultural comet to economic recovery. Art enthusiasts from around the world now come for more than the cream cakes. The original kitchen is the award-winning Kitchen Restaurant. One of the featured events is a tour of the collection ending with a nourishing bowl of soup in the Kitchen. The following soup is one I consider appropriate to serve after an outing in a gallery.

Pollok House in Glasgow has transformed their original kitchen into a fine Kitchen Restaurant now below the museum.

# CURRIED CARROT, ORANGE, GINGER SOUP

*This soup is in honour of Van Gogh, an artist with carrot/orange/ginger hair. The Auberge Ravoux in Auvers, his last home, lists on its menu a cream of carrot soup from Crécy, a town noted for its high quality carrots. Use the best you can find or pull some from the garden.*

*A soup fit for an art gallery.*

**INGREDIENTS**
1 tablespoon butter
1 tablespoon oil
3 shallots or 1 medium onion
8 carrots approximately 7 inches long
4 cups chicken or vegetable stock or enough to cover
two thirds cups of freshly squeezed orange juice
grated zest from one orange
1 inch piece of root ginger
1 teaspoon ground cumin
1/2 teaspoon hot curry powder
salt and pepper to taste

**METHOD**
1. Melt butter and oil together in a large, heavy soup pot.
2. Stir in the finely chopped shallot or onion.

3. Scrub or peel the carrots. Grate them in small batches in the processor or on a fine-holed hand grater.
4. Toss with the softened onions.
5. Peel and grate the root ginger. Add it to the pot along with the curry powder and cumin.
6. Pour in the orange juice and the stock.
7. Simmer gently covered for 30 minutes.
8. Add salt and pepper to taste.
9. Garnish with sprinkled orange zest.

May be blended if a smooth soup is preferred.

Intrigued by the odd sounding name of the city's main shopping venue, Sauchiehall Street, I asked Aunt Esther what she knew about it.

"Your dad was a bartender in one of the pubs there. But I hear that there are also a few very nice tea rooms. One of them that's been on the street for donkeys' years is called The Willow Tea Room because the word *Sauchiehall* means *a damp place where willows grow*. I doubt that it's still there."

Fortified by a slab of chocolate cake at one of the other "very nice tea rooms" Aunt Esther had recommended, we walked over to the Tourist Information Office to ask them what they knew about the original Willow Tea Rooms. The guide proudly explained that tea rooms were originally conceived by a tea merchant, Stuart Cranston in 1875. He started by charging customers a few pence to sample his imported tea leaves at a small table. His sister, Kate Cranston picked up the concept and raised the art of taking tea to aesthetic heights. Her avant-garde tea rooms became the toast of the town, largely due to her artistic union with Charles Rennie Mackintosh. She commisioned Charles and his wife Margaret to design every aspect of her building on busy Sauchiehall Street in his spare linear style. The couple designed every detail – from the outdoor signage to the cutlery and lamps, even weaving *The Willow* motif into the name and onto a gesso panel by Margaret, inspired by Rossetti's sonnet, *all ye that walk in willow wood*.

Kate's astute aptitude for business coupled with the Mackintoshes' lyrical fantasies brought a combination of imagination and daring to the table, resulting in a chain of thriving tea rooms that set standards across the continent. More than crumpets were dispensed with the tea. Glaswegians now had an alternative to the pubs for meeting with friends. These subtly radiant white, silver and pastel interiors continue to dispell the northern gloom of Glasgow. Mackintosh and Cranston had brought their sense of style and beauty into the workplace and made a lasting difference to an industrial city. This unique mix came to be known as *The Glasgow Style*.

# RICH CHOCOLATE CAKE

*Charles and Margaret Mackintosh preferred pale cakes, such as meringues and sponges, because they matched the decor of their tearooms. David has no such food aesthetic and orders chocolate cake at every tea stop in Glasgow. I have tried to duplicate the rich flavour of these cakes by substituting a dark roasted coffee for the usual liquid. You do not get a mocha taste. It just deepens and darkens the cake. Because it has a frosting on the outside, a filling of fresh fruit is advised between the layers. Happy Birthday David.*

**INGREDIENTS**
Cake batter
1/2 cup unsweetened cocoa
1 cup of hot dark roasted Kenyan coffee
1-1/2 cup sifted all-purpose flour
1/2 teaspoon baking powder
1 teaspoon baking soda
1/4 teaspoon salt
1/2 cup of unsalted butter at room temperature
1-1/4 cup granulated sugar
2 large eggs at room temperature
1 teaspoon pure vanilla extract
Filling
1/4 to 1/2 cup of three berry jam - raspberry, blueberry, strawberry - or cherry jam

1 tablespoon of Kirsch liqueur

1 pint of fresh raspberries

Frosting

4 ounces semisweet chocolate, either chips or squares

1/3 cup of 10% cream

1/2 cup of unsalted butter

1 cup icing sugar

## Method

1. Butter two 8 inch springform cake pans. Line the bottoms with circles of parchment paper.
2. Preheat the oven to 350F.
3. Whisk hot coffee into the cocoa. Allow to cool.
4. Sift dry ingredients together.
5. You will need an electric beater to achieve the smooth texture and incorporate air for a light batter in this next part of the preparation.
6. Cream the butter until fluffy. Gradually beat in the sugar until smooth.
7. Add the eggs one at a time, beating well after each addition.
8. Add the vanilla and continue beating at top speed for several minutes, making sure you scrape the sides of the bowl.
9. Using a lower speed, blend in alternating quarter cups of the flour mixture and then the cocoa liquid, ending with the remaining flour.
10. Divide between the two pans. Bake for 30 minutes. Test by inserting a fine skewer. It should come out dry.
11. Allow cakes to cool in the pans before running a knife around the sides and removing onto racks for further cooling.
12. Place one layer on a flat serving plate at least 2 inches wider than the cake.
13. Thin jam of your choice with some Kirsch.
14. Paint the surface layer of cake with just enough of the jam to make an adhesive for the fresh berries.

15. Arrange raspberries in circles, covering the cake. Set other layer on top.
16. If you prefer, you may at this point paint the top with jam and circle with raspberries. If you want a real treat go for the icing as follows.
17. Put a stainless bowl and beaters into the freezer to get really cold.
18. Over medium heat, melt the chocolate in the cream whisking until smooth.
19. When this mixture has cooled down, transfer it to the chilled bowl.
20. Cream the icing sugar with the butter in another bowl.
21. Beat in the cold chocolate until a spreadable thickness is achieved.
22. If it is not firm enough, chill in the frig a few moments and beat again.
23. Frost the sides and the top of the cake.

Stylistic signage for one of the Cranston/Mackintosh Willow Tea Rooms.

Our last day in Glasgow we took the boat down the Clyde to Dunoon where the bronze Highland Mary still gazed out over the harbour wistfully toward Ayr and her Rabbie. David and I walked the same seaside promenade where grandma Annie had strolled with her hand clasped firmly around mine on holidays years ago. Because the Cowal Games were in full swing, every tearoom was jammed with kilts and bonnets, so we sat on the pier to eat our fish and chips from newspaper wrappings and watched the Empress of Canada pulling out on its return trip to Montreal. She had dropped us off less than two weeks ago but we had already caught up on our past and felt that our future had taken a turn for the better.

The pier at Dunoon, where the steamers docked with holiday makers from Glasgow further up the Clyde.

# Chapter Five

## TAKING THE HIGH ROAD

We tramped across the moor through three foot-high purple heather until we came to a crystal brook for a tea and sausage roll break.
Journal entry, Spittal of Glen Shee, September 12, 1968

    Living in the confines of the van that first week brought us close to divorce. Here we were for the next nine months in a space half the size of the average bathroom. Fortunately, once we organized the essentials, stashed everything else under the back seat, and moved as little as possible, we became happy as clams in our VW shell. Behind the front passenger seat was a doll-sized sink and food storage cupboard. When the side door slid open, a tray could be popped up on the side of the van to hold the two-burner stove that we had bought in Glasgow. It ran on a small blue tank of butane gas that was readily available all along our proposed route. Behind the driver's seat hung a table which could be flipped up onto a leg when needed. We used this table for writing and competing in card games at night as most meals were taken perched on the suitcases outside the van staring at the ever-changing scenery. As I had neglected to pack either cookbooks or utensils, we did more snacking than dining on the upended ivory Samsonites for the first few months. Our eating habits hadn't progressed much beyond the familiar fare of our British backgrounds at this point as we happily tucked into plates of fish and chips, beans and chips, pies and chips, Spam and chips, eggs and chips. On fast track to a heart attack.

David at our campsite on the summit of Arthur's Seat, Edinburgh, looking toward the Firth of Forth.

Looking down from the Castle on Princes Street Gardens and the train station, Edinburgh.

Our first night on the road we had dinner on the top of Arthur's Seat near Dunsapie Loch with gulls circling the van. Edinburgh spread around us, a rugged, regal capital which owes its distinctive peaks and valleys to glacial pressures. At one end looms The Castle Rock, an ancient keep that is more than a tourist attraction since it is still the home of the Scottish division of Her Majesty's Army. At the other end is the 251-metre summit of Arthur's Seat, the eroded remnant of a long-extinct volcano, on which we were munching our meat pies. These two outcroppings are connected by a historic backbone, The Royal Mile, a jammed cluster of sixteenth century tenements with its haunted narrow wynds or laneways. On that sunny September day in 1968 we could see it all from the door of the van, from the Georgian Crescent of New Town to the tempting glimpse of hills and sea beyond. As darkness obliterated the view, we pulled the yellow and brown checkered curtains in a complete circle around the van windows, creating a bedroom on top of the world.

Down on the streets of the capital the entire world was dancing to the swirl of one thousand pipers. Wherever there was a stage, in churches or concert halls, a performance was in progress. During that week we were camped on top of the world's grandest Arts Festival - plays, music, spectacles were spread at our feet. Edinburgh was the first course of a remarkable nine month cultural banquet on which we still feast.

Admission must have been very reasonable because even on our tight budget we attended a performance of the Scottish Symphony, led by composer-conductor Benjamin Britten in the Usher Hall; Ibsen's *When We Dead Awaken* in the Assembly Rooms and J. M. Synge's *Playboy of the Western World* in yet another venue.

The next morning breakfast rolls were eaten on the edge of the Firth of Forth, crunching along the beach on a bed of mussels before the tide came in. We lunched on Granny Smith apples, treacle scones and Scottish cheddar in a gazebo in Pittencrieff Park, a lush garden of globe thistle and coreopsis, Andrew Carnegie's gift to the people of Dunfermline.

We spread out a supper of thin slices of Silverside beef and wholemeal bread on the crags of Stirling Castle. An entire year in which every meal offered a different view was truly a moveable feast. Pity we were snacking rather than savouring at this point. If I had been more knowledgeable about food preparation, I might have tried steaming a dish of clams or mussels open on our gas burner. Surrounded by seafood and no idea what to do with it. That was about to change.

Cramond Inn, at the mouth of the river Almond where it enters the Firth of Forth, site of our first food epiphany.

*September 5, 1968*

Edinburgh had offered a feast of film, theatre and art, but in a small Roman village on the outskirts of the city we experienced our first food epiphany. In the ancient village of Cramond, we scrambled among the bits and pieces left by early Roman conquerors then sat awed in a cool stone kirk. After being attacked by two enormous swans at the edge of the river, we felt a bit peckish and stumbled into The Cramond Inn, a low white-washed building, scarlet geraniums cascading from its leaded windows.

We threw budgetary caution to the winds and dined under oak beams on plump mussels in a creamy shallot wine sauce, followed by herb-roasted chicken. In front of a peat fire in the lounge the waiter served two small white cups of black espresso with a film of heavy cream on top. The scales fell from our tongues and we had a glimpse of life beyond Spam. This meal set standards for ambience, service, and comfort which, like Wordsworth's daffodils, we have frequently recollected in tranquillity. In a warm fuggy haze we walked hand-in-hand around the back of the Inn to stare across the Firth of Forth, silvered by the sky's night lights. Tomorrow we would cross it on the steel-girded bridge which marked our real entry into the countryside.

# MUSSELS IN A CREAMY SAUCE

*In the restaurant, the mussels were served out of their shells, bathed in a cream soup consistency sauce. A less formal bistro presentation presents them in their shells with a more liquid cream and broth mixture. I have experimented with both options over the years.*

### Ingredients
1 kilo - 2.2 pounds of fresh mussels - ample for two people - smaller mussels are sweeter

For the steaming broth:

1/3 cup thin leeks or shallots chopped

1/4 cup chopped onion

1 large clove of garlic chopped

1 cup of white wine

1 bay leaf

3 sprigs of fresh parsley with stems

5 whole black peppercorns

For the light cream sauce:

strained mussel broth from the pot

1/2 cup of 35% cream

1/2 teaspoon of fresh tarragon, minced

2 teaspoons of lemon juice

minced parsley for garnish

For the alternative thick cream sauce:

2 egg yolks
2 tablespoons of butter
2 tablespoons of flour

## Method
Cleaning the mussels:
1. Scrub them thoroughly to remove any mud or sand.
2. Soak for a few hours in a gallon of cold salted water. Change the water at least twice.
3. Pull or cut off pieces of dried seaweed or "beard". These are the byssus or filaments that mussels use to attach themselves to rocks. As a child, I pulled them from seaside piers.
4. Discard any that are even partially open. Keep those that are tightly closed.

### Steaming them open:
1. In a large stainless steel pot with a lid place the wine and seasonings from the first list.
2. Add the mussels. Put on the lid and bring to a boil. Adjust the heat to a steady simmer.
3. After 5 to 8 minutes, the shells should be opening.
4. Transfer opened mussels with a straining spoon to another pot.
5. Strain the broth through a cheesecloth-lined sieve into a small bowl.

For the light bistro sauce:
6. Pour the broth back into the steaming pot. Heat to near boiling.
7. Whisk in the cream, tarragon and lemon juice.
8. Divide the mussels, still in their shells, between two wide-rimmed soup plates.
9. Pour creamed broth over them, sprinkle with parsley and serve with slices of baguette.

**FOR THE THICKER CREAM SAUCE:**

1. Remove the mussels from their shells. Reserve in a bowl.
2. In a heavy pan, melt the butter and whisk in the flour to make a roux.
3. Beat in the egg yolks and cream and tarragon off the heat.
4. Whisk in the strained mussel broth and lemon juice. Keep stirring over medium heat until the desired thickness is achieved. If too thick, thin with a little hot water.
5. Taste for seasoning.
6. Stir the mussels into the sauce.
7. Ladle into fine soup bowls. Garnish with a thin slice of lemon or herbs.

*Don't expect the restaurant menu to be the same forty years on.*

*September 8, 1968*

The narrow gravel walkways in Pittencrieff Park, lined with black-eyed Susans and scarlet dahlias, circle the walls of a ruined castle where in Scottish lore, "The king sits in Dunfermline town drinking the blood red wine." The king who drank the wine (and spilled a lot of blood) was Robert the Bruce. His bones lie under the pulpit in the sanctuary of the abbey, topped by a full-length brass plaque. A charwoman dusting the intricately carved pulpit told us that she keeps Robert shining with Brasso. This former capital is the burial place of seven Scottish kings and the birthplace of the philanthropist Andrew Carnegie.

Yet I devoted the space in my journal to the description of a green jug in the window of an antique store. Straight-sided, with a pewter top and brown glazed interior, this handsome pitcher triggered my love of serving pieces from the past. Folly to start on a buying spree when our living space was four feet by six feet, especially for items that hardly qualified as essential camping gear. If I don't justify right now my mania for collecting old kitchenwares, I'll be apologizing every time we buy another piece on this trip. Grannie McColl did not have much in the Glasgow kitchen, but what she had was simple, sturdy and durable. The basic utensils were the kail or broth pot and the griddle. They had sustained families, hanging on chains since the days of cottage peat fires. During the 1950s and 60s the quality of kitchenwares deteriorated, as we filled our shelves with bright plastic geegaws. Then I read William Morris' dictum, *Have nothing in your houses that you do not know to be useful or believe to be beautiful.* In 1968, Britain was a treasure trove of kitchen relics from estates and cottages waiting for me to rescue them from small secondhand stores.

These simple domestic objects could reveal aspects of social history. A creamware plate that I once purchased at an auction, came with this note taped onto the back: *"Plate belonging to wedding set of my great, great grandmother, Susan Yorke, grandma Winnett's mother, who was born about 1840, youngest of seven children. Plate approximately 1820 - 1825 at least."* A family's history came with the plate. A delicate scrap of lace had a message pinned to it: *handmade by my grandmother in Honiton, one of their best lacemakers.* Objects resonated vignettes of home life.

This green jug that had caught my fancy may have been used by the housekeeper in the grand country estate, Hopetoun House, near the Forth Bridge to serve warm milky drinks during the blitz. On the practical side, old kitchenwares cost less than fine porcelain or sterling silver. They are more available and can be used, as opposed to merely admired. As we had virtually zero disposable income and liked warm milky drinks, we bought the jug.

This historic Scottish town displayed a winning retail format. Position a tea room and an antique store in close proximity to a cathedral. After admiring Norman pillars, crawling around naves, tombs and cloisters, visitors are in the correct frame of mind to purchase a piece of the past and have a cuppa. Review the events of the day as you sit surrounded by the hospitable clutter of a silver three-tiered cake stand, laden with thinly sliced sandwiches, biscuits, cake, and a plate of something warm - crumpets, or scones. On arriving in a town, it became a habit to head for the abbey, whose spire came to symbolize the comforts of a warm teapot and china cups.

# TOASTED TEA CAKES

*We bought these from the bake shops, split and toasted them on a fork over our camping gas ring, then smothered them in dairy butter.*

### Ingredients
1-1/2 cups of hard unbleached flour
1/4 teaspoon salt
1/4 teaspoon allspice
2 ounces of butter
2 teaspoons of active dry yeast
2 teaspoons of fruit powdered sugar
1/2 cup of whole milk
3/4 cup of currants
1/4 cup of mixed peel

### Method
1. Have all ingredients at room temperature.
2. Warm the milk. Stir in sugar and yeast. Leave it to proof for about ten minutes until it bubbles.
3. Meanwhile, sieve together flour, salt and spice.
4. Cut butter into cubes and rub it into the flour until it becomes pea size lumps.
5. Toss the currants and peel into the flour mixture.
6. Pour the yeast mixture into a well in the centre of the flour.

7. Mix with a wooden spoon to form a ball of dough.
8. Turn it onto a floured board. Knead until it feels smooth and elastic.
9. Cover with a loose cloth and let it rise for about an hour.
10. Preheat the oven to 400F and line 2 baking trays with parchment paper.
11. Cut the dough in half, then quarters then eighths. Shape these pieces into balls. Transfer 4 each to the baking sheets and flatten them with your hands.
12. Cover with clean cloths and leave to rise again for 15 minutes in a warm spot.
13. Paint surfaces of the cakes with some warm milk and bake for 20 minutes in a hot oven. Do not let them darken too much.

*Put the kettle on to boil. Split while slightly cooled and lather with butter.*

*September 9, 1968*

On the road to St. Andrews we pulled the van over to the shore of Loch Leven, drawn by the allure of a brooding castle on a wind-battered island. In true Homeric tradition, we were rowed over the choppy waters by a one-eyed ferryman into a variation of Hades. This bleak island had been a personal hell for Mary Queen of Scots, held captive here in the dour stone keep of Sir William Douglas for ten and a half months, during which time she suffered a miscarriage and was forced to abdicate in favour of her young son, James. A servant helped her to escape by concealing her under the boatman's seat. She fled her grey, desolate island prison only to end up with her head on the block at Fotheringay Castle by command of her cousin, Queen Elizabeth I.

The castle on the island of Loch Leven where
Mary Queen of Scots was held captive.

# MARY QUEEN OF SCOTS SOUP OF BITTER GREENS

*Scots cookery books give recipes for a soup in this queen's name, rich in almonds, eggs, and chicken. They claim the ingredients are in recognition of her mother's country, Lorraine in France. I felt her isolation and sorrows to be more reflective of the following soup which I base partially on my conception of her surroundings. There was a garden of greens in the castle grounds, which might have grown sorrel and tarragon. The shallots and onion are a nod to her mother, Mary of Guise from Lorraine. She probably would not have had access to the other ingredients, but we do.*

**INGREDIENTS**
3/4 pound spinach leaves
1/2 pound sorrel leaves
1 large potato
1/4 cup butter
1/3 cup chopped shallot
2/3 cup chopped onion
3-1/2 cups chicken or vegetable stock
several sprigs of fresh French tarragon
salt and pepper to taste
1/2 cup of 10% cream

## Method

1. Wash the greens thoroughly, especially if from the garden.
2. Peel and chop the potato, shallots and onion.
3. Melt butter in heavy bottomed soup pot of at least 2 quart capacity.
4. Sauté the potato cubes, chopped shallot and onion on medium heat until they are soft but not tinged with brown.
5. Trim thick stalks from ends of sorrel and spinach.
6. Cut leaves into thirds.
7. Place all of them on top of the sautéed vegetables. Don't be concerned about the amount as they will shrink down quickly.
8. Pour on the warm stock.
9. Season with the tarragon and salt and pepper to taste.
10. Simmer gently for about 30 minutes.
11. After the soup has cooled, blend the ingredients either by passing through a food mill or using an immersion blender in the pot.
12. Swirl in the cream.

From our campsite on the North Sea we could barely see St. Andrews, shrouded in mist. Seemed like the perfect day to visit the old cemetery near the Abbey. As we spiraled up the stone stairway of St Rules Tower, the iron handrail emitted strong electric shocks. Even the thick walls were charged with static electricity, probably made by the wind from the North Sea whistling through the tower. The eerie view of a thick fog rolling in through the upper slits reminded us of Mary Shelley and Dr. Frankenstein's experiments involving jolts of electricity to stimulate life. The elements motivated us to picnic on the horizontal tomb slabs in the deserted Abbey grounds. During a highly wrought sausage roll lunch we read appropriate verses on Death by James Shirley and other Jacobean poets.

David recited Byron's *Ocean Stanzas* on the rocks beneath the Castle where we watched a family gathering winkles when the tide was out, as I had done as a child. On forays to Scotland's rocky salt-sea beaches, we'd gather winkles off the rocks, usually in lashing rain. After a quick boil, these little snails were skewered out of their shells with a straight pin. It was a strange addiction for a six-year old, but the strong briny flavor primed me to become a fan of escargot when we reached France. On a recent trip to Paris, the waiter at Le Dome, an old Hemingway haunt, brought a small bowl of these little winkles as an appetizer. A silver foil-covered cork bristled with straight pins. As I coaxed the tight black corkscrew out of its shell, the briny whiff of the Scottish sea was transported to Montparnesse.

*September 11, 1968*

St. Andrew's was still shrouded in fog on the drive toward the Tay Bridge over to Dundee where we stopped to buy a delicious fruit and almond Dundee cake, in memory of a scene from a 1961 Cary Grant movie. He enters a country house drawing room, saunters toward the tea table groaning under piles of scones, cucumber sandwiches, ginger cakes and inquires in that clipped tone, "What, no Dundee Cake?" On the banks of the River Dee we pulled the van over and toasted Cary with a slice of Dundee cake and a thermos of tea.

Tomb stones in the mist swirling around the ruins of a 12th century cathedral in St. Andrews.

# DUNDEE CAKE

*On tea trolleys or in shop windows, Dundee cake with its circles of blanched almonds, holds pride of place. My Aunt Margaret worked for a Glasgow bakery, so I asked her for a basic list of ingredients. She recited off the fruits that had been included forever, then for method, referred me to a collection of Scots favourites printed just after the war ended, when such luxuries became possible again. Make sure you buy best quality, fresh ingredients.*

**INGREDIENTS**
Make sure all are at room temperature.
1-3/4 cups all-purpose flour
pinch of salt
1/2 cup of dark raisins
1 cup of white sultana raisins
1 cup of currants
2/3 cup of peeled ground almonds
3/4 cup of mixed chopped candied peel
1/2 cup of glacé cherries
grated zest of 1 small orange and 1 small lemon
1/2 pound of unsalted butter
1-1/4 cups of pale brown sugar
5 large eggs
1 teaspoon baking soda
1 teaspoon milk
3/4 cup of whole blanched almonds

## Method

1. Set for a slow-baking oven - 300F.
2. Line an 8 inch round by 2-1/2 inch deep cake pan with 3 layers of parchment paper to prevent fruits from scorching.
3. Wash the syrup off the cherries and pat them dry. Grate the peel off the citrus fruits.
4. Toss all the currants, raisins, sultanas, cherries, diced candied peel, grated peel together by hand in a large mixing bowl.
5. Sift the flour twice.
6. Cream the butter. Beat in the sugar 1/4 cup at a time.
7. Whip the eggs in a separate bowl.
8. Add 1/4 cup flour alternately with a small amount of the eggs to the creamed butter and sugar, beating well after each addition.
9. Fold in the fruit, ground almonds, salt, until all amalgamated.
10. Dissolve the baking soda in the teaspoon of milk and stir it into the batter.
11. Spoon into the prepared pan.
12. Smooth the top in order to set the whole blanched almonds in concentric circles all over the surface.
13. Bake for 2-1/2 to 3 hours. Cover the top with a piece of foil if it is browning too quickly. Test by inserting a skewer in the centre. It should come out clean.
14. Cool for several hours on a rack. Store, wrapped in foil in a tin.

*September 11, 1968*

In Blairgowrie, the gateway to the Highlands, David bought a couple of tickets to a variety show in the town hall entitled, *A Breath of Scotland*. After the tenor emoted his way through *The Star of Robbie Burns* and *Bonnie Dundee*, the fellow sitting beside me deemed the performance "unadulterated corn."

The next day brought us a true breath of Scotland. Before long we were humming last night's tunes as the van skimmed the narrow grey ribbons of road in the Highlands. The windshield had become the screen in a magic lantern show, flashing scenes of heart-stopping beauty on a rare day when the sun was out and the highland breezes carried the scent of heather in through the side vents. As the van rolled over the bare tracts of moor, we entered the domain of the eternal. Overlapping, desolate mountains fade to infinity in mist. Scotland's melancholy landscape bypasses the mind and speaks directly to the emotions. Tone and contour are the striking features - giant, massed mounds of brown, mixed with the purple of heather and burnt orange, the colours of a fine Scottish tweed. During our days in the Highlands we were too exhilarated to care much about regular meals, contenting ourselves with grazing in bucolic settings with the long-haired cattle. Drams of single malt Scotch were held under crystal mountain streams to catch a splash of pure water. The route was so intoxicating that we had to pull over to ruminate in five different lay-bys on the thirty odd mile stretch between Blairgowrie and Braemar.

The fisheries and smoking houses that dot the Highlands inspired our picnics. There is now an oyster bar at the head of Loch Fyne offering local products from surrounding waters. They smoke salmon, trout, mussels, eel and mackeral. Marinated Loch Fyne herring and locally landed crab and lobster round out a fine menu with dry Burgundian white wine or premier grand cru Champagne. Most local fish mongers sell smoked kippers, smoked salmon and smoked trout. We developed a van-friendly sandwich filling to carry in a haversack on walks into the hills.

# SMOKED KIPPER KEDGEREE SANDWICH

*A proper dish of kedgeree is flavoured with curry and topped with egg in some form. Since we enjoy this combination, I adapted it to a spread that could be made in the van with a bowl and a wooden spoon.*

### Ingredients
2 slices of smoked kipper (for two people; adjust for your group)
1 teaspoon lemon juice
1 tablespoon unsalted butter
1/2 teaspoon curry powder
2 boiled eggs
wholemeal or other hearty brown bread

### Method
1. Remove skin and bones from the kipper.
2. Flake it in a bowl with a fork.
3. Squeeze in the lemon juice and the curry powder.
4. Beat in the butter using the back of a spoon pressed against the bowl until a spreadable consistency is achieved. If you have access to a food processor, so much the better.
5. Slice and butter the bread. Spread on the filling.
6. Slice the hard boiled eggs and lay them on the spread.

Back in those hills of heather, beside a clear stream with a kipper sandwich, we could satisfy the hunger of the heart as well as the hunger of the moment.

At the Spittal of Glen Shee we threw an apple, tea and biscuits into a haversack and rushed down through the purple heather into a green valley, until we reached the banks of a whisky-pure stream at the foot of amethyst mountains. A quiet spot cushioned with thick grass and sweet heather was perfect for a tea break. We camped by the River Clunie just outside of Braemar. The sheep were rounded up by two black and white collies, even the stragglers who had wandered to the River for a drink had been herded safely into their stone-walled pen. As the night closed in on all sides of this desolate spot, we pulled the yellow and brown checkered curtains closed and opened a bottle of port, happy in the cocoon of the van.

David walking into the domain of the eternal.

# SHEPHERD'S PIE

*The van stopped often for the herds of black-faced sheep that took over the single lane roads, in no hurry to get from one side to the other. Sheep farmers must be the most patient men on earth. No wonder they enjoy returning home to the farmhouse for their favourite meal. I only make this farmhouse favourite when there is at least one cup of meat left on the bone from a roast leg of lamb.*

### Ingredients
1/2 cup of cubed carrot
1/2 cup of cubed turnip
1 tablespoon butter
1/2 cup of chopped onion
1 teaspoon of flour
3/4 cup of stock from the lamb bones or an herbal stock
1/2 teaspoon salt mixed with 1/2 teaspoon thyme and rosemary leaves
2 tablespoons chopped parsley
1 cup of cooked lamb cut into cubes
3 potatoes
a knob of butter for mashing
1/2 cup celeriac
3 tablespoons of buttermilk

### Method
1. Preheat oven to 350F.
2. Steam the carrots and turnips and celeriac

3. Boil the potatoes while preparing rest of the dish.
4. Melt the butter in a large skillet.
5. Cook the onion gently then stir in the flour to make a roux.
6. Pour stock over and whisk smooth.
7. Stir in herbs, vegetables and seasonings.
8. Add the cooked lamb. If mixture is too dry, dribble in more stock.
9. Mash the potatoes with cooked celeriac and a knob of butter or buttermilk.
10. Spread the lamb filling into a rectangular baker. For this amount I use a 7 inch by 5 inch by 3 inch enamel ashet, an old-style baking pan with a lip all around, ideal for pastry topped meat pies. This one will be topped with a blanket of mashed potatoes.
11. Smear a little butter on top before baking in the medium oven for about 30 minutes.

*Serve with green peas.*

Our main traffic hazard on highland roads.

# Chapter Six

# ROAD TO THE ISLES

*The old gent who owns the estate, wanders around in his kilt
with a gun in one sock and a dagger in the other,
stalking invaders to his privacy.
Journal entry, near Elgin Cathedral, September 17, 1968*

Suddenly the Highlands become a bit tamer along the stretch of road from Braemar to Ballater, not less beautiful, just less awesome, more countrified. It is known as Royal Deeside because the road follows the River Dee and Queen Victoria declared "This dear paradise" to be royal when Albert bought Balmoral Estate in 1852. He renovated the castle as a Scottish baronial holiday home for their family which increased steadily each year. This prolific couple granted royal warrants which are still proudly displayed on the shops in the area.

Enjoying a slice of Dundee cake and a thermos of tea on the banks of the River Dee.

# VICTORIA SANDWICH

*Almost every bake shop window throughout Britain features one of these sandwiches of jam between rounds of sponge or yellow cake. Usually the jam is raspberry, but I wanted to give a feeling of the Queen's highland home and chose blackcurrant jam, the deep purple of royalty. Brambles or blackberries grow wild in this region, benefitting from the long hours of daylight.*

### INGREDIENTS
3/4 cup of soft unsalted butter
1 cup of fine fruit powdered sugar
3 large eggs at room temperature
1-1/2 cups of self-raising flour
a jar of blackcurrant (or your choice) of jam
1/2 cup of confectioners sugar

### METHOD
1. Preheat oven to 325F.
2. Butter the sides of two 8 inch cake tins. Line the bottom with parchment paper.
3. Cut the butter into cubes and beat it until light yellow and creamy using a heavy spoon, a set of beaters or (my choice) the steel blade of a processor.
4. Incorporate the sugar, 1/3 cup at a time.

5. Whisk the eggs in a separate small bowl.
6. Add alternate amounts of the egg and flour to the sugar and butter, beating well after each addition.
7. Transfer the batter to a four cup glass measuring cup. You will have almost three cups.
8. Pour half of the batter into each prepared tin.
9. Tap the tin on the counter to eliminate air pockets and insure even distribution of the batter.
10. Bake in the centre of the oven for almost 30 minutes. Sides of the cake should have shrunk away from the pans a little. Top should be smooth and hopefully even.
11. Set baking tins on wire racks to cool.
12. Reverse cakes out onto the racks to finish cooling.
13. Warm the jam slightly, stirring in a little cassis liqueur or syrup if it needs to be thinned.
14. Layer one cake with jam. Place other on top.
15. Place a paper doily on cake. Sprinkle icing sugar through a sieve over the doily to make a pattern when paper is removed.

*This cake takes pride of place on the tea trolley, but if you wish to serve it as a more regal dessert, pour some cassis, black currant liqueur, into a flute of champagne. A Kir Royale befits a Victoria Sandwich.*

*September 12, 1968*

Braemar Castle was more like a real home than a three hundred year-old fortified keep. Once through the impressive stone doorway, the ticket attendant directed me to the kitchen.

"Take the service stairs down to the old servants' quarters built into the salients of the outer wall. When you reach the flagstones at the foot of the stairs, make a sharp right."

These precise directions from the ticket attendant brought us into the original barrel-vaulted kitchen. On one wall was a French cooking stove, still operational, that had prepared a hearty breakfast for Queen Victoria when she stopped overnight on her way to the Highland Games at Balmoral. Warm hearths emanate a security, a sense of permanence, sadly missing in efficient galley kitchens. The graduated set of white porcelain bowls and worn wooden spoons had been used to nourish entire households. In the golden years before fitted cupboards, hutches in these classic country kitchens were filled with pewter and blue-patterned dinnerware. They were completely free of what William Morris called, "useless fripperies." In one corner, a hollowed tree trunk served as the bowl for a very large mortar and pestle. A scrubbed pine table stood ready for the cook to prepare pheasant pies. I itched to bake bread, stir a vanilla custard, turn a joint on a spit to make up for my ration-book upbringing. These kitchens represented a lost way of life. Less susceptible to the changing fashions of the drawing room, they offered a return to basics many of us were looking for in the sixties. A sense of poise, stillness, logic reigned, attributes seemingly missing in the turbulent world of our time. I added a page of inventory ideas to my notebook in case we ever ended up with a kitchen of our own on this scale.

Braemar Castle, near Balmoral, has two restored kitchens, one with a French stove which made porridge for Queen Victoria.

# COUNTRY HOUSE PHEASANT PIE

*Many years passed before I fulfilled the urge to prepare a pheasant pie. On one of our yearly return visits, we rented a sixteenth century cottage in Hertfordshire. On misty days, a pheasant sat on the stone wall where brambles flourished. A small butcher's shop in the vicinity sold these birds that had lived in the English countryside since Roman times. For my first attempt, I chose to roast the bird and asked the butcher to recommend appropriate seasonings. "Choose flavours of the season that complement game." To me that meant sage, apples, chestnuts, wild mushrooms and juniper berries.*

*One of the vendors in our local London, Ontario market offers pheasants each fall. Now with a kitchen equipped to bake a pie, I recalled the basic ingredients from that first attempt and incorporated them into a more ambitious recipe - fit to present to the gentry upstairs.*

### INGREDIENTS

one 2-1/2 pound fresh pheasant will serve four in this pie filled with other ingredients

24 hour advance seasoning mixture:

a sprig of fresh sage or 1/2 teaspoon dried

the same quantity of thyme

a scraping of nutmeg

1 teaspoon of juniper berries - sort out any that are withered or shrivelled

1/2 teaspoon coarse salt

1/2 teaspoon whole black peppercorns

**FOR THE STOCK:**
bones and wings from the pheasant carcass
1 small onion halved
1 small carrot scrubbed and cut into thirds
1/2 stick of celery with some leafage
5 black peppercorns
1 bay leaf
2 sprigs of parsley

**FOR BRAISING THE PHEASANT:**
2 slices of smokey bacon
1 or 2 tablespoons of oil
1 tablespoon Calvados - apple brandy
2 cloves of garlic, finely chopped
1/2 cup white part of leek cut in 1/4 inch slices
1/2 cup of celery cut same size
1-1/2 cups of above stock

**FOR VEGETABLE CONTENT IN THE PIE:**
2 tablespoons butter
6 cremini mushrooms cut into quarters
6 chestnuts cut into quarters
1 large apple, peeled, cored and cut into 12 wedges

**FOR THE CREAM SAUCE:**
liquid from braising pan
1/4 cup of 35% cream
1 teaspoon cornstarch
1/4 cup of stock
salt and pepper to taste

**FOR THE CRUST:**
savoury version of pastry made with shortening as given on page 211.
or
2 sheets of phyllo pastry
or
prepared frozen puff pastry

**METHOD**
For the day before preparation:
1. Chop the neck and wings off the bird. Remove the thighs. Split the carcass, separating the breasts from the bone using a deboning knife. Discard any excess fat and skin. Lay the meaty bits on a platter. Place all bones and wings into a pot to make the stock.
2. Pound the juniper berries in a mortar to release their fragrance. With the pestle, blend in the other herbs and spices.
3. Rub all sides of the thighs and breasts with this mixture. Cover with plastic wrap and refrigerate overnight.

**PREPARATION OF STOCK:**
1. Put all of the ingredients listed in the stock section in the saucepan with the bones.
2. Cover with water. Bring to a boil then simmer for at least 1 hour.
3. Cool then refrigerate if being held overnight.
4. It is preferable to make this the day before, then remove the fat from the surface and strain before using in the recipe.

**FOR BRAISING THE PHEASANT:**
1. Bring out all ingredients, including pheasant, to come to room temperature one hour before starting to cook.
2. Set oven to 325F.

3. Use a large stove-to-oven sauteuse pan with lid - 12 inches across by 2 to 3 inches deep.
4. Cut bacon into 1/2 inch pieces and fry gently in the sauteuse pan. Once fat is rendered, add a bit of oil to brown the bird.
5. Pat any excess herbs off the surface before browning the thighs and wings on all sides.
6. Pour brandy into the pan and allow to boil for a minute.
7. Distribute the chopped garlic, celery and leeks around the pieces in the pan. Sauté a few more minutes.
8. Bring stock to a boil and pour 1-1/2 cups over the pheasant and vegetables. Set the rest aside.
9. Place covered pan into the heated oven for 45 minutes.

**PREPARING THE PIE VEGETABLES:**
1. Melt 2 tablespoons of butter in a 12 inch oval cast iron enamelled au gratin dish.
2. Sauté the pieces of mushroom, chestnut and apple until coated in warm butter.
3. Remove the cooked pieces of pheasant from the braising liquid.
4. Cut the meat from the bones, being careful to watch for any small splintered pieces of bone. The legs of these birds have a fan-shape grouping of very long, fine bones that you must discard.
5. Cut the flesh into bite-sized pieces and place them in the au gratin dish with the buttered vegetables. Sprinkle on some salt. Toss gently together.

**PREPARING THE SAUCE:**
1. Strain the liquid from the braising pan through a sieve set over a saucepan.
2. Discard the solids.
3. Heat the liquid while stirring in the 1/4 cup cream.
4. Dissolve 1 teaspoon cornstarch in 1/4 cup of reserved stock.

5. Whisk into the saucepan until a napping consistency is reached.
6. Taste for seasoning.
7. Pour over the pheasant and vegetable pieces in the oval pan.
8. Cover the pie filling with one of the suggested pastry toppings.
9. Bake for about 25 minutes until the crust turns golden.

The panelled rooms upstairs seemed cozy rather than costly, as you might expect in a private residence. The artist, Gustav Doré had stayed there in 1878 and left several watercolours hanging in its halls. The one of the castle, with a rainbow arched over the fluttering standard, emphasizes the fairy tale proportions of the rounded turrets. It is thought that he included wisps of the castle's ghosts in this painting. Several sightings have been recorded.

A second Victorian kitchen has been added, complete with furnishings and utensils. We could have happily moved in.

As it turned out, Braemar was the highland town to which we would return many times due to my one ancestral claim to culinary fame – shortbread. When our family first arrived in Windsor, Ontario in 1950, five of us were housed in my paternal grandfather's renovated attic. There were no cooking facilities up there. The downstairs kitchen for the household was a six-foot square box, which did not produce a single memorable meal on its spindly-legged electric stove. Family life evaporated. In the fifties and sixties the watchwords in domestic design were efficient, sleek, clinical, minimalist. Kitchens were considered galleys where slaves worked, no place for the modern woman. Cooking utensils were hidden; they were a sign of clutter, bad taste. Our new elderly blood relatives had trouble understanding our sense of displacement. They had rescued us from the slums of Glasgow, only to have their ungrateful grand daughter show disdain for the fake plaster fireplace in the livingroom, with its pair of Chinese figurines.

But grandpa Grant did give my domestic skills a nudge by initiating me into the rite of kneading Scottish shortbread. Three hundred and sixty-four days of the year we spread sickly white margarine that came in a plastic bag with the orange dot in the centre, onto equally unappetizing pale bread. For one day a year, in the week leading up to the New Year, butter was king. An entire pound of it was hand-rubbed with rice flour and fruit powdered sugar to make wonderfully rich shortbread. I was allowed to prick the pattern with the tines of a fork.

# GRANDPA GRANT'S SHORTBREAD

*Every Scottish family has handed down its own variation of this recipe through the generations. In the years when we operated a retail store, we distributed hundreds of grandpa Grant's printed shortbread recipes every Christmas, along with wooden presses and fluted tin cutters.*

*My grandmother recited the following over the telephone several years after her husband's death.*

### Ingredients
1 pound unsalted butter
1 cup rice flour
1 cup fruit powdered or castor sugar
3 cups all purpose flour

### Method
1. Set oven to 300F.
2. Grandma's verbal instructions were to rub the rice flour into the butter first. Generally in baking, butter and sugar are creamed together first and you may follow convention here if you wish. I have checked several Scottish cookbooks and a few do follow grandma's method.
3. Beat in the castor sugar until smooth and creamy. Fruit powdered sugar can be found on most grocery store shelves. It is a different consistency from icing sugar, more like super fine granulated.
4. On a wooden board, incorporate by hand one cup of flour at a time.

Knead the dough for a total of 15 minutes. It is possible to complete the first several steps in a food processor, but some hands on with the flour is recommended. The shortbread is ready when it comes away from the board without sticking. More flour may need to be sprinkled on during kneading to obtain this creamy, smooth finish.

5. This versatile dough offers the cook many baking options. The easiest most traditional method is to line a couple of baking sheets with greaseproof paper and pat or roll the dough into a 1/2 inch thickness. Crimp around the edges by pressing down the back of a fork. Pierce the surface in symmetrical lines with the tines of the fork. Cut into finger shapes. Bake in a slow 300F oven for 30 to 40 minutes. It should be removed pale, not browned.
6. As soon as it is out, recut the finger lines as it will be hard to do when cooled.

To make shortbread cookies, chose cutters in heart, star, or leaf shapes. Roll the dough about 1/4 inch thick.

Bake on greaseproof paper-lined pan for about 15 to 25 minutes, depending on sizes. Monitor the baking process carefully. They may be dusted with fruit powdered sugar or garnished with bits of ginger or dried fruit, stuck in while still warm.

Recently, while kneading the New Year's batch of dough, I started thinking about the historic connections between France and Scotland. I reached for a madeleine pan, a gift from the year before, rolled the dough into small balls, pressed them into the shell shapes and baked a tray of Scottish memories of the Auld Alliance.

Tips for the Successful Use of Wooden Moulds
1. Rub a new mould lightly with unflavoured vegetable oil a few hours before using.
2. Chill the dough slightly.
3. Dust the mould with flour and castor sugar.

4. Shape a bit of the dough into a ball that will press down to be approximately 1/2 inch thick and a little larger in diameter than the size of the mould you are using.
5. Do not roll the dough out flat. Pressing down on a ball of dough makes a deeper impression.
6. Press firmly until edges of dough appear around the sides of the mould.
7. Trim with a fluted cutter or sharp knife.
8. Lift off the mould. If the dough sticks, tilt the mould at right angles to the board and bang sharply to knock out the shape.
9. If it does not co-operate, just scrape it up, re-knead and try again with another light dusting of flour. Fortunately, shortbread dough benefits from kneading, unlike pastry dough.
10. Once you have a tray full of successful imprints, prick the edges with a fork and chill the whole tray for a short while if you wish to help set the designs.
11. Moulds vary in size from 2 inches to 10 inches. Baking time will vary correspondingly, from 20 to 40 minutes. Remember, pale is preferred.

The baker's challenge is to imprint shortbreads with a wooden thistle pattern. Years of searching for the traditional hand-carved thistle shortbread presses brought us back to Braemar and The Woodcarvers Shop in the 1970s. Jamie's workbench straddled a gurgling mountain stream. Every day he gazed down a valley of firs shrouded in mist as he carved thistles into discs cut from tree trunks. One afternoon as Jamie, David and I were placing an order for his carved porridge spurtles and presses, and toasting everyone's health in pure single malt whisky, we heard a hullabaloo outside his door. "Och, don't bother yerselves," said Jamie. "It's just the Queen Mum passing by again." Deeside has maintained its royal connections.

The thistle carver's workbench staddles a stream.
A cat keeps him company.

*September 13, 1968*

Six a.m. Saturday morning found us on the Commercial Quay of Aberdeen's Fish Market waiting for the unloading to begin. Seagulls were waiting too, on the salt–encrusted railings of the docked trawlers. But there was nary a fisherman to be seen. A young man in a dress suit sauntered by and offered the critical piece of information,

"We only work a five-day week."

Nothing for it but to pitch camp for the weekend and be in position Monday morning for another six a.m. rise. The boats had just chugged into harbour when we arrived, about fifty of them down each side of the Albert Basin. The rising sun cast a surreal pinkish–orange glow over the mounds of silver fish layering the quay. Out of the holds in hefty wicker baskets came endless rivers of halibut, haddock, sole, whitings, herrings, anglers, dogfish and rarer varieties identified by a booklet presented to us by a guide on the dock. At 7:30 a.m. the auction started. The boxes of fish disappeared on to trucks waiting to take them to tables in London and Glasgow. The Aberdeen Fish Market Publicity Association had compiled a little pamphlet of recipes which we added to our van collection.

The fishing fleet at sunrise in Aberdeen harbour.

# FISH CASSEROLE

*This recipe is made for two people but is easily doubled. Fresh fillets of white fish are more expensive now than North Sea oil.*

**INGREDIENTS**
1/2 pound wild caught fillet of haddock
1-1/2 tablespoons of butter
2 leeks
1 tablespoon of flour
1/2 cup of light fish or vegetable stock
1/2 cup of milk
1/2 teaspoon of finely minced parsley
1/4 teaspoon seafood seasoning of your choice - a pinch each of salt, celery seed, paprika, pepper
4 slices of tomato
2 potatoes
1 cup of peeled and cubed celery root
butter and warm milk for mashing

**METHOD**
1. Preheat oven to 300F.
2. Melt butter in an oval enamelled iron au gratin dish that can go from stove to oven.
3. Wash the white part of the leeks, slice thinly, toss in butter.

4. Sprinkle on the flour and stir it in to make a roux (thick paste).
5. Warm the milk and stock then stir into the au gratin off the heat to make a smooth sauce.
6. Add the seasonings.
7. Dry the fish with a paper towel and nestle it in the sauce.
8. Surround with slices of ripe tomato.
9. Heat it on the stove top then cover with foil and place in the oven for about 20 minutes. Check with a fork to make sure fish is flaky.
10. Meanwhile, boil the peeled potatoes and celeriac.
11. Mash in butter and warm milk and season with salt and white pepper.
12. Serve the fillet with sauce and tomatoes around it and a scoop of potato purée to accompany.

The catch ready for immediate auction and shipping.

At a rate of between four and seven tons of fish being hauled up each week day it is no wonder that the sea began to show signs of depletion. But a richer treasure lies below the seabed. Aberdeen is now the base that services the North Sea oil drilling rigs. Recently, a lady from Aberdeen told me that they now have to buy fish from Australia for their breakfast tables.

*September 16, 1968*

When we entered Lossiemouth, a herring port on the Moray Firth, its small stone houses and shops were shuttered. We camped on a desolate stretch of beach enclosed by mountains and mist reminiscent of the Hebrides or Skye. I started humming the overture from *Brigadoon*. It's the type of village where you'd expect to find Flora MacDonald walking through with a wicker basket of fish over her arm. But Lossiemouth has not been allowed to sink into myth. The RAF jets roaring overhead every five minutes dispel any sense of towns lost in highland mists. They certainly turned David's crank and had him hopping in and out of the van all through breakfast. As soon as our gear was stowed, we drove toward the base to investigate. The road runs directly under the landing approach and there was some concern that the jets' wheels might scrape the roof of our van. There is a golf course on either side of this road and those golfers duck more than they swing. We asked the lady in the newsagent's shop if the constant roar bothered the community.

"The townsfolk no longer hear the noise as it has been with us since 1938. This is Ups and Downs week. They're breaking in new pilots."

The caravan park in Lossiemouth borders on a magically changed spot. Findhorn Garden, at the edges of the town, has become a Mecca for anyone with a mystical reverence for growing vegetables. In the early 1960s, a trio of believers in the wholeness of nature, (including Dorothy Maclean from Guelph) transformed this land on the edge of the North Sea into a world famous producer of enormous, healthy cabbage, squash, and leeks, great soup ingredients. We asked one of their members who toured us around the grounds,

"How did you manage to change a windblown, sandy site into this lush garden?" He pointed to seven towering piles of vegetation in various stages of decay.

"Compost is our magic ingredient. On the first pile we throw large stalks, uprooted plants. Everything gets turned and rotated through each section until our final rich dirt is the consistency of chocolate cake. This black gold nourishes the plants that feed our community." Horse manure from local farmers also helped this early ecovillage take root. The enriched soil is heaped high in raised beds whose sides are supported by logs.

We had absorbed an important lesson in maximizing resources - work with nature, not against it. Both the pilot training and the productive gardens benefit from a shared natural phenomenon. This part of the British Isles gets more hours of sunlight than any other, ideal for growing plants or training pilots.

# COMPOST SOUP

*David grows our vegetables in a pesticide-free community garden. Because the city rototills the plots every year, whatever produce left at season's end goes into the compost piles. Toward the end of September, he comes home carrying a basket of organic vegetables that produce a different soup every year. This soup reflects a vintage harvest.*

### Ingredients
1 tablespoon of vegetable oil
1 tablespoon of butter
2 leeks
1 large potato - 1 cup chopped
3 carrots -1 cup chopped
1 cup cubed yellow turnip
4 - 5 cups vegetable/herbal broth
2 cups of cauliflowerettes
2 cups fresh, juicy, diced tomatoes
1/4 cup chopped parsley
salt and pepper to taste
1/4 cup of cream (your choice)

### Method
1. Melt oil and butter in your soup pot.
2. Toss thinly sliced white of leeks in the oil and butter.
3. Add the prepared potatoes, carrots and turnips. Coat all lightly with oil.
4. Pour on enough of the warmed stock to cover.
5. Simmer for 15 minutes.
6. Add the cauliflower and more stock. Simmer 5 minutes.

7. Add the tomatoes and parsley. Gently simmer for another half hour.
8. Purée the soup leaving some chunky pieces for texture.
9. Taste for seasoning and whirl in some cream if you wish.

David watching for the clouds to clear from the top of Ben Nevis.

Our van camped at the base of Ben Nevis.

*September 18, 1968*

If you pass Loch Ness without sighting Nessie, don't be disappointed. For decades, expeditions have been patrolling this lake, the deepest and longest in the Great Glen, a wide fault line separating the highlands from the Lowlands. We took a three and one half hour cruise of this Loch to investigate the legend. Castle Urquhart, a twelfth century ruin, juts out into the deepest part of the Loch, with measureless caverns beneath it. For many centuries, this was the stronghold of the Clan Grant, my father's family name. When I told a friend about the many sightings of the creature reported near this spot, he replied,

"Well Ann, you always did like animals,"

We explored the castle on foot the following day, stopping to chat with "sighters" seated with binoculars and cameras mounted atop a Nessie expedition van. They reported encouraging signs of monster activity.

Soon a more evident black monster, Ben Nevis, rises out of the fields of claret and orange gorse. The sunset produced an eerie strip of neon orange on the bleak side of Scotland's highest peak as we pulled into a campsite at his feet. Before darkness set in, the mist cleared twice allowing elusive peeks at his rounded crown. Tomorrow we are going to try to climb him. In the black of night a trip to the ablution hut almost made me change my mind. The brute towered over our little van, his sprawling black hulk shrouded in a blanket of cloud. He glowered down daring us to try. In an attempt to wear us out during the night, the wind blew, not in a steady blast, but in powerful gusts every ten minutes, rocking the van enough to cause concern. We had parked diagonally across the mouth of the valley in Glen Nevis so that the wind hit us full force as it tunnelled through.

The next day, we barely reached our training heart rate about a mile up the "easy" climbing path on the gentle side of Nevis, before cold rain and lowering clouds made any effort to continue foolhardy. We retreated to Inverness and the comfort of shopping at the butcher, baker, ironmonger and greengrocer. It was another chance to have a chat with some friendly independent merchants. The butchers surrounded by carcasses of meat hanging against the cool white tiled walls, go out of their way to be courteous and helpful. One of them overheard me admiring a white porcelain ham stand on his marble counter. After he carved off some fresh slices of their own smoked ham, he asked, " Would you like one of those stands to take back to Canada?"

When I nodded "Yes please", he climbed up into the rafters above the shop and handed this unusual gift down to us. The van was getting a bit crowded, but we found a safe spot for it nestled among the books. It now takes pride of place on our kitchen counter when a significant-sized ham is part of the buffet. We bought a jar of Cumberland Sauce to accompany the ham.

It was near this town that the Duke of Cumberland, in the mid-eighteenth century, decisively defeated Charles Stuart at the Battle of Culloden. He routed any sympathizers, burning farms and earning the name Butcher Cumberland. Perhaps that is the origin of the name of the condiment that is served with cold meats and wild game.

Loch Ness investigation team on watch for the monster.

# CUMBERLAND SAUCE

*It's handy to keep a jar of this preserve around. It is the ideal condiment for any cold meat. A spoonful adds distinction to the gravy for game meats like venison. And the jar we bought at the butcher's shop turned our cold ham sandwiches into a highland feast.*

*It is essential to use a fruit-rich jelly as opposed to one with too much sugar.*

### Ingredients
1/3 cup of port wine
1 tablespoon brown sugar
2 teaspoons of stem ginger confit
large pinch of cayenne
1-1/2 teaspoons Dijon mustard
1/2 teaspoon allspice
salt to taste
a few turns of the black pepper mill
zest of 1 orange
1/3 cup of orange juice
zest of 1 lemon
1 tablespoon of golden raisins
1 cup of red currant jelly

## Method

1. Simmer the first group of seasonings for 10 minutes while you prepare the citrus fruits as follows:
2. Cut into fine julienne strips just the yellow part of the citrus rinds.
3. Blanch in small pan of water for 5 minutes to remove bitter taste.
4. Drain and set aside.
5. Squeeze the orange juice.
6. Stir the juice and rinds into the pot of seasonings.
7. Stir in the currant jelly and ginger conserve until melted.
8. Add raisins.
9. Simmer for 15 minutes.

*This is traditionally a thin napping sauce. It will thicken slightly stored in the frig in a screw top jar, but do not expect a jelly.*

*Setember 21, 1968*

Failure to reach the summit of Nevis, strengthened our resolve to hike through "The Valley of Death", Sligachan Glen on the Isle of Skye. Armed only with a haversack of sandwiches, we plunged into a gorge where glacier marks on the crags are still evident. The rocky path disintegrated into bog but we continued, lured on as though by the power of the place until we came to the ridge of a gigantic valley, surrounded by The Black Cuillins, stark, jagged lifeless peaks lit by primeval shafts of light. Discretion and encroaching evening turned our steps back to a cozy white inn at the entrance to the valley, where we nursed a pot of coffee and a plate of oat cakes in front of a fire in the lounge.

I buy baking supplies from a small stall in our local market. When I asked the lady behind the counter for oats to bake cakes similar to the ones eaten on the Isle of Skye, she surprised me by declaring that she was related to the MacLeods who have lived in Dunvegan Castle for over 800 years. She has been in correspondence with Lady Flora who invited her to come for a visit. The original Miss Flora was a MacDonald who in 1745 aided Bonnie Prince Charles in his flight from the mainland to refuge in her family home.

A narrow path leading into the Black Cuillins on the Isle of Skye.

# MISS FLORA OATCAKES

*These are ideal camping biscuits, packed with strength-giving oats, easy to store, and baked over an open fire. The ingredients are basic; the method can be tricky. The secret is to sprinkle extra oatmeal on the ball of dough, on the rolling surface, on the baking pan. This ancient procedure has been passed on like folklore. It is still made by a grannie on an iron griddle in many a highland croft. It adapts easily to all the mod cons.*

### INGREDIENTS
1 cup of rolled oatmeal
1/4 cup of oatmeal ground finer for sprinkling
1/4 teaspoon salt
1/4 teaspoon baking soda
2 teaspoons melted bacon fat
3 tablespoons hot water or more if needed

### METHOD
1. Preheat the oven to 350F if you do not have an open fire going.
2. Place 1 cup of oatmeal in a processor or blender to cut the flakes into smaller pieces.
3. Whirl in the salt and soda.
4. Pour the fat and water into the centre and blend until a stiff paste is formed.
5. Sprinkle rolling surface with finer ground oatmeal to knead the

paste into a ball.
6. Shape into a round circle and roll it out to 8 inches diameter. Cup your hands around the perimeter to keep the edges tidy.
7. Cut the circle (called a bannock) in half, then quarters, then eighths.
8. Sprinkle a 10 inch flat cast iron fry pan or griddle with fine oats.
9. Carefully use a spatula to move the triangles onto the baking surface.
10. Bake on a flame for 15 minutes then finish crisping in a moderate oven, or bake in the oven for the entire 25 minutes.

We enjoy them warm with strawberry-rhubarb jam, or a crisp apple and some soft cheese.

After fording mountain streams and crunching along six miles of rocky path that dissolved into a bog, we felt that we deserved to pamper ourselves. So we sat down to a bracing highland meal in the dining room of the Royal Hotel, Portree, then booked into a spotless white cottage for the night.

*September 23, 1968*

While waiting for the ferry at Ballachulish, I asked an old highlander, "What is the name of the hills in the distance?"

"Those are the paps of Glencoe."

"What are paps?" I asked naively. He stared fixedly at my shirt front and replied,

"Wee breasts."

Soon we were driving through these foothills into the deep-cut Glen of Weeping. Every traveller approaches this spot with reverence. We fortified ourselves with corned beef on the banks of the River Coe before plunging into the scene of a historic tragedy. In 1692, members of the Macdonald Clan were massacred by troops under the command of a Campbell. The perpetrators of this brutal slaughter had enjoyed the hospitality of the Macdonalds for a week before murdering them in their beds. We cowered into the sleeping bags, aware of our solitude in this desolate tragic site.

The old gentleman who had explained the meaning of paps back at the ferry told us we could camp anywhere in the Glen. When I inquired about the necessary facilities he replied,

"Och lass just lift your kilt in the heather."

So it was, in the dead of the night under a billion brilliant stars I stepped out of the van surrounded by the terrifying black pyramids, the savage almost vertical slopes of the Three Sisters of Glen Coe. It was so intimidating I almost forgot to lift my kilt.

*September 26, 1968*

The Trossachs is an area that could be called Scotland in miniature. It packs in a sampling of every one of its scenic charms and is close enough to Glasgow for my uncles to bicycle out on Sunday afternoons. Loch Katrine, in its midst, inspired Sir Walter Scott to write *The Lady of the Lake* and *Rob Roy*. More prosaically, it supplies Glasgow with water. I pulled out the poetry book and read,

> *And when the Brigg of Turk was won,*
> *The headmost horseman rode alone.*

A quick map check confirmed that we were standing on The Brig o' Turk, at the end of which was a tearoom and an antique store. The kilted owner caught our Canadian accents right away. "I was stationed at Camp Borden in Ontario for several years" he explained. " Now I'm in the process of selling off all my stock. It's time to retire." We could have ended the trip right there, bought the lot, and still be operating a business in the Trossachs. As it was, we contented ourselves with the purchase of three framed 1800s lithographs of Santa Sophia, with an authentication cetificate from the Victoria and Albert Museum. Even in the wilds, we continued to cram things into the van.

On the banks of Loch Lomond, we picnicked on delicious red salmon sandwiches, full soft fat cheese, and apples. After a walk along the banks, we cut through a field, thick with green clover and circled by stone fences smothered in bramble berries ripe for the picking.

Spot the van on a typically empty road in the Trossachs.

*September 27, 1968*

We rolled back into Aunt Esther's welcoming arms carrying with us the curse of the camper – a serious head cold. Electric blankets, a blazing hearth and tea in bed put us right for a family outing October 1, which included Uncle Joe, Aunt May, Aunt Esther, and cousins Josephine and Margaret. Everyone bundled into the van for a jaunt to Largs, a holiday resort along the coast. The day was brisk, bright and cheery with a salt-fresh gust blowing over the promenade.

Uncle Joe knew of a good fish and chip shop where he got seven fish suppers to bring back to the van where tea was brewing. As we sat surrounded by my re-found family, David remembered that Largs was his father's favourite seaside town. It was a suitable spot to wrap up the Scottish part of the trip.

The euphoria of this first month on the road had obliterated any thoughts of career plans. Yet in an oblique way, September in Scotland turned us in a new direction. This rugged country had called up ancestral spirits, people of independence and determination. Poets may have inspired the journey, but now other critical faculties were being sharpened. Below stairs tours of historic castles developed a passion for sturdy, simple kitchenwares and the tales they told of the past. After one month, food made with honest ingredients was beginning to have an appeal (although we still couldn't pass a fish and chip shop).

Josephine, the youngest family member in the group photo on the following page, sent us a Christmas card December 2010. She now has a daughter about the same age as she was then.

A family outing to Largs - cousin Josephine, Ann, Aunt Esther, Aunt May, Uncle Joe.

## Chapter Seven

## A NATION OF SHOPKEEPERS

> To walk down York's cobbled shopping streets
> is to step into a time machine.
> Journal entry, October 2, 1968

On the drive down to London from the Borders, we had the opportunity to check out Virginia Woolf's observation that English cathedrals stand in a perfect garden of their own. In York, Lincoln and Peterborough her description was accurate, not only for these northern towns, but as we were to discover, also throughout the rest of the country. The great cathedrals of Europe usually open directly on to bustling streets. Their English counterparts created a closed, comfortable, ecclesiastical world around themselves, thus the term, cathedral close. It provides the perfect breeding ground for booksellers, publishers, antiquarians, and tea shops. Travellers on the continent take refuge under the striped awning of a cheery cafe, luxuriating in the sun while a waiter in a long apron pops the cork on a bottle. In England we huddled under the shadow of the cathedral spire, wrapped our cold hands around a steaming pot, and gave our woollens a chance to dry in this enclosed world of damp tweed. I wondered if I was exaggerating the relationship between churches and tea rooms until I read the words of Bishop Ronald Knox,

The medieval Shambles in York.

who donated 6,000 pounds for the construction of a new priests' chapel in Oxford. He instructed the architect to design plans that would allow it to be turned into tea rooms later on, which has in fact been its fate.

Because of their proximity to the ancient centre of any town, we could rely on these small retail comfort zones being housed in buildings of architectural interest. We criss-crossed the country aiming for cathedral towns, admiring the finer details of church gothic in the mornings. By the afternoon, buttresses, spires and chancels had been abandoned for what poet John Betjeman called, "chintzy cheerfulness" where we examined our latest book purchase as Ceylon leaves steeped in a brown betty under a knitted tea cozy in front of us.

As soon as we crossed the border separating England from Scotland, we left the country of brave hearts and entered the country that Napoleon had condescendingly called, "a nation of shopkeepers". York was our first exposure to a city with an original medieval shopping core - cobbled streets, white column Georgian houses and large plane trees. We passed under the preserved Micklegate set in the thirteenth century wall that surrounds the city, crisscrossed Stonegate and Petergate, distracted by print stores, rare book stores and PUBS, the other institution that flourishes south of the border. Their counters were loaded with inexpensive, hearty lunch treats. Raised meat pies, grilled fat sausages, a wheel of Stilton and Cheddar, pigeon casserole, treacle tart, apricot crumble. Our favourite pub fare was a Ploughman's Lunch - chunky bread, a wedge of cheese with pickle or chutney.

# GREEN TOMATO CHUTNEY

*In October, the garden yields a basket of unripened tomatoes, perfect mixed with fall apples and a large Spanish onion in aromatic spices.*

**INGREDIENTS**

8 cups of green tomatoes, blanched peeled and cut into 1/2 inch pieces
6 cups of cooking apples, peeled, cored and chopped the same size as the above
2 cups of Spanish onions, chopped
2 cups of chopped green peppers
1/3 cup of medium hot red pepper, seeded and chopped (wear plastic gloves)
2 cups sultana raisins
3 cups of white wine vinegar
3 cups firmly packed brown sugar
2 teaspoons each of tumeric, whole cumin, whole black mustard seed
1 teaspoon each of ground fenugreek, ground ginger, ground cloves, ground allspice, whole coriander
2 cloves of garlic, minced
2 teaspoons salt
2 teaspoons crushed black peppercorns
2 tablespoons pickling spice

## Method

1. In a large stainless steel heavy-base pot, combine the second group of ingredients to slowly dissolve the sugar and release the great fragrances of the spices while you prepare the first group.
2. Stir the chopped vegetables and the sultanas into the vinegar mixture.
3. Simmer uncovered on a low heat stirring frequently until a thick consistency is reached. About 1-1/2 hours should do the trick.
4. Taste to check seasonings.

Preparing the jars:
1. Sterilize 10 (8 ounce/250 ml) jars by running through the dishwasher then sitting them on a baking tray in a 225F oven for 15 minutes. A large stainless spoon and a wide-mouthed funnel should also be sterilized.
2. The metal lids can be boiled in a small saucepan. Screw bands just need a wash.

Filling the jars:
1. Spoon chutney through the funnel into the jars, pressing it down to eliminate air pockets.
2. Fill to within 1/4 inch of the top. Cover with the sterilized new lids and tighten down with the metal rings.
3. Wipe jar clean. Store in a cool dark spot. Make sure you mark the date on a label so that you consume within a few weeks or refrigerate if open. I do not have confidence in aged preserves.

Not only is this the perfect relish to serve with curries, it is great with slices of cold chicken or turkey.

In the shadow of the great Minster lay The Shambles, the name given to twisting narrow lanes whose timbered Tudor shops lean over as though chatting to each other. This street has evolved from the earliest butchers' and fishmongers' stalls that were called shambles. You can still see the low, wide wooden window ledges where produce protruded out tempting the passing crowd. The life of these ancient premises has been extended with tourist-related merchandise. At one end of this medieval street in a green square a young boy turned the handle on a nickelodeon. The flower shop behind him spilled blossoms out onto the cobbles.

In the middle of a downpour, within the protected radius of York Cathedral, we bought a newspaper package of hot, just fried, haddock and chips and carried it into a snug little bookshop whose back room was warmed by a glowing coal fire in a black Victorian iron grate. Book shopping in Canada had been confined to the university book store, a range limited to our studies. Now we could buy with the abandon of obsessives. Before you could say "Trollope" we had the desk piled with the start of an old book collection. In the ensuing months, David built up a respectable little library, starting here with Bunyan's works illustrated with steel engravings.

The villages, towns and cities of England in the 1960s still maintained enough of a main street presence to provide an education in Victorian and Regency shop fronts. Their bow front windows, side doors leading to a residence above, gilt lettering or decorative signage, all impacted our sensibilities. To go through a front door with a polished brass handle was to enter a lost retail world. Tall mahogany showcases, filled with unique merchandise, a cat curled on a long wooden counter, all presided over by eccentric sales people. Our imaginations fed on this fantasy shop keeping. It was more like playing store than working.

On that glorious second day of October, David parked the van beside the River Ouse so that we could picnic on its banks under an avenue of maples. Shafts of sunlight filtered through onto piles of spilled gold. Our travels through these northern cathedral towns were tinged by an autumnal glow enhanced by the lack of other traffic.

# A GINGERBREAD PICNIC IN YORK

*Yorkshire natives have a fondness for a soft, sticky gingerbread, traditionally made with ground oatmeal and molasses. Called Parkin, this spice bread is associated with Guy Fawkes Day, named for a Yorkshire man who tried to blow up the Houses of Parliament. Four hundred years later, it is still made in northern English kitchens all year round. On that picnic, we enjoyed the taste of ginger in a more conventional, drier cake, accompanied by a wedge of Wensleydale cheese. I have adapted an old recipe from a cookery instruction book that came along with new McClary stoves in Canada of the 1940s. Gingerbread became a new-world culinary tradition.*

### INGREDIENTS
3 tablespoons softened butter
1/2 cup brown sugar
1 beaten egg
1-1/2 cups flour
1/4 teaspoon salt
1-1/2 teaspoons ginger
1 teaspoon cinnamon
1 teaspoon baking soda
1/2 cup plain yogurt
1/2 cup molasses (treacle is a tasty alternative)

**METHOD**

1. Butter the pan and set oven to 350F.
2. Either by hand with a wooden spoon and a large bowl, or using an electric mixer, cream together the butter and sugar.
3. Whisk the egg separately then beat into the mixture.
4. Sift all of the dry ingredients together. Stir molasses into the yogurt.
5. Incorporate the flour mixture into the creamed mixture alternately with the yogurt and molasses. A couple of spoonfuls of flour, a few tablespoons of liquid, a bit more flour, some liquid, more flour, etc. beating well after each addition.
6. Spatula evenly into the prepared pan.
7. Bake at 350F for 35 to 40 minutes.

The road to Lincoln ran straight through a time tunnel of russet leaves, across the fells, the flat Lincolnshire plain that had a profound effect on the writings of Tennyson. The guide book promised that a statue of the poet stood in front of the great cathedral whose honey-coloured spires rose through the greenery of the town's highest hill. Our road passed through a Roman arched gateway up historic Steep Hill, lined with twelfth century mullioned shop fronts, ending at the cathedral close. On this idyllic Sunday afternoon, the townsfolk in tweed suits, were sauntering on a green common surrounded by dignified red brick Georgian houses in front of the cathedral doors. Lunch was on the cathedral grounds under a statue of Tennyson and his dog.

David lunching under a statue of Tennyson and his dog in front of Lincoln Cathedral.

# HERBED PORK PIES

*Lincoln is noted for the quality of its pork products. A couple of millennia ago, while Roman soldiers were building the gates to the city which still stand, Roman women were teaching the Brits how to stuff baby pigs with a finely chopped mixture of herbs. The slice of herbed pork loaf between brown bread we ate beside Tennyson, is one of the legacies of the invasion of Britain. The versatility of pork products allows scope for the creative cook. We enjoy it encased in a flaky rich pastry.*

### Ingredients

1/2 pound plain ground pork (breakfast sausage squeezed out of its casing would work)
1/2 cup finely chopped onion
1 tablespoon of vegetable lard or oil
1/2 teaspoon fennel seeds
1 tablespoon minced sage leaves
1 teaspoon of lemon thyme (worth cultivating)
1 tablespoon of minced parsley
1 large clove of garlic, minced
1 teaspoon of fresh rosemary leaves, chopped
1/2 teaspoon salt
8 whole black peppercorns
4 frozen vol au vent cases (or use your own flaky pastry)

## Method

1. Preheat oven to 400F.
2. Heat oil or lard in fry pan over medium temperature. Cook onions until soft but pale.
3. Break up the minced sausage using a wooden fork as it browns in the pan.
4. While the sausage is cooking, pound the herbs, pepper, salt and garlic in a mortar.
5. Stir it into the cooked meat and onions. Let sit while you prebake the pastry cases for 18 to 20 minutes.
6. When you remove them from the oven, turn the temperature down to 350F.
7. Carefully lift off the tops of the vol au vents using a fork.
8. Spoon the meat mixture into the cases, pushing down gently to fill.
9. Sit the tops on the filling. Return to the oven for 5 minutes to heat through.
10. Serve with chopped brussels sprouts or green and yellow beans.

Margaret Drabble in her *Literary Landscapes* attributes the melancholy, languid aspect of some of Tennyson's poetry to the fact that he was born in Lincolnshire amid misty horizons. But on this brilliant day of high adventure it was more appropriate to read from his spirited *Ulysses*:

> *I am a part of all I have met;*
> *Yet all experience is an arch where thro'*
> *Gleams that untravell'd world whose margin fades*
> *For ever and for ever when I move.*

The horizon as seen that day from the heights of Lincoln Cathedral seemed limitless to us. David explored the chapter house and cloisters while I sat in a small side chapel whose stone window ledge held earthen pots of pale purple Michelmas daisies. We walked back down the steep hill to examine those eight hundred year-old storefronts more closely. The pace of these towns encouraged the enjoyment of small civilized pleasures.

We forced ourselves to leave this peaceful town in order to reach Peterborough before nightfall. With a history that can be traced back 6,000 years, the jewel in its crown is the finest Norman cathedral in the country. It began to seem as though cathedrals were to England what mountains had been to Scotland. This was our third gigantic pile of masonary in as many days. But we had personal associations with this one. The remains of Mary Queen of Scots, whose prison we had recently visited on Loch Leven, had lain here until her son James had them removed to Westminster Abbey when he became James the First. And its lower stained glass windows were executed by William Morris, the Pre-Raphaelite poet-craftsman whose work I had admired in Victorian English lectures.

A blazing sunset made us feel adventurous. We aimed the van towards London and reached it as the moon appeared.

At this point, we booked into a small London hotel for a week, but this account will continue with our van tour of the country and leave the London adventures until the end.

Canterbury Cathedral close. Notice the booksellers.

## Chapter Eight

## ALONG THE SOUTH COAST

After buying two tickets to the opening night of John Gielgud in *40 Years On*, we spread out lunch on the lawn of Brighton's Royal Pavilion. Journal entry for Canadian Thanksgiving Day, 1968

The Aldgate underground stop let us off a few blocks north of The Royal Mint and the St. Katherine's Docks, near the spot where Ald Gate, one of the original entrances in the eastern section of the ancient wall around the City once stood. The Father of English literature lived from 1374 for twelve years over this thoroughfare. During that time, Geoffrey Chaucer, served as Controller of Customs to the very busy Port of London, with offices on the Thames at Wool Quay. His duties included the supervising and auditing of the collectors' accounts, to make sure the king was getting his full revenue on exports of leather, hides and wool. A more adventurous aspect of his job was to apprehend illegal smugglers and earn some of the monies due on seized goods. The Crown granted him a salary, bonuses and annuities. But the significant part of his payment was the leasehold of a set of spacious rooms over this Aldgate where we now stood looking at remnants of its foundation. Every morning and evening a colourful flow of London traders and farmers bringing produce from the fields, would pass literally under Chaucer's feet through gates that still performed the intended function of fortification for the city. If you were making a pilgrimage to Canterbury, you would pass under Chaucer's lodgings (while he was upstairs writing about you), because this was the road that led south across the old London Bridge. He died October 25, 1400, still writing pilgrims' tales.

On this site, October 12, 1968, we found a post office where we sent letters back to Canada informing relatives that we were heading for the shrine of St.Thomas à Becket. A lusty musical production of *The Canterbury Tales*, seen the night before at the Phoenix Theatre, reminded us that the pilgrims had gathered at The Old Tabard Inn on the south bank of the Thames before setting off. We found a replica of the Inn on Talbot Yard, just off the Borough High Street, where we quaffed a pint and tried to remember our Chaucer lectures as we steered the van south past countless other coaching inns, pubs and hostels set up to accommodate travellers on pilgrimage.

Chaucer was writing his Tales while King Richard II was compiling one of Britain's first culinary manuscripts. Almost every one of Chaucer's pilgrims reflected this increased interest in food in his stories. In *The Cook's Tale*, Chaucer makes it clear that you would not want to eat anything this man made. *The Franklin's Prologue* is particularly descriptive of a 14th century foodie. He is described as Epicurius' own son whose groaning board was always set for a feast. His house was never without a meat pie, prepared according to medieval versions, very different flavours than our modern pies.

# OLD ENGLISH SPICED BEEF LOAF

*The ingredients for a beef loaf were originally pounded in a large mortar, thus the resulting thick paste was called a mortrew. When it crossed the Atlantic on the Mayflower, the spices were replaced by herbs and it was rechristened, meat loaf.*

INGREDIENTS
1 pound of topside sirloin
3 strips of bacon
1/2 cup of finely minced onion
1/2 teaspoon ground allspice
1/4 teaspoon ground cloves
1/4 teaspoon mace
1/2 teaspoon ground ginger
1 crushed bay leaf
a pinch of cayenne
1 teaspoon coarse salt
5 turns of the black pepper mill
1 minced clove of garlic
1 egg
2 tablespoons of port wine
1/3 cup of very finely ground almonds

## Method

1. Allow several hours for the following mixture to sit before you turn on the oven.
2. Do not buy already ground chuck. Have a butcher grind the topside or whirl cubes in the processor until it is finer than store-bought ground. Or you could pass it through an old-fashioned meat grinder, should one be at hand. Place in a bowl.
3. Remove the rinds then cut the bacon into small cubes.
4. Mix it into the beef with the minced onion and the ground almond.
5. Put all of the spices, garlic and seasonings into a mortar and grind together with the pestle to form a paste.
6. Whisk the eggs with the wine in a separate small bowl. Blend into the mix in the mortar.
7. Incorporate this mixture thoroughly with the beef.
8. Cover the bowl with a plate and allow to stand for two hours in a cool spot to allow the flavours to blend.
9. Preheat the oven to 325F. Set a 2 inch deep pan with water on a rack in the middle of the oven to act as a water bath for the beef loaf.
10. Butter an 8 inch by 4 inch loaf pan.
11. Give the mixture a few turns before spooning it into the pan. It should be about half full. Brush a little melted butter on the surface.
12. Bake in the middle of the 325F oven for 1-1/2 hours.
13. The loaf will be surrounded by liquid. Lift it out with a slotted spatula. Set it on a small oval platter to cool and firm before slicing. You will get eight one inch thick slices.
14. Serve with mashed turnips and steamed broad beans. A spoonful of the green tomato chutney on page 140 goes down a treat.

We turned west toward Canterbury in time to receive the benediction of a spectacular sunset through the Cathedral stained glass. In order to allow enough time to explore the city properly the next day, we pitched camp at Whitstable on the North Sea. Waves washing over a beach of smooth brown pebbles, right up to the van's wheels, woke us at day break. In the dark of night, we had parked just a few feet from the sea. David started a painting of a small green boat beached near us while I set off to find out if Canterbury still retained some of the medieval atmosphere of *The Canterbury Tales*.

The entrance to the Cathedral Close through Christ Church Gate sets the tone of this place of pilgrimage. Saint Augustine established the site as a place of worship in 597 AD. The Cathedral Bookshop just outside the close confirms the timeless connection between books-publishers-ecclesiastics.

Once inside the cathedral, the pilgrims' presence was evident in the deep crevices worn into the massive stone steps that led to the martyred Becket's shrine. Hundreds of thousands of worshippers' feet had ground down the impressive slabs sent by the Normans from France for the building of Canterbury in 1070. Although Henry VIII had stripped the jewelled glory and the martyr's shrine, Becket still reigns here, in the stained glass window executed shortly after his death and in his spirit.

The route along the south coast of England is charged with emotions, personal and historical. It was difficult to travel this southern stretch of the English coast without thinking of the fragility of the defenses in the Second World War, just a little over twenty years earlier. Stark stone bunkers and jagged cement entrenchments were grim reminders of a near run thing. That beach of brown pebbles on which we had camped was very near a landing spot, where in 1940 my father, George Grant, was brought back from Dunkirk. On that unforgettable beachhead, under bombing and machine gun fire, he had waded out to a British ammunition ship during the evacuation.

At Hastings we tramped dispirited along a promenade lined with souvenir shops, fish and chip stands, and amusement galleries, in a futile attempt to conjure up the significance of the place. One of this island's most pivotal battles was waged here in 1066 when the Norman William defeated the English Harold. We later discovered that the actual site where the Normans conquered Britain lies six miles inland. It is said that if you stand receptive on this field of battle, under certain cicumstances you can hear the combatants communicating across the millennium. French cuisine came ashore with the conquerers, making a dramatic initial impact when William's cooks and stewards set up a formal banquet table on the battlefield before they waged war for the British crown. I stood in silence, listening for the sounds of small birds roasting on spits, or chefs sharpening carving knives.

# NORMAN ROAST OF PORK

*Calvados, cream and a fondness for roast pork were introduced to the English court by their Norman conquerers. One of our favourite everyday dishes is pork cutlets in apple cider. The following recipe I devised for formal dinners or when a battle is won.*

INGREDIENTS
3 pound loin or shoulder pork roast
2 tablespoon oil for browning
a soffrito (flavouring mixture) made of the following:
a medium onion
10 fresh sage leaves
3 stems of parsley
2 cloves of garlic
1/2 stalk of celery with leaves
1 teaspoon of coarse salt
several grinds of black pepper
1/2 teaspoon of whole fennel seed
2 tablespoons oil for cooking the soffrito
1/2 cup of apple cider
1/4 cup of Calvados apple brandy
1 teaspoon of grainy mustard
1/2 cup of cream

## Method

1. Bring the meat from the refrigerator and let it come to room temperature. May take an hour.
2. Preheat oven to 325F.
3. Make the soffrito by whirling ingredients in a processor or chopping together in a heap on the cutting board with a mezzaluna or large chef's knife.
4. Heat the oil in a casserole that will go from stove to oven. Turn the pork to brown all sides.
5. Put the meat on a platter. Wipe brown oil out of pan.
6. Warm fresh oil to sauté the soffrito until soft and fragrant.
7. Set the meat on top of the herbal mixture.
8. Pour on the cider and bring close to a boil.
9. Put covered pot into 325F oven.
10. Baste at least twice with the liquid that accumulates in the pan. Take a temperature reading after two hours. It should reach an internal temperature of 185F.
11. Remove the roast to a warm platter and let it rest while making the sauce.
12. Strain juices from the pot into a small saucepan. Throw away herbs and veg mix.
13. Pour apple brandy into pan to swirl and scrape up any brown residue.
14. Add warm pan juices.
15. Whisk mustard into the cream. Incorpoate slowly into sauce.
16. If too thin, add a beurre manié (a tablespoon each of butter and flour mixed).
17. Taste for seasoning.

An excellent accompaniment is a red cabbage, onion and apple casserole. See *Woodfield Cooks*, page 190.

*October 12, 1968*

Brighton, true to its name, was gloriously sunny with a clear blue sky. The campsite grass was vivid green, thick with dew, and we were ready for the seaside city of sin. Brighton had enjoyed a reputation for gaiety and brilliance ever since the Prince of Wales made it his place for a romantic rendezvous in 1783. By the time he had become Prince Regent in 1815, he commissioned John Nash to transform his villa into the exotically gay Royal Pavilion. Onion-shaped domes, pinnacles and minarets created an Indian palace on the English seaside, the most extravagant chinoiserie interiors ever built in Britain. We tried to imagine the future George IV and his secret wife, Mrs. Fitzherbert, hosting soirées for the beau monde under the dramatic dragon chandelier in the banqueting hall.

The great kitchen provided roasted sides of beef for these upstairs galas. The entire centre wall held a walk-in fireplace, spits all in working order, with papier maché pigs eternally turning. This lofty space, with a skylight upheld by four copper bamboo poles topped by palm fronds, set seriously high standards for kitchen design in my eyes. For anyone raised in the era of aluminum saucepans, the "waterless" cookware, it was dizzying to stand surrounded by metres of French catering copper. Graduated sizes of saucepans and their lids, once the property of the first Duke of Wellington lined the huge open cupboards. Rectangular roasters, huge tureens and elaborate moulds by the dozen sat alongside a bain-marie that could keep more than a dozen pans of sauce warm by surrounding them with a hot water bath. Use of this quality of cookware became possible with the introduction of the closed range - a large rectangular stove, freestanding, completely enclosed, with solid state cast iron burners. The Prince Regent was so proud of these outstanding facilities that he would invite his noble guests down to inspect his kitchen of wonders.

Brighton Pavilion.

# SKATE POACHED WITH CAPERS

*A pan designed to poach an entire turbot has to be the most dramatic piece of copper cookware. With triangular wings like a stealth bomber, it is several feet across. Another fish with an interesting shape is the ray or skate. An Irish friend, visiting us in Britain on a later trip, bought ray wings from a fishmonger in Codicote and poached these skate pieces in an ordinary skillet.*

### Ingredients
2 or 4 skate wings depending on size of your largest skillet
1 teaspoon of white vinegar
1 teaspoon lemon juice
salt
2 tablespoons butter
1 tablespoon chopped parsley
1 tablespoon small capers

### Method
1. Poach the fish in shallow water with a dash of vinegar and salt. Do not allow water to boil. If fish is thin, about 5 minutes should do it.
2. It is normal for this fish to be viscous. Use a wide spatula to lift the skate wings out. Allow them to cool before removing the skin and residue.
3. Make beurre noir (black butter) by melting it slowly until it is dark brown (not really black).

4. Sauté the fish briefly in the butter.
5. Toss the parsley, drained capers and lemon juice over the fish.
6. Heat for a moment.
7. Best served with plain boiled potatoes and green beans.

This visit to the royal kitchen converted me to a copper collector, on the watch for any culinary bits and pieces that might be available. The initial glow faded with the realization that it was ruinously expensive. Later in our career, I came to understand that the seductive copper glow turns black with the application of heat and the interior tin lining wears off. In our age of efficiency, it is decidedly inefficient. But every kitchen deserves a warming piece of copper to beam us back to a time before prefab meals.

Our first opportunity to scout out bargains was in The Lanes, Brighton's maze of seventeenth century cottages now housing curiosity shops, bookstores and antiquarians. Although we enjoyed strolling its red brick lanes and taking tea in the intimate squares, we found that decades of earlier tourists had beaten us to the copper bargains. But the area was an outdoor gallery of whimsical shop signs. A painted panel of a Walrus, Carpenter and Oysters hung over the entrance to a seafood restaurant, echoing Carroll's ships and seas and sealing wax. Cabbages and Kings struck us as the perfect name for a business that might sell kitchen utensils (cabbages) and antiques (kings).

Fish sellers and restaurants in Brighton.

# OYSTER CASSEROLE

*We did not sample any of Brighton's seafood restaurants on that first visit, but on a subsequent visit, we did enjoy a proper oyster luncheon there one Easter Sunday with a friend, Ron, following the Latin Mass at St. Bartholomew's Church, Brighton. When Ron lived across the street from us in London, he would invite us over on Christmas Day to salute the season with a festive glass of Campari and orange juice followed by his oyster casserole. I have tried to remember the ingredients from many Christmases past.*

**INGREDIENTS**
To serve four:
1/2 cup uncooked wild rice
1/2 teaspoon salt
1 cup of fresh oysters, shucked with their liquor
chicken stock to bring liquid up to 1 cup
1 cup cremini mushrooms, chopped
1/4 cup of chopped shallots
1-1/2 cups of crumbled saltine crackers
1/2 cup of melted unsalted butter
an additional 1/4 cup of butter

## Method

1. Preheat oven to 350F.
2. Wash the wild rice in several changes of water. Drain in a sieve.
3. Bring 2 cups of water to a boil. Add 1/2 teaspoon of salt.
4. Stir in the rice then cover and adjust to simmer for 30 to 40 minutes. Do not peek or disturb the rice but monitor the heat so that it does not boil.
5. Shuck the oysters, taking care to collect all of the liquor in a cup. You can buy shucked oysters in their liquor, packaged by Mac's in B.C., available in Ontario grocery stores. Add enough stock to the oyster liquor to make a cup.
6. Crush the crackers to a fine texture using a rolling pin or a food processor.
7. Combine the crackers with the melted butter.
8. Sauté the chopped mushrooms and shallots in 2 tablespoons of butter.
9. Butter a 4 cup oblong covered casserole generously with butter, saving some to dot the top.
10. Toss the mushrooms, shallots and 1 cup of the buttered crumbs with the rice.
11. Layer half of this mixture in the bottom of the casserole.
12. Lay the oysters on top evenly.
13. Spoon the remaining half cup of rice mixture over them. Finish with the remaining 1/2 cup of crackers.
14. Dribble the cup of liquid over the casserole. Add a few knobs of butter to the top.
15. Cover and bake for 20 minutes. Remove cover to gratinate for 10 minutes.

It was a joy to wake up in our campsite, the Municipal Gardens, to the clearest, bluest sky with a full sun evaporating the heavy dew from the sloping green fields surrounding us. Last night the sea lashed the promenade, but this morning we could take a bracing walk along the shingle beaches which sweep eastward beneath the chalk cliffs, collecting some samples of the black rocks that studded the white cliffs.

In the evening, the Royal Pavilion came to life for a special event. Lights from the lotus blossom chandeliers shone on the scarlet and yellow silk wallpapers. Through the tall French doors I could watch tuxedos twirling with evening gowns around the pearl-inlaid piano. Caterers were carrying trays of hors d'oeuvres. Long white tables were being set up in the Banqueting Hall with a delicate green wreath pattern of china, centred with a pale pink rose. Liveried waiters popped the corks from stacked cases of champagne. That's how to throw a party! Feeling like orphans locked outside in the storm, we retreated with a bag of chips down to the VW parked at the darkening sea where Matthew Arnold echoed our thoughts: *Ah love, let us be true / To one another!* For the world did seem to lie before us on this darkening plain like a land of dreams. We took ourselves off to dreamland on a foam rubber mattress in the back of a van.

*October 14, 1968*

    The Duke of Norfolk, Earl Marshall of England is the man in charge of the ceremonials for coronations, royal weddings and funerals. We sat on a mound of ivy facing the moat surrounding his restored Norman Castle. It dominates the Tudor village houses in this south coast town of Arundel where we experienced the highlight stop on our cross-country Tea Tour. A large wooden cutout of a teapot called us into Belinda's Tea Rooms, a Lewis Carroll sort of place, where eccentricities were the norm. You wouldn't be surprised to find the Mad Hatter and his entourage sitting at a table amidst the crush of gently used teapots, creams and sugars that threatened to tumble off the shelves under the bits of brass and copper hanging from the blackened beams. A lady in cap and gown ushered us into a small back dining room where she seated us at a round walnut table circled with ladder-backed rush seated chairs and benches covered in a rose chintz. Behind us on a carpeted stairway sat two congenial dogs staring longingly at our lemon sponge and jam roly poly. One was a brown Airedale, the other white with a brown eye that I swear was winking at us. All around were shelves filled with old crockery, clocks, mugs and cups for sale. At the back of the shop in a patio garden, tea tables were set in an aviary filled with bluebirds. The whole interlude left a lasting mark on us. A pair of brass candlesticks from the shelf that ran along the top of her walls, sits on our mantlepiece now, proof that Belinda's wasn't a dream and that a soft sell approach really works.

# MAIDS OF HONOUR

*This traditional little tea cake befits the home town of the Earl Marshal. It is his office which is responsible for royal weddings. This old "receipt" was sent to me forty years ago by an elderly English lady who knew her way around teashops.*

INGREDIENTS

These amounts should produce approximately 18 tarts in 2 inch fluted tins.

You are best using the rich version of the versatile pie pastry on page 211 or a square of packaged puff pastry.

1/2 cup (4 ounces) ground almonds

2/3 cup fine castor sugar

1 egg at room temperature

1 tablespoon self-raising flour

2 tablespoons heavy cream

1/2 teaspoon pure almond extract

1 teaspoon of fine lemon zest

1/4 cup of thin slivers of almonds for garnish

METHOD
1. Preheat oven to 350F.
2. With the steel blade of a food processor, thoroughly blend all of the ingredients, except the last item. Introduce one ingredient at a time,

until a creamy, smooth paste is achieved.
3. Brush the tartlet tins with butter.
4. Roll out the pastry as thinly as possible. Use a 2-1/2 to 3 inch crimped cutter to make the tart shells. Gather up unused portions and reroll when necessary.
5. Spoon the filling into the cases leaving a bit of head room as they will puff up. Sprinkle on a few almond slivers.
6. Bake in the middle of the oven for 20 to 25 minutes.
7. Remove to a rack to cool before loosening the edges carefully with a knife.

At Her Majesty's Dockyard in Portsmouth you can board Nelson's flagship, The Victory for a guided tour (by an able seaman) of all the decks. The rows of cannons and the captain's quarters may be impressive, but the living conditions for the sailors were frankly appalling. The cat o'nine tails with its ends dipped in lead seemed an unnecessarily harsh form of punishment. No wonder they were allotted a small tot of rum daily.

That evening we sat under kegs of rum suspended from the black beams of Ye Old Whyte Harte, a sixteenth century pub in the village of Hamble. Our campsite was a particularly lonely, bleak place on the sea, so The Whyte Harte's old world hospitality and blazing log fire was all the more welcome. The heavy beams above us were from ancient ship's timbers. From a seat set in the inglenook fireplace you could study the massive iron fireback bearing the Royal Arms CR or GR. I wasn't sure which. The publican cleared up the mystery:

"It reads Charles Rex, 1668. The Inn was built in 1563. Look up inside the chimney at the ironwork hung for smoking bacon and suspending kettles. This was also an escapeway for smugglers leading to the room above." Shades of Daphne Du Maurier's *Jamaica Inn*.

In keeping with the situation, we ordered mead (Queen Elizabeth I's favorite tipple), blackcurrant wine, English farmhouse cheddar and crusty bread. As the candles glowed on the worn oak tables, Dutch seamen chatted with locals, nursing their pints on the settle by the fire. On this bleak night the open hearth and warm congeniality convinced us that we were part of the company of wayfarers who had passed through here since 1563.

# HONEY MEAD

*Any drink that has been fermented since the iron age is bound to have many variations. This is not a recipe as much as an ingredient list, a reflection of the availability and preferences of the myriad flavours used to brew a batch of mead over the years.*

liquids: water
sweeteners: wildflower honey or sugar or corn syrup
fermenting agents: wine yeast or champagne yeast.

In the beginning, only these basics were used. Depending on where you lived and how wealthy you were, one or two of these flavourings could be added.
herbs: attar of roses, damask rose petals, rosemary (indicating love and remembrance)
spices: ginger, cinnamon, vanilla, cloves, nutmeg
fruits: apples, strawberries, blueberries, mulberries, grapes, zest of lemon, zest of orange
Irish Moss, a seaweed used as a stabilizer

The skill is in the choosing. Never all at the same time.

*October 18, 1968*

In Exeter, the local cinema was showing Thomas Hardy's *Far from the Madding Crowd*, an appropriate title for this corner of the coast. The large screen was filled with images of a countryside we had just passed through. Black and white collies continue to round wayward sheep into stone pens on the rolling green downs. That morning, under a downpour, we had crouched by the slabs at Stonehenge where Tess had been captured asleep on the fallen central stone.

Although severe bomb damage had obliterated many of the town's old shops, a welcoming light shone from the diamond-shaped window panes of the Elizabethan Mol's Coffee House, protected under the shadows of the twin Norman towers of Exeter Cathedral. At a padded window seat, overlooking the cathedral close, our discussion of Julie Christie's portrayal of Hardy's fickle heroine, Bathsheba, was lubricated by a proper local spread. I was forming a padding of my own from the chocolate rolls and Battenburg cake.

Stonehenge in the rain.

# DEVON CREAM TEA

*The tray arrives at your table with a crystal jar of fruit jam, a bowl of thick cream, warm scones and a pot of tea. I have experimented with several scone recipes and definitely prefer this lighter version, more like a Southern biscuit. The processor method transfers it from Hardy's century to ours.*

**INGREDIENTS**
2 cups all purpose flour
2 tablespoons sugar
3 teaspoons baking powder
1 teaspoon salt
4 ounces of chilled unsalted butter
3/4 cup 10% cream

**METHOD**
1. Preheat oven to 425F.
2. Sift the sugar, baking powder, salt and flour together into the bowl of a food processor.
3. Arrange slices of the cold butter on top. Process with an off/on motion until coarse mixture is reached.
4. Slowly pour in the cream as the blade blends it together.
5. Remove dough to a floured counter top.
6. Knead it five or six turns.
7. Roll dough out to a 1/2 inch thickness.

8. Use a 2 inch metal cutter to cut into circles. Gather the remainder of the dough for a second roll. I get 24 two inch biscuits out of this recipe.
9. Line a baking sheet with parchment paper.
10. Bake in the centre of the oven in batches of 12 for 10 or 12 minutes.

This recipe can of course be done by hand in a bowl with a pastry blender or fork.

Sir Francis Drake's statue on the Hoe where he watched the approach of the Spanish Armada.

At a nearby bookstall, David scored a truly rare find – two leather bound volumes of Dante's *Divine Comedy* illustrated by Gustore Doré for one pound each. The VW was in danger of becoming a book mobile. But a very classy one. These volumes are all bound in crimson or tan leather, softened by years of handling. Titles and authors' names appear in gilt, usually with an illustration etched onto the front of the cover. No dust jackets. Many of them still sit on our book shelves. My market purchases were more practical, influenced by Hardy's austere vision – a stone hot water bottle. Cold nights in campsites were approaching.

*October 19, 1968*

Plymouth is historically the gateway to the New World. A simple stone archway marks the spot from which the Pilgrim Fathers sailed on the Mayflower in 1620. Heavy bombing during the Second World War necessitated a considerable amount of rebuilding. This city of new beginnings opened a small door of opportunity for us with a product as basic as the Pilgrim's prayer for daily bread. At a vendor's stall near the sea, I unearthed a round wooden breadboard and knife. This particular board was a gently worn circle of beech with the word BREAD carved around a perimeter design of leaves. The knife had a matching carved handle and a scalloped carbon steel blade that was still efficiently sharp. It would be perfect to cut the wholemeal loaves that were a daily struggle in the van. And I had a feeling that Europe would not be sliced bread territory either.

"What price is this board and knife?" I hesitantly inquired of the grey-haired saleslady who was very involved in her afternoon tea ceremony. Her terse reply "one pound" had me reaching for my change purse. She offered me a cuppa and became voluble.

"Now this set here is definitely an antique. No doubt about it. Look at the sheen from years of bread sitting on the board. But should you ever find yourself in the market for a new one, a firm up in Sheffield still

Carving bread boards at Bramhall Woodware Co.

makes them."

The pedigree of these humble pieces of kitchenware was easily confirmed by checking the Illustrated 1869 *Mrs. Beeton's Book of Household Management* purchased in Hatchards' rare book department. The identical breadboard was illustrated on one of her pages as essential equipment for the kitchen.

Several years later we visited Bramhall Woodware Co. in Sheffield to place a large export order. David had decided to become a wholesaler of unique, hand made British goods and these traditional wooden boards fitted the bill perfectly. In the showroom, glass cases displayed samples of boards with deep intricately carved borders, made in Victoria's days when labour and materials were cheaper. Wood carvers still stood at benches with chisels and planes surrounded by piles of thick wooden discs waiting to be turned.

Over the years, we imported hundreds of these knives and boards into Canada. Many brides received them as gifts for their new homes and we encouraged the giver to inscribe the couple's names and the wedding date on the back of the board. Decades from now, in Vancouver or on Prince Edward Island, in a roadside antique stall, a young couple might unearth a warmly worn board on which they will cut their homemade bread for another generation.

# A HEFTY BROWN LOAF

*When we returned to Canada, I was hesitant to try baking a proper yeast loaf, so I cut my bread-baking teeth on variations of the traditional soda bread. This old-fashioned round loaf suits both me and the old round bread board perfectly- no yeast, no waiting, no kneading, just quick eating, warm with butter and jam.*

### INGREDIENTS
8 ounces of unbleached brown or wholemeal flour
1/2 teaspoon sea salt
1/2 teaspoon baking soda
1/2 teaspoon cream of tartar
1 ounce of cold unsalted butter
1 tablespoon of molasses
1/2 cup of sour cream, buttermilk or yogurt

### METHOD
1. Preheat oven to 400F.
2. Sift the dry ingredients together into a bowl.
3. Cut in the butter or crumble in by hand.
4. Stir the molasses into the sour cream.
5. Make a well in the centre of the dry ingredients into which you pour the liquids.
6. Incorporate with a large fork or spoon until a soft mass is achieved.

7. Do not knead the dough or fuss with it too much beyond getting it into a smooth round ball about 7 inches by 3 inches. The soda starts to work as soon as it is introduced to the liquids so the quicker the better. A little more liquid may be required to get the dough to hold together.
8. Place on a piece of baking parchment or a smear of butter on a baking sheet.
9. Cut a deep cross on the top with a sharp chef's knife.
10. Bake at 400F for 25 to 30 minutes.
11. Let it cool down a bit to allow the texture to firm up before cutting.

This bread is a good accompaniment to a wedge of cheddar cheese and some chutney (page 140).

A very steep cobbled street led from our parking lot campsite down to the sea in Clovelly.

The van barrelled through timeless green tunnels.

The van barrelled its way through the green time tunnels of England's hedgerows. At Clovelly one October night, we walked down four hundred steep feet from our parking lot (where we had permission to spend the night) to the harbour. A fishing boat anchored a short distance out on the Bristol Channel, was brightly lit. We watched its beams reflect in the bay as we sat on the beach, listening to the pebbles being rolled back and forth by the waves. A small white dog, with a head too big for its body, had followed us down and kept us company until his place was usurped by a Persian cat. She insisted on trying both our laps as we rested on a long wooden bench at the base of the cliff. Halfway back up the cobblestone main street, we stopped, hypnotized by the lights from the fishing boat still bobbing in a black midnight sea. By the time we had climbed up to New Inn, we were ready for rum and a hot Cornish pasty.

On a rugged crest of the Cornish coast at Tintagel, a fierce wind blowing all the way from Labrador, tested our ability to stay upright on the legendary site of King Arthur's Castle, which straddles two jagged peaks with the sea crashing in between. Over the misty Vale of Avalon, Arthur was carried to rest in the Abbey of Glastonbury. We followed his route.

The legends came alive as the brilliant late afternoon sun made the scarlet ivy flame against the great stone arch of the Glastonbury Abbey ruins. Arthur and Guinevere's bones lie under the break in the archway where blue sky looks down on the grassy knoll that once was the high altar. Suddenly a hooded monk and a scarlet-cloaked figure fluttered amongst the masonry. We assume it was a theatrical group soaking up the atmosphere. Maybe not.

## Chapter Nine

## INLAND

*The Bishop of Bath and Wells has a moated palace,
stocked with ducks and swans who are clever enough to ring a bell
by the drawbridge to have their bread flung out.
Journal entry, October 22, 1968*

The air of mystery hung in misty patches of fog along the route to Wells. A white haze hovered low over fields where the occasional pheasant strutted along the top of the stone fences. At dusk we struck camp in Wookey Hole where our suspicions were confirmed by a pamphlet David picked up in the campsite office – Visit Wookey Hole Caves, Home of the Witch of Wookey. These caverns measureless to man are considered by scholars to have inspired Coleridge's Kubla Khan on his two visits there in the company of William Wordsworth.

The surroundings may have spooked us, but the campsite itself was thankfully rooted in the material world - hot water, baths, washing machine, dryer, grocery store. Basic conveniences, but luxuries to road travellers in late October. We took advantage of them all before venturing into The Caves of Mystery and History. Floodlights penetrated the still pools of bottomless green water. On cue, a squadron of bats zoomed overhead. If it hadn't been for the promise of history, I would have been out of there in a flash. Our guide, sensing mutiny, launched into tales of neolithic skeletons, and the remains of Roman-British and medieval cave dwellers. The caves have also yielded a rich harvest of valuable coins, jewellery and kitchen utensils. He had finally caught my interest.

"Students on archaeological digs have long recognized that the humblest fragment of pottery or section of a cutting instrument can reveal as much about a lost civilization as a more spectacular piece." Here was justification for my hoard of old kitchenwares on a scientific level, more convincing than personal whimsy. We could claim to be domestic archaeologists.

The stalactites hanging from the roof of the caves, are the stars of the show. It took millions of years of steady dripping to develop one of these elongated formations, then Alexander Pope shot several off in a few seconds to cart back to his grotto at Twickenham. Those eighteenth century poets took their interior decorating seriously.

In a section of the caves, the temperature is right to store large wheels of cheddar cheese.

In honour of the Witch of Wookey we assembled ingredients for a cheddar fondue. Our largest pot on the gas stove became a cauldron which we stirred carefully as night fell on the Wookey Hole campsite.

# CHEDDAR CHEESE FONDUE WITH ALE

*A flameproof earthenware pot or enamelled cast iron, a stirring stick and a gas ring are essential for cheese fonduing. The thick earthenware is a slow, even heat conductor, less likely to scorch melting cheese than metal. But if you are limited to metal, set your pot in a skillet of water, creating a double boiler effect. The herbal properties make this a White Witches' brew.*

**INGREDIENTS**
1 pound of English cheddar cheese
3 tablespoons flour
1 clove of garlic cut in half (for protection against evil spells)
2 cups of English pale ale
a pinch (an eighth of a teaspoon) of several magic herbs (according to your tastes and needs):
dry mustard stimulates the nerves
fennel seed for vitality and courage
celery seeds aid in treatment of arthritis, rheumatism and gout
chopped comfrey leaf protects travellers from negativity
a dash of Worcestershire sauce
a generous pinch of baking soda
a loaf of crusty bread
boiled potatoes

**METHOD**

1. Grate the cheese and toss it in the flour to coat.
2. Rub the sides of the pot with the garlic.
3. Bring the ale to a simmer.
4. Add the cheese by handfuls, stirring well with a wooden spoon to incorporate each addition.
5. Stir in your choice of seasonings.
6. Add the baking soda last. It is the potion that adds volume and aids digestion.
7. Keep more ale handy in case mixture becomes too thick.
8. In addition to dipping bread and potatoes, you could try wedges of crisp apple.

*October 24, 1968*

As a break from damp campsites, we took rooms in a warm townhouse in Bath, which had a curious built-in bath, complete with a stone perch.

Early Britons had enjoyed the curative waters, but the Romans turned The Baths into a commercial success. The shivering troops discovered radium-rich hot pools, the Sacred Spring, that spout hundreds of thousands of gallons of 120F water daily from a rift in the earth's surface. They were so appreciative of this gift from the gods, they constructed an elegant spa, complete with columns and statues that are still reflected in the restored pools. The Great Bath for centuries lay under the King's Bath and was not discovered until a workman poked through to the pool in 1878. Since their restoration, visitors have gravitated to this ancient spa.

Considering that we had sampled baked goods in just about every tea shop in Britain by this point, a regimen at the waters seemed appropriate. The recommended sequence of steps to follow for the cure include a soak in the soupy pale green waters of the Roman Baths, enjoy a light lunch, drink a tumbler of mineral water in the Pump Room. We skipped the first stage and headed straight to the delicious luncheon of grilled trout and plum tart served among the statues of the Caesars who stare continuously down on the calm pool.

# ROMAN BAKED TROUT

*During their time in Britain, the Romans introduced the Celts to the wide use of their island's bountiful fresh herbs in food preparation. This is my conception of a dish the conquerors might have enjoyed putting together. It contains olives, garlic and wine (the Italian influence) and old-fashioned English green aromatic herbs.*

### INGREDIENTS
1/4 cup of chopped onion
1 clove of minced garlic
1 tablespoon of olive oil
8 black olives, pitted and halved
1/4 cup of dry white wine
2 trout fillets
1 tablespoon each of chopped chives, parsley and sweet cicely - if this anise flavoured herb is not in your garden, substitute dill or fennel leaves
coarse salt

### METHOD
1. Preheat oven to 350F.
2. In an oval stove-to-oven au gratin, heat the oil and sauté the onion and garlic until soft.
3. Chop the herbs together with the salt. A crescent-shaped mezzaluna

is the perfect utensil for mincing herbs on a wooden cutting board or in a wooden bowl.
4. Add the herbs to the onions. Pour in the wine and simmer for a few minutes.
5. Press the fillets down on both sides in the au gratin mixture, finishing skin side down.
6. Sprinkle the olive halves around the fish.
7. Cover with foil and bake for 10 minutes.

Boiled new potaoes are a fine side dish.

The regimen's recommended tumbler of mineral water is sipped on Chippendale chairs at a round walnut table in the Great Pump Room. The name of the room is derived from the marble font in the bay window constantly dispensing therapeutic warm water. The attendant handed us each a tumbler of magic minerals, which we dutifully carried back to our table.

While the mineral waters were helping our digestive system, the refinement of the room was reshaping our psyches. David read Punch magazine as I recorded descriptions in my journal of the antique sedan chairs, long Chippendale benches, and enormous crystal chandeliers.

The next day was exactly the type that would have made the early Romans long for Naples – dreary, dark and drizzling. We retreated back to the Pump Room, settled at a table by the fireplace in time for "elevenses," coffee served with slices of Bath loaf. A French Huguenot refuge, Sally Lunn, arrived in Bath in 1680, and started baking the original bread in Bath's oldest house, a pre-Georgian building with records going back over 500 years. Her kitchen, in the foundation of the building, rests on Roman stones and shows indications of an early open hearth. You can still sample Lunn's buns in the tearoom here and tour the kitchen museum below, with the wood-fired oven set into the stone wall.

# BATH SWEET BREAD

*Any recipe more than 300 years old is bound to have many variations. Our landlady explained the significant distinction between Sally's simple lemon-flavoured yeast bread, and the Bath Buns which evolved filled with bits of fruit and sprinkled with cream. In style, the following version tends toward the sweet egg breads of the continent, such as the French brioches. I prefer to emphasize the light, lemon flavour, and omit any other bits and pieces. This way, the toasted slices are more versatile.*

INGREDIENTS
For proofing the yeast:
2-1/4 teaspoons of active dry yeast
1/4 cup of warm water (100F)
1 teaspoon sugar
For batter:
2 cups plain white flour
2 tablespoons granulated sugar
grated zest of a whole lemon
1 egg
1/2 teaspoon of pure lemon extract
4 ounces soft butter

## METHOD

1. Preheat oven to 350F.
2. Mix batter ingredients so that they will be ready to receive the activated yeast.
3. You may use the traditional bowl and spoon or a food processor bowl and blade.
4. Sift the flour into the bowl. Fold in the sugar and grated zest.
5. Beat the egg. Whisk in the lemon extract. Incorporate into the centre of the flour.
6. Beat in the softened butter which has been distributed in knobs.
7. Stir yeast and sugar into warm water. Let stand in a warm place for 10 minutes. As soon as the mixture doubles in volume, it is ready to use. If it is not used in time, it will become inactive.
8. Make a well in the centre of the flour mixture. Pour in the yeast and incorporate thoroughly until you can remove the dough with your hands.
9. Knead for a few minutes on a floured board.
10. Place in a lightly buttered bowl. Cover with a clean cloth and allow to rise for 1/2 hour to 1 hour. It should almost double in size.
11. Knead again, making two small loaves, either round or rectangular, depending on your choice of tins.
12. Place loaves in lightly buttered tins, loosely cover and leave for 1 hour.
13. Bake in the middle of the preheated oven for one hour. A finished loaf should sound hollow when tapped. Baste the tops with melted butter during the last 15 minutes.
14. Set on a rack to cool.

Serve toasted with butter or plain with a mild cheese or fish spread.

The Royal Crescent in Bath.

The Palm Tree Trio was playing Gilbert and Sullivan, whose trademark plot-lines bore a resemblance to our trip - topsy turvy. A distinguished retired gentleman in tweeds at the neighbouring table broke his toe-tapping to lean over and ask, "Can you name this piece?" His question seemed so much like a radio quiz scenario that I stifled a giggle before confessing ignorance.

"It is the overture to Patience, one of my favorite G & S operettas." The D'Oyly Carte Company had opened their new Savoy Theatre in 1881 with this production which was based on over-the-top aesthetics of the period. G & S had incorporated several of the trend-setters of the London scene: Oscar Wilde, walking down Piccadilly with a lily; the greenery-yallery of Morris papers; the maidens descending the Golden Stairs in Burne-Jones' painting.

The old gent probably felt we needed to be directed toward the finer things in life, because he launched into a mini architectural lecture on the glories of Bath.

"The Royal Crescent is the best proportioned street in the country. Thirty Georgian Bath stone houses fronted by an arc of 114 Ionic columns. Nothing to beat it. Except maybe The Circus, three segments of the circle typifying the Greek orders – Doric, Ionic and Corinthian. The rain has stopped. Go have a look."

Without his gentle prodding we would have missed John Woods and son's tours de force. Each of the three sections of eleven houses that arc around to form The Circus must have shone pure and clean when Jane Austen stood on the grass in the centre just fifty years after they were built. She would have recognized that this was more than just a pleasing arrangement of old stones. A visionary had shaped this space and done a great job of it. The harmony that resonates serenely through the centuries, both here and on the Royal Crescent, enforced our admiration of classical architecture. Bath encouraged us to restore Canadian heritage buildings for our home and our workplace.

# CREAMED SALMON SANDWICHES

*During a farewell picnic lunch under trees turning to gold in Bath's Victoria Park, we saluted the elderly gentleman who was passing on nuggets of information to naive visitors as he sipped his aqua vita and listened to the topsy-turvy repertoire of Gilbert and Sullivan. Whenever we were in a spot requiring a little elegance, I'd make these sandwiches that can easily be transformed into party hors d'oeuvres. Our Bath picnic qualified.*

### Ingredients
4 ounces of smoked salmon
2 ounces of unsalted butter
2 ounces cream cheese
1/4 teaspoon of pepper
a pinch of cayenne
1 tablespoon lemon juice
a few snips of fresh chives

### Method
1. Flake the salmon with a fork in a bowl.
2. Cream in the butter and then the cream cheese.
3. Blend in the pepper and lemon juice.

If you are making this in a kitchen with a food processor just whiz all the ingredients together, saving the chives to garnish your fingers of rye bread, telling your guests they have been piped with poisson fumé.

For our picnic, we spread it on slices of Sally Lunn's bread, purchased at her original bakeshop.

# Chapter Ten

## TOWNS and GOWNS

*An elderly gent on a bicycle asked if we had seen Addison's Walk.
Our "No" brought an admonition.
"Oh but you must; it is the pleasantest part of Oxford.
I shall charge you if you don't." He chuckled as he rode away.
Journal entry, The Botanic Gardens, Oxford, November 5, 1968*

Oxford was still a city on two wheels, friendlier, more accessible. We had no sooner parked the van at a b&b before a gowned undergrad pulled up on his bicycle.

"Helloooo, visitors are you?"

"Yes, we've just arrived."

"In that case, why not see the best first. This is my college, Christ Church, the largest, most magnificent in the university. And the richest, as that custodian with the bowler hat collects an admission fee from visitors. You just stick close by me."

He threw his bike against an ivied wall and led us on. We passed under stone walls clad in scarlet virginia creeper to enter the fifteenth century cloisters of Christ Church Cathedral.

"This archway used to be blocked in by Cardinal Wolsey, builder of the college, but we can go through it now."

Our guide led us up a flight of stone steps on the west side of the cloisters to Christ Church Hall. Visitors are rarely admitted to this grand dining hall with its rows of dark oak tables, carved and gilded hornbeam roof and gilt framed portraits of college notables keeping an eye on the students' table manners. The food served in this hall had at one time been prepared in one of the country's most historic kitchens. Cardinal Wolsey had his priorities in the right order. He instructed the builders to complete this mammoth kitchen before Henry VIII pulled the financial plug on his career as Chancellor. Wolsey's red-tasselled hat is flung like a banner across one corner of the the Great Kitchen at Christ Church College. I wondered how the cooks liked preparing tapioca pudding under its shadow. Three huge ranges along the high-ceilinged walls stood ready for the fowl and game dishes enjoyed in the hall. Carroll set an episode of Alice in the cavernous kitchen, where a large turtle's shell hanging over the stoves probably brought to mind his story of Mock Turtle Soup.

"Do the meals that they serve you now measure up to the grandeur of this medieval kitchen with its huge copper cauldrons?" I asked our new friend.

"No, they're a bit institutionalized, the standard sausage and mash, steak and kidney pud, custard and prunes. Now if it's the legendary Brideshead luncheons you're thinking of, you should aim to be invited to a don's chambers. Roast pheasant served on 400 year-old college silver by a scout in white gloves, soufflé and fine wines, very decent."

I doubted we could push our luck that far but I was becoming interested enough in food to find out more. The colleges, like fine restaurants, had been noted for their specialities of the house. Our friend said that Christ Church favoured wild fowl. Venison was the meal of choice at Magdalen, no doubt inspired by the herds of deer grazing in the meadows around it. Merton favoured dressed crabs and hare soups.

# VENISON PÂTÉ

*Ontario lawns do not generally have deer grazing on them. But venison meat is accessible at three farm-outlets within a twenty mile radius of us. In this recipe, I use it in strips down the centre of the terrine to add texture and flavour to the standard ground veal and pork. Covered rectangular or oval terrines are available, but you can manage with a narrow loaf pan. The amounts given require two six-cup baking pans, 9 inches by 4 inches.*

### INGREDIENTS
Marinade for the venison:
1 pound of venison meat from the leg or shoulder, cut into thin strips
1 teaspoon of juniper berries, crushed
1/2 teaspoon of black peppercorns, crushed
2 cloves of garlic, minced
1 teaspoon of dried thyme
1 tablespoon lemon juice
1 tablespoon olive oil
1/4 cup of Madeira

### METHOD
1. Combine the prepared seasonings with the liquids in a bowl that will accommodate the meat.
2. Stir together then toss in the deer strips. Cover and refrigerate 6 to 8 hours or overnight, turning several times.

## Ingredients

For the body of the terrine:

1 pound ground veal

1 pound ground pork

1/2 cup of ground venison (remainder bits from cutting the strips) The steel blade of a processor will work fine for grinding the meats.

1/2 pound or 1 cup of ground pork fat back (available from a butcher who specializes in pork products)

1-1/2 teaspoons whole pink peppercorns

1/2 teaspoon of ground allspice

10 scrapings of nutmeg

1-1/2 teaspoons salt

2 cloves minced garlic

2 whisked eggs

1/4 cup chopped shallot

1 tablespoon butter

1/4 cup Madeira

zest of an orange, blanched

1/2 cup of dried cranberries

8 or 9 whole bay leaves

enough pork fat back flattened into sheets to line the terrines

## Method

For assembling and baking the pâté:
1. Preheat the oven to 350F.
2. Lift the strips of venison meat from its marinade using a slotted spoon so that some of the herbs and spices adhere.
3. In a large bowl, thoroughly combine the ground veal, pork, ground venison, ground pork fat back.
4. In a small bowl, whisk the eggs then blend in all of the herbs, seasonings and spices, except the bay leaves.
5. Incorporate into the big bowl of meats.

6. Sauté the shallots in melted butter until soft. Add the Madeira and simmer several minutes.
7. Stir into the main mixture.
8. Fold in the orange zest and cranberries.
9. Press slices of pork fat against the sides and base of the terrines.
10. Pat an inch or so of meat mixture into the bottom of the terrine.
11. Lay three rows of venison strips down the meat.
12. Press on another inch of mixture. Add another row of deer strips. Finish with the meat mixture. Smooth the surface and lay three whole bay leaves along the top.
13. Depending on the sizes of your pans, you may have enough to make one or two more terrines. Lay strips of fat on the top.
14. Cover the pan tightly with foil and put on a snug lid.
15. Set the pâtés in a pan large enough to keep hot water half way up their sides while baking.
16. Bake in the lower half of the 350F oven for 1-1/2 hours.
17. Lift the covers to see if the juices surrounding the meat are clear or yellow (done) as opposed to rosy pink (not done).
18. Remove from the water bath. Set a weighted shape on top of the foil to press the pâté down while it cools. I fill a plastic bag with pebbles so that it takes the shape of the meat loaf.
19. Refrigerate the pâtés in this weighted container, with their juices around them. They will form a jelly.
20. The next day, remove meat, scrape away fat and jelly, replace meat in a covered container or wrap in plastic to store in the refrigerator. I would use it within a week or freeze for future use.

Back in the Cardinal's kitchen, two workmen were replastering the bricks behind the huge fireplaces, which gave every appearance of having been the only source of heat since the sixteenth century. Even now, the room was ten degrees lower than the outside temperature. We escaped to the warmth of the lanes that weave between the colleges, still hung with climbing roses and ivy, in spite of the lateness of the season.

Our research led us through an unassuming doorway off the High Street where we found ourselves in the square block city market of fishmongers, game stockists and marmalade vendors who have been supplying head table since Isaac Newton's day. This was Oxford's indoor market, servicing town and gown much as it has done for centuries.

The High Street Oxford set in the countryside.

The next day, while in a phone booth trying to get directions to the Lamb and Flag for dinner, I noticed David chatting with a young man leaning nonchalantly on his handlebars.

"Hi, I'm Peter White, a fellow Canadian, presently at Oxford researching the philosopher Locke in preparation for my doctorate thesis. The best place for dinner in this part of the country is The Bear in Woodstock - sixteenth century building, great food."

After getting directions and agreeing to meet him the next day for a guided tour, Peter pedalled away and we set off on a Bear Hunt. Heading south on the A 34, the night sky was lit by fireworks and bonfires. The ancient autumnal need for a fire festival has been re-channeled into burning Guy Fawkes in effigy every November fifth, the day he tried to blow up the parliament buildings in 1605. The drama of the evening absorbed us until we realized after passing Blenheim Palace, that we should have taken the A 34 to the north. It was worth retracing the route, as The Bear in Woodstock turned out to be a singular experience. Sherry in the fire-lit lounge, duck à l'orange in the panelled dining room; coffee in armchairs, another meal for the memory bank. A silver moon and streaks of fireworks, reflected from grey slate-gabled shops that lined the cobbled Cotswald street, lit the night when we finally staggered outside, amazed that the simple act of eating could be so pleasurable.

Deer graze on the grounds of Magdelan College.

# SPICED CITRUS DUCK

*There is a poultry farm near our city that specializes in whole ducks and geese as well as individual parts. If I am re-creating our romantic dinner for two, I buy a pair of duck thighs or breasts. If company is coming, a whole duck is needed. This recipe can be adapted for either.*

**INGREDIENTS**
2 duck thighs
1 large clove of garlic
6 whole juniper berries
1/2 teaspoon of Chinese five spice powder
1/2 teaspoon coarse salt
a few grinds of black pepper
1/2 teaspoon of olive oil infused with lemon

For the sauce:
1 tablespoon of honey or maple syrup
1 tablespoon of grated fresh ginger
1 tablespoon Grand Marnier
the juice from 1/2 an orange and 1/2 a lemon
1 tablespoon of peel (no white) from an orange and a lemon
2 tablespoons fruit powdered sugar
2 fresh figs

## Method

1. Pat legs dry and bring to room temperature.
2. Pulverize the whole juniper berries in a mortar. Blend in the minced garlic, spices, seasonings and lemon oil to make a paste.
3. Prick the fat on the duck in several places with a sharp fork.
4. Rub the oil/spice mixture on the meaty side.
5. Set oven to 450F and allow duck to sit for about half an hour to absorb seasonings.
6. Place duck, skin up in a shallow roasting pan in the hot oven for 15 minutes to draw out the fat. Reduce oven heat to 350F.
7. Pour off fat. Turn duck over and set in a lower temperature oven for 20 minutes per pound.
8. Meanwhile, prepare the sauce. Peel just the top zest off the orange and lemon, leaving the white pith. Cut it into matchsticks (about 1 tablespoon each fruit). Boil them in a little water for 10 minutes. Drain.
9. Boil the sugar in 1/4 cup of water to make a light syrup. Poach the strips of zest in it for 5 minutes.
10. Squeeze the juice from the 1/2 orange and 1/2 lemon.
11. Combine the honey, juices, zests, grated ginger and Grand Marnier to heat in a small saucepan.
12. Test the duck with a sharp knife to see if juices run clear.
13. Remove legs to a warm platter while you pour off excess fat and deglaze the pan over a hot burner with the prepared juice mixture. Add several slices of orange and the figs cut in half.
14. Return the legs to the pan and baste them with the sauce.
15. Return the pan to the oven for 5 minutes to let the glaze warm through.

Peter met us in front of Saint Christopher's guesthouse the next morning for a tour that held pleasant surprises for the three of us. The travellers' saint stayed with us all the way. At the Sheldonian Theatre the curator, standing alone in the centre of this rotunda, gave us an impromptu lecture on the design of the building by Wren, the type of presentations given in the hall, and how the degrees are conferred.

At a secondhand bookstore, Peter found a book on Liebnitz,

"I've been searching on two continents for this volume. It is no longer published and is a key work in the preparation of my thesis."

He celebrated with a very uncanadian little jig on the High Street then broke into song: "O frabjous day! Callooh! Callay! He chortled in his joy! Let's really enter Lewis Carroll's world. I can actually take you through the looking glass."

Peter had access to Christ Church Library, where his wife, Molly, was a librarian. She had taken her degree at University of Toronto and was pleased to give Canadians a behind-the-scenes tour.

"Lewis Carroll, really Charles Dodgson when he kept rooms in this college, stood at this window looking down on young Alice Liddell, the daughter of the Dean, playing on the grass below with her sisters. Yesterday I gave a talk to a group of school children and caught their interest with our current display."

Molly led us over to a long library table on which were spread out the original designs for the famous Alice in Wonderland books with those perfect illustrations by Tenniel.

After chatting with Molly for a bit, I recognized Charles Dodgson as another author who had bridged the gap between fact and fantasy. He took a first class degree in mathematics at Christ Church, where he spent the rest of his life, rising to become a member of the Governing Body. In Oxford he wished to be known as the author of An Elementary Treatise on Determinants, not as the author of Jabberwocky. One afternoon, when he was engaged in writing, a lady visited his rooms, "

"Oh, are these to be some more nonsense verses?" she asked.

"No, it is not funny - it's about Euclid", sternly replied the author of Alice.

Although he preferred to keep math in a separate chamber from myth, this spinner of theorums and fairy tales did not suffer from a personality split. His imaginative use of words was based on a solid logic that could lead the reader through a maze of absurdity to a reasoned conclusion. He had a logician's love of puzzles, riddles, and conundrums. His pseudonym is a good example of how his mind worked. He translated his first and middle names, Charles Lutwidge, into Latin - Carolus Lodovicus - then reversed them when anglicized into Lewis Carroll. Critics of James Joyce acknowledge that his Finnegan's Wake owes much to Jabberwocky.

Any reader of the Alice adventures will notice that she takes a great deal of interest in matters of eating and drinking. Dodgson makes the point of telling us that she was particularly fond of orange marmalade. No coincidence that his brother actually made and sold marmalade on a large scale. Charles even got into selling jars at nine pence each in the Common Room where he was Curator. From his verses, The Lobster Quadrille and Turtle Soup, we can assume that Dodgson himself enjoyed the pleasures of the table. Then there is the kitchen of the infamous Red Queen and her trial to determine who stole the tarts.

The twin towers of All Souls College.

# THE QUEEN OF HEARTS' TARTS

*Because these are the Red Queen's tarts, we'll use red berries and bake the tartlet shells upside down, of course. You will need two trays of 12 each mini-tartlet forms, each 2 inches wide, a crimped edge pastry cutter, also 2 inches, and a 1 or 2 inch heart-shaped cookie cutter.*

### INGREDIENTS
a pint of fresh strawberries
1/2 jar of strawberry jam (the Queen prefers homemade)
one half of the following pastry recipe page 211
mild oil for basting the inside and outside of the tartlet tins

### METHOD
1. Preheat oven to 375F.
2. Put aside 24 of the smallest berries then thinly slice the remainder.
3. Melt the jam slowly in a small saucepan. Add the strawberry slices. Simmer.
4. Turn the tartlet tins over. Brush the backs of the tins with oil.
5. Roll out the pastry and cut 24 circles, 2 inches wide.
6. Drape each pastry circle over the backs of the tins.
7. Prebake the pastry shells in the oven for 10 minutes.
8. Meanwhile, cut 24 hearts out of thinly rolled pastry.
9. Place them on a baking sheet which has been lined with parchment paper.

10. Remove the tart shells and set the tray of hearts in the oven for 5 minutes. Set your timer.
11. Lift the pastry shells off the baking tin. Turn it over and oil the inside of the tins around the edges.
12. Set the delicate pastry forms on the tartlet shapes. Do not press down. You are just stabilizing them. This may sound fussy, but it works, and is much easier than trying to dig fruit-filled pastry out of metal tins.
13. Spoon 2 or 3 slices of strawberry from the jam pan into each pastry shell. Do not include much of the jam liquid at this point as it will boil out over the edges.
14. Top each tart with a whole berry, pointed end up.
15. Baste the berries gently with melted jam.
16. Hope your timer warned you to take the heart shapes out of the oven by now. Stick one in each tart beside the berry.
17. Bake the completed trays for 10 minutes.
18. If the jam hasn't bubbled out, these tarts will lift onto a serving plate easily once slightly cooled. Add a bit more jam glaze if you wish at this point.

No wonder the Queen was furious when the knave ran off with these little beauties!

# VERSATILE PIE PASTRY

*Depending on the proportions of fat used, this pastry can be adjusted for traditional apple pie, French fruit tarts or rich flans. I always make this amount as the unused portion freezes well and it is good to have a back-up if someone steals your tarts. Basic procedures remain the same for all pastry making:*

*Have all ingredients very cold.*
*Work quickly.*
*Chill dough for a few hours prior to rolling.*

### INGREDIENTS
for two 9 inch shells:
2 cups pastry flour
1/2 teaspoon salt or sugar (depending on the filling)
4 ounces of shortening
2 ounces of butter (reverse these amounts for a richer crust)
5 to 6 tablespoons of ice water

### METHOD
1. Place flour either in the bowl of the processor or in a mixing bowl.
2. Add salt or sugar if a sweet crust is desired.
3. Cut shortening and/or butter into cubes. Drop into bowl.
4. Work quickly to cut fat into flour until granules are the size of navy beans. Or whirl machine with off/on rapid motions.

5. Dribble in ice water with machine running until pastry just forms a ball. Stop immediately.
6. Sprinkle a little flour on parchment or wax paper. Wrap the ball of dough and refrigerate.
7. Cut it in half to roll out on floured surface.

The richer butter and sugar pastries are preferred for open fruit tarts such as apricot, pear, plum, and berries.

Savory quiches and meat fillings are usually baked in a crust made with a higher percentage of shortening or without butter. As are the traditional covered apple pies.

Molly had to pry us away from yet more Carroll memorabilia by enticing us, "Now I'll show you a secret hiding place." We followed her into a back room of the library where John Locke's escritoire is stored.

"I keep digestive biscuits in one of its pigeon holes on the theory that close personal proximity might help Peter in his thesis research."

The philosopher's desk was probably the most unique bread box we'll ever see. In this environment, The Mad Hatter's party arrangements no longer seemed fanciful.

*November 8, 1968, Cambridge*

We squeezed in among students eating and drinking Elizabethan style at long bare wooden tables under a balcony at The Turk's Head Inn, Cambridge, a popular carvery. More students filled the gallery above which circled three sides of the room. Two undergrads on our left were tackling the relevence of Swift and Pope's satires to the current political situation. The fellow to our right, tackling a roasted chicken, introduced himself.

"I'm from Boston, name's Herb. Back home I'm the head of the Sociology Department at a Private School, currently enjoying a sabbatical study period."

We chatted about the Nixon-Humphrey presidential race in the U.S. It seemed so remote from this micro world of art, learning, and roasted wild fowl. For the first time on this trip we wanted to be here as students. I pumped Herb for some insider information on life at the colleges.

"I have rooms at Clare, that's the one with the curved wrought iron gates. Films about college life give the impression that we live in book-lined suites. Actually, my space is little better than a bed-sit."

"What do you do about food prep, or is this your regular eating spot?"

"We do have access to a very basic kitchen facility called a "gyp" room, little more than a sink in a corner. A housekeeper, called a bedder, keeps our rooms tidy."

Now the van was beginning to look good.

"It all sounds rather meagre."

"There are posh sets and dinner in the great halls can be impressive when the undergrads wear their gowns to dine at long polished tables set with candles and antique college silver. Take a stroll around Trinity courtyard if you want a whiff of that atmosphere."

Virginia Woolf presented two sides of college life in her book *A Room of One's Own*. In a lecture given to Cambridge women at Newnham College in 1928, she compared a luncheon in rooms at a richly endowed male college - sole in cream sauce, partridges with condiments, thinly sliced roast potatoes, a confection of spun sugar, liberal accompanying wines of the correct hues -with a dinner at Fernham, a relatively new ladies' college later that same evening - brown gravy soup, dried beef, yellowing brussels sprouts, prunes and custard, washed down by jugs of water. She then carries the obvious comparison further by telling us that "a good dinner is essential to good conversation. One cannot think well, love well, sleep well, if one has not dined well."

A vindication of the importance of the kitchen if there ever was one. Endowments of proper kitchens and chefs is therefore as important as grants for libraries.

A book browser's paradise.

# SOLE IN CREAM SAUCE

*Proper Dover sole is not readily available fresh in North America. Our grocers stock frozen fillets, members of the flounder family. Do not let that stop you from trying whatever recipe for sole in a cream sauce appeals to you - the Kitchen is the Room of Your Own. You can do them in a Mornay sauce, gratinée them with cheese, garnish them with mushrooms, potatoes, and so on. Since this is a delicate fish, I prefer to treat it gently, so that the flavour survives the cooking.*

**INGREDIENTS**
4 small fillets of sole
1/4 cup water mixed with 1/4 cup milk
1 bay leaf
2 sprigs of parsley
salt and white pepper
1-1/2 teaspoons of butter
1/3 cup of thinly sliced small leeks or large green onions (1/2 inch diameter)
1/4 cup of heavy cream
1 tablespoon of lemon juice
a sprinkling of paprika

**METHOD**
1. Preheat oven to 350F.
2. Sauté the sliced leeks in melted butter in an oval gratin dish or oven-proof pan.
3. Lay fillets on top of the leeks and season to taste.
4. Warm water, milk, bay and parsley before pouring it over the sole. Bring to just below a simmer on top of the stove.
5. Place in the oven uncovered for about 8 minutes, depending on the thickness of your fillets.
6. Boil the heavy cream for a few minutes to thicken slightly.
7. When fish is at flaking consistency, remove with a slotted spatula to a warm platter and pour cream over. Sprinkle lightly with paprika if desired.

Best served with plain boiled potatoes and steamed spinach. But it's your kitchen.

That evening at The Turk's Head we had dined well and felt a companionable glow as we retired with our new friend to the red plush lounge in the bar, where over coffee he gave us a suggestion that made the next two evenings memorable.

"Pick up some tickets for the Dryden Society's theatricals at Trinity Hall Theatre. You'll be in for a treat."

The plays to be presented in Trinity Hall Theatre were from the school of the absurd, but presented by The Dryden Society, they attracted a traditional group, sophisticated in dress and in manner. The tall fellow, who took our tickets, striking in a dark blue three-piece suit, waved us in with assurance. We felt pretty smug too, for we ended up seated beside the theatre critic for a major newspaper. It amused me to try to figure out what he was scribbling down during Ionesco's *Chairs*. We purchased tickets for the next night's performances of *Krapp's Last Tape* and Joe Orton's *Erpingham Camp*. As student fans of contemporary theatre in Windsor, we had often crossed the Detroit River to attend plays by Pinter and Beckett presented by Wayne State University. But the Orton play would be a unique production - Prince Charles, a student at Trinity College that year, was to play the padre.

We arrived in the courtyard of Trinity a good half hour before the performance as seats were not reserved and we anticipated a sell-out. But the cast were going through a last-minute rehearsal, so we ambled around the Great Courtyard of Trinity College on an unseasonably warm November evening. At the time, Prince Charles had rooms on a staircase adjoining the statue of the first Queen Elizabeth. A.A. Milne had been a student here and had bequeathed the original manuscript of *Winnie-the-Pooh* to Sir Christopher Wren's Library. Candlelight glowed through the leaded windows of Tudor Hall where black-gowned dons dined under the double hammer-beamed ceiling. A large portrait of the founder, Henry VIII, dominated the panelled wall behind the high table. The Chapel was closed for evensong, but we could hear the music in the vestibule, where under statues of its renowned graduates, Newton,

Macaulay and Tennyson, I peered through the keyhole in the massive wooden doors at rows of glimmering candles illuminating the gold cross on the white-clothed altar.

A mob was lined up at the theatre door on our return. Fortunately, the queue was for tickets. All we had to do was flash ours at the same dapper doorman and reclaim our front row seats next to the critic. Every seat and all available standing room was taken. We were eager to see how Joe Orton's outrageous kitchen sink drama would unfold within this bastion of tradition. His plays deal with the working class, as opposed to those who swagger around in smoking jackets waving long cigarette holders on west end stages.

The experience of viewing HRH on stage from the front of a small crowded lecture theatre was instructive. He had the right tone of voice and elevation of manner required to play the not-too-religious padre in this satire of holiday camps. The ludicrous scenes, in which he laced the director of the camp into a girdle and received a cream puff in the face, carried an added frisson due to his future post as the head of the Church of England. Many of the lines bear a heavier ironic load when delivered by the heir to the throne. "We must not allow the seeds of anarchy to gnaw at the established order," carried a portent even Orton could not have imagined. David commented that the experience would give Charles practice at role-playing in the life he has to lead. Why would a student prince have subjected himself to this role of public humiliation? If he only knew what lay ahead, he might have opted for the theatre of the absurd, rather than the world of the absurd. I wonder if Prince Philip had told him that waiting to become monarch would be a long haul.

As a representative of my highschool student body in the late 1950s, I was sent with other students to meet the Queen and Prince Philip while the Royal Yacht Britannia was anchored in the Detroit River. The Prince asked me, in a fatherly fashion, what I wanted to be.

"A lawyer," I replied.

"That will be a long haul," he said with a chuckle.

He was practising being a parent.

## Chapter Eleven

# HEADING NORTH

> At that moment, the road to Windermere seemed the one to take.
> The scenic beauty confirmed Wordsworth's wisdom
> in choosing this area for his retreat.
> Journal entry, The Lake District, October 28, 1968

Darkness closed in on the van earlier every night now. Yet the road still held an allure. Touring season had passed and we were solitary travellers. In spite of it being close to November, several farms posted signs indicating that they would welcome campers. The Red Lion at Bishop's Norton sounded like a pub, but it was a working farm with a small pond, surrounded by ducks, geese, and yellow goslings, just facing the spot where the farmer's wife told us to park for the night. Black rabbits and kittens scurried up and down the path. In this sheltered spot, a gentle drizzle fell through the last rays of the sun. As I stood making soup at the sink in the van, the front window was suddenly filled by a full spectrum rainbow, rising out of the forest and ending in the garbage pail at the gate of the campsite.

"You know what they say about the end of the rainbow?" I rushed down to the pail of kitchen scraps, bent in and pulled out a blue enamel candleholder. "This will be needed with darkness coming earlier every night now." Not exactly a pot of gold, but certainly an indication of the good fortune that followed us through these northern cities.

A Roman Wall completely encircles Chester.

A typical cozy English bed and breakfast.

*October 25, 1968*

Gloucester scored a double-header - a Tudor building housing an antiquarian bookshop below and a restaurant tucked under the eaves above it. Narrow stairs tilted with the building up to an intimate space where black oak floors were so angled that the cake trolley found our table by gravity. The aged waitress, tottering behind it, creaked towards us carrying (for safety reasons) the ubiquitous dark brown pots of tea and toasted crumpets swimming in butter. I increased my girth at the tables upstairs while David augmented our library with a leather-bound 1793 copy of Dr. Johnson's Dictionary and Marlowe's *Faust* from the fine collection downstairs. These rare early books were going for less than the price of a weekend newspaper in those days. By the flickering light of the Coleman gas lamp in the van that night we looked up Dr. Johnson's definition for oats.

*October 27, 1968*

Chester, from the Roman Castro, a fortified camp, is England's only completely walled medieval town. The surrounding countryside can be seen from all directions as you walk this perfect two mile rampart. The River Dee embraces it in a graceful semi-sweep. Here we were introduced to another variation on the shopping street, The Rows, galleried arcades raised a few feet above the road, have offered pedestrians protection from traffic and weather since medieval times. Two-tiered columned walkways could be considered early stylish forerunners of our street plazas. Timbered buildings with gables and leaded windows attract customers and ease the stress of sterility in the work place for the staff.

Because of a heavy rainfall, half of the town was window-shopping under the arcade with us. A walnut portable writing box with brass inlay sat open in one of the curio shop windows. We convinced ourselves that two travelling scribblers definitely needed an eighteenth century folding laptop - for composing verses and writing this journal in the van. During a recent spate of electrical blackouts in our corner of North America, it was one laptop that could still be used for writing.

When the rain eased a bit we climbed to the walkway at the top of the Roman wall and made a circular tour of the town to orient ourselves with the cathedral, playing fields and city centre. Fortified walls were the earlier form of visitor orientation centres or scenic lookout platforms and we made the complete circuit under a cascade of wet yellow leaves.

This evening was to be what we had affectionately begun to dub, "a romantic splurge night." We would chose one of the dressy outfits wedged in the van's tiny closet, and carry it into our b&b. Liberal use of blissful hot water made us human enough to sit in a proper diningroom with candles and develop our growing appreciation for fine food. Tonight's cookery experience included Wiltshire chicken and white wine in the candlelit Roman Room. These evenings ended in a real bed with an eiderdown under the eaves of a proper red brick bed and breakfast. The van does have its limitations.

# WILTSHIRE CHICKEN BRAISED IN WHITE WINE

*Chicken thighs are the most seductive part of the bird, moist and full of flavour. A simple braising is our current favourite preparation. It can be done on the stove top or in a moderate oven.*

### INGREDIENTS
2 plump chicken thighs
salt, pepper and lemon juice
2 tablespoons of sage herbal butter (see page 241)
1 shallot chopped
4 cloves of garlic
1 tablespoon of olive oil
1/2 cup of white wine

### METHOD
1. Loosen the skin by inserting a finger underneath and working it down as far as possible.
2. Rub the thighs with a mixture of salt, pepper and juice.
3. Warm the olive oil on medium low heat. Gently turn the chopped shallots in the oil.
4. Crush the whole garlic cloves, but do not chop.
5. Add to the oil for just a few quick turns. Try not to colour.
6. Brown the chicken thighs in the skillet, being careful not to burn

the seasonings.
7. Remove chicken so that you can clean off any excess browned oil.
8. Return chicken to pan and pour in the wine. Cover and simmer for 25 minutes.
9. If the sauce becomes too thick, dribble in some more wine or chicken stock. A syrupy texture is preferred.

Serve with parslied rice and green peas. Don't forget to spoon out the garlic cloves which have melted and become unctuous.

The season was closing in. Every open campsite now was a bonus. North of Lancaster we pulled into one of the nicest sites of the trip, a farm in a natural clearing in the heart of the wilds of Westmoreland. In a small pond facing the van, we watched ducks diving as black rabbits scurried up and down the path. A goose perched on a tree stump seemed intent on keeping an eye on us for the night. A rainstorm had splattered the acrylic roof in the washroom with brilliant russet and yellow leaves, an image revived for me years later by those thick acrylic spoon rests of the eighties. Although the washroom facilities seemed like a cement bunker from the exterior, there was a charming walnut swivel mirror on the porcelain ledge beside the wash basin.

The quacking ducks woke us the next morning for our drive up the A6 toward Aunt Esther's. Then I spotted a road sign "Windermere 8 mi." It had been our intention to beeline up to Glasgow, empty the van at Auntie's flat and regroup for winter on the Mediterranean. But travelling with no commitments allowed us the freedom of detours. We swung the van down the road toward Windermere and entered the spellbinding world of the Lake District. Wordsworth's poetry lies around every bend in the road.

Dovecot Cottage at Rydal Mount remains as it was when the poet lived there with his sister Dorothy and later his wife Mary. The stone floor, tallow candle moulds and copper boiler are testaments to his credo "plain living and high thinking." A tin box that Wordsworth used to carry his sandwiches into the hills on his long walks, reminded us of our picnics. The floor level slopes upwards as the house has been excavated into the hill with the front entrance lower than the back. This complete naturalness of the spot was echoed in the freedom accorded to visitors. The trusting guide invited us to sit at Wordsworth's desk and lounge on his divan. She must have considered us kindred spirits for she launched into some Wordsworthian details that surprised us, including the fact that at one time he picked up a bit of spending money by distributing postage stamps in the Lake District.

The drive along the shores of Lake Grasmere was accompanied by my readings from the romantics as we viewed the scenery that had inspired them in the royal hues caused by autumn's chill. On the route back to the main highway we pulled in at the sign of the White Horse Inn for lunch. A blazing coal fire cheered the white washed, black-beamed room. We carried our pints and smoked trout platter over to a red velvet window seat, which looked out over a misty heath crowned by a high barren mound.

# POACHED TROUT ON BROWN

*The trout may have come from one of the lakes. It certainly was fresh. The inn served it on a slice of soda bread with a spoonful of mustard-mayo and a watercress garnish.*

INGREDIENTS
2 fillets of lake trout
poaching court-bouillon:
a stalk of celery, halved
a carrot, halved
a small onion studded with 4 cloves
3 sprigs of parsley
1 bay leaf
1/2 cup of white wine
juice of half a lemon
6 peppercorns
water to cover

For presentation:
fresh watercress
1/4 cup of mayonnaise
1 tablespoon of Dijon mustard
soda bread

### Method

1. Bring the court-bouillon ingredients to a low boil in a small fish poacher or oval baker for 20 minutes.
2. Put the fish in the bouillon. Make sure the liquid barely covers the fillets and keep them at a bare simmer for about 5 to 8 minutes, depending on thickness and size. The flesh should be firm and flake when removed from the liquid.
3. Remove fish and drain.
4. Stir the mustard into the mayo.
5. Serve on the bed of watercress accompanied by the bread, or on the bread accompanied by the cress. Mustard-mayo spooned on top.

You can turn this into an appetizer by creaming the flaked trout with the mayo, spreading on toast or crackers, topping with a smidge of cress or fern of dill.

*October 30, 1968*

It is only a few hours drive from the Lake District to Glasgow where we shed the flights of poetic fancy for the city of reality. Aunt Esther's hearth was very welcoming after a second month on the road. She rose from her chair next to the hot water heater to greet us warmly as usual.

"I hope yer no coming home wi a cold again."

"No, we're getting tougher. Any mail?"

"Sit doon by the fire. I'll just put on the kettle tae boil and bring it in."

The box of slides that we had taken of our Scottish tour in September seemed like pictures from a past life. October's drive around England had offered exposure to architecture, history, literary giants, kitchens the size of ballrooms dripping with copper cookware, rare book stores and antique finds. A rich harvest that autumn.

The November snow fell on Cathkin Braes, the hills above Aunt Esther's housing scheme, signalling us that it was time to prepare for the trip back down to London for Christmas.

The book collection, the kitchenwares collected on the trip around Britain, were boxed and stashed under Aunt Esther's bed.

This month, stripped of the gold of autumn, the hills of the border country were frosted, the trees stark. Bonfires illuminated the bare fields on this sobering drive South.

We rented a flat at 50 Cranley Gardens London SW

## Chapter Twelve

## SWINGING LONDON

> In Canada House on Trafalgar Square
> you can sit in a wingback chair by a fireplace
> to read Canadian newspapers.
> I took one look and ran out to sit on the steps of the National Gallery
> to watch the passing scene.
> Journal entry, November, 1968

 

We drove past Marble Arch, flood-lit from below and moon-lit from above, steering the van north towards the university district and Montague Street. This long row of four-storey eighteenth century houses faces the British Museum and joins Bloomsbury Square with Bloomsbury Gardens. We pulled up in front of several small Edwardian hotels, black doors framed in archways, brass handles and doorplates gleaming under the glow from iron gas lamps.

The Lonsdale was run like a tight ship by ex-military personnel. The Colonel made sure the silver breakfast service was gleaming and the grandfather clock in the hallway kept accurate time. The efficient staff wore black uniforms with spotless white aprons and caps. After checking in, we resisted the urge to fall into a real bed to take a late night stroll down Shaftesbury Avenue checking out the theatre marquees.

To be seated at a breakfast table, set with a white linen cloth in front of a long window, justified the expense of this brief hotel interlude. Montague Street took its name from the family that owned the land on which the British Museum now sits. While working our way through a silver rack of toast spread with marmalade, we peered out at the dome of its famous reading room, barely visible behind the iron railings that surround the Museum through the heavy curtain of fog and rain. The temptation to stay here was strong, but we couldn't afford the hotel for a month. We walked through the connecting green link formed by St James Park, Green Park and Hyde Park, to the Tourist Bureau and inquired about finding a flat for November and December.

"We'd like someplace airy, with long windows overlooking a traditional London street with space to park a camper. Not a bed-sit. We need a proper kitchen please. And it has to be very reasonable."

Instead of showing us the door, they directed us to a firm with the endearing name of Universal Aunts. One of these "aunts," Mrs. Torres-Cable, took our measure in a glance and recommended we try a Mrs. Bacon in Cranley Gardens, a Masterpiece Theatre version of a London street with white pillared Regency town houses just off Old Brompton Road in SW7.

*November 11, 1968*

Our Cranley Gardens flat lay north of the currently hot street, King's Road. Just down the street from the house one hundred years earlier, Frances Palgrave had compiled Palgrave's Golden Treasury of Lyrical Poems. Tall sage green curtained windows looked out on a leafy street of white neo-classical terrace houses. A columned portico provided an imposing Italianate entrance. Our sitting room had the prerequisite gas fireplace, flanked by easy chairs and book shelves. The van even had a parking spot in a South Kensington mews behind the flat, once storage for horse-drawn carriages. Mrs. Bacon set the tone for her neighbourhood.

"Whenever I see anyone littering the street I tell them, We don't do that in SW7."

We were eager to measure up, but were aware that change was eroding these London neighbourhoods. The elegant town houses no longer operated as one household with two social stratas, downstairs help serving upstairs occupants. Now they were genteel rooming houses full of students from the far-flung corners of the Commonwealth, such as Canada.

The kitchen was sufficiently equipped to test out the many new dishes we had tasted on the road. Provision shops in the area were more than a match for these kitchen challenges. A few streets to the north, along Old Brompton Road, gilt-lettered signage from the last century on their windows still identified the established butchers, fishmongers, bakers and greengrocers. The route home from the South Kensington underground stop lay past this supply row, allowing us to pick up dinner fixings at the last minute. These small purveyors were so pleasant, I usually preferred to turn grocery shopping into a morning's entertainment.

At the corner of our street, the fruit and vegetable store displayed its cabbages and apples at outdoor stalls. Strings of red peppers, onions and garlic soon gave our South Ken kitchen some continental flair. Mr.

Hicks, the butcher greeted us with a hearty "Good morning, Sir, Good morning, Madame," then did his best to produce the exact cut of meat from the carcass hanging on the wall. Mr. Mac, the fishmonger, cleaned two lovely trout for our dinner, then we crossed the street to buy a bottle of white wine from the well-stocked cellars of a reputable wine negotiator. The chap who sold me the camembert warned that it could not be eaten for another day until it had softened. The scale of these businesses and the exchange of pleasantries turned shopping from a boring routine into an instructive adventure.

To the south lay the Fulham Road and King's Road, the main streets of Chelsea where the small antique bits and pieces we had picked up in our tour of the provinces for five shillings were on display for thirty. We figured you could almost pay for a trip by buying wisely and in quantity. It came as no surprise when we later met many dealers who did just that for a living.

The historic traditions of the city were in creative fusion with a youthful energy that was breaking out after the austerity of the fifties. The bright pink wildflower, called London Pride, bloomed in the bomb sites that scarred the edges of the city. New walls of highrises loomed over the recently uncovered Roman Wall. Covent Garden hawkers still bellowed bargain prices on fruits and flowers around Inigo Jones' Piazza. City businessmen would cross old London Bridge for the last time this year, wearing top hats or bowlers and swinging their tightly furled umbrellas. It would be dismantled during our stay and sent to Arizona. In these pre-Diana years it was still permissible to admire royalty as they went about the city opening fêtes and attending concerts. BBC voices were broadening as Cockneyfied accents became acceptable. The Beatles' image dictated hair length and width of pant flare while they were re-writing musical history. Pop art dominated billboards, album covers and the underground. Cheeky young authors like John Osborne, Alan Bennett and Kingsley Amis were challenging the establishment and we caught their first stage presentations.

The city was a shopper's paradise in this decade, with many of the original Victorian and Edwardian establishments operating along side brilliant new entrepreneurs like Terence Conran. His first Habitat store opened in 1964 on the Fulham Road and instantly swept aside the dust and fustiness of typical houseware departments, allowing air, space, light and a sense of adventure to sweep the retail scene. We wandered in just to buy a tea towel and were enthralled by the totality of his vision – from the masses of fresh white tulips crammed into square glass vases, to the rustic baskets bristling with wooden stirrers - everything was dictated by a clean sense of design and a respect for the objects that were offered for sale. The air space was not sullied by elevator muzak. A high-tech system delivered the Fab Four in step with the hip clientele. No comparison can be made between this first stylish version of warehouse shopping and today's vast arenas of cheap goods consumers now prowl lured only by the lowest price.

The entire concept struck me as brilliant. The colour scheme had been taken from French country kitchens, stark white walls in contrast with terra cotta tile floors. Earthen pots from France and Spain were stacked in tottering towers. Serious knives, cleavers and meat hammers covered the surface of chunky butcher blocks. The product mix ranged from Victorian tin toys to bold Marimekko fabrics from Finland. Conran introduced the now popular display techniques: "Put all of the stock on the showroom floor" he decreed. Like a Mondrian canvas, this mass merchandising in brilliant blocks of colour elevated warehousing to an art form. The style that we take for granted now was started by Conran and no one has ever done it so well. Today, Habitat stores can be found in Paris, New York and other major capitals. England eventually knighted him for revolutionizing the home design industry.

Conran had started out with a small restaurant called The Soup Kitchen. He never lost his interest in good food and eventually combined architectural preservation with fine restaurant dining, as in Bibendum and Tower Wharf. An aspect of Habitat's agenda was to educate their customers in the use and care of the utensils imported for their kitchenwares departments. Caroline Conran composed a series of little pamphlets providing recipes and usage tips for utensils. We bought a moulin-legumes (food mill) once we discovered how useful it would be in a spartan kitchen.

Artist consulting with bobby in Trafalgar Square.

# CELERY SOUP

*Before electric blenders or processors appeared, cooks relied on hand food mills to turn a pot of boiled vegetables into a creamy purée. They have three discs: the fine-holed is perfect for keeping seeds out of a raspberry sauce. Medium-holed disc makes a skinless tomato coulis.*

*The large holes can handle mashed potatoes. A boon for campers who meal prep in a van. The same procedure can be followed with asparagus, peas, squash or other vegetables.*

### Ingredients
4 cups of celery
2 shallot bulbs, peeled and minced
3 tablespoons of butter
3 cups of chicken or vegetable stock
1/4 cup fresh coriander
salt and white pepper to taste
1/2 cup of light cream (optional)

### Method
1. Melt the butter and slowly sauté the minced shallots over low heat.
2. Wash the celery bunch then trim the ends. Cut the stalks into 1 inch pieces, including the tender leaves from a couple of them.
3. Toss the celery bits in with the butter and shallots until coated.
4. Add the stock. Simmer for about one half hour or until tender.

5. Stir in the chopped coriander.
6. Fit the food mill with the largest hole disc and set it over a bowl or pot.
7. Turn the handle to purée the mixture. The blade will hold back any tough membranes.
8. Transfer a ladle of stock to a small bowl. Stir in the cream if using to acclimatize it to the heat.
9. Pour into the cooling soup.
10. Reheat gently when ready to serve.

If you wish a light soup or broth, for instance for an invalid, omit the cream. This method with cream is best followed for a variety of vegetable soups - carrot, asparagus, pea.

We took the tube up to Carnaby Street, a legend in contemporary times. Up until 1957, it was just one of the many narrow, unassuming streets in the bohemian area of Soho. After John Stephens opened his first stylish clothing shop for young men the boutique crowd rushed in. In the mid-sixties it set the scene for a mod capital discovering the mini and rock and roll. By the time we got there, it was a bit too brash and tasteless. Union Jacks were draped over storefronts crammed with repeated flag motifs on mugs, plates and trays. The velour clothing looked cheap and tatty.

A conservative at heart, I felt more comfortable around the corner in Liberty's Tudor-style premise on Great Marlborough Street. The wood timbers that are the hallmark of the Tudor period, came from two old British men-of-war. Bolts of their trademark cotton prints and Morris patterned materials lie under carved walnut beams and chandeliers. Liberty's had set the trends in home decoration right from its 1875 opening on Regent Street. Their carpets and china from the Orient drew an arts clientele including Rosetti, Morris and Burne-Jones. But it was their designs on fabric that most influenced the aesthetic movement with Art Nouveau swirls in greenery- yallery tones. Unable to afford one of the heavy silk scarves that every Sloane Ranger tied under her chin, I headed to the housewares' floor.

Their kitchen gourmet department was ahead of its time. European implements of good design made from quality materials, heavy striped butchers' aprons, sturdy chopping blocks, wooden stirrers, mortars and pestles, pottery and coloured glassware, all displayed on antique fixtures. David bought a brass-handled corkscrew to open the dinner wine and to make an essential start on a basic travelling utensil kit. I bought a wooden pair of ridged butter hands, a mezzaluna and a mortar and pestle. Traditional kitchenwares break down my resistance precisely because they represent a homey, secure family environment where an imaginary grandmother shows me how to chop herbs, pound garlic and hold the wooden forms in my small hands to fashion elegant balls of ridged butter for the Limoges butter plates at the dinner table. Pure fancy.

# HERBED BUTTERS

*A variety of fresh green herbs can be preserved frozen in butter with other seasonings, ready to swirl into a sauce or top meat and vegetable dishes.*

## Ingredients
1/4 pound of unsalted butter for each herb you chose
1-1/2 tablespoons of just one of the following culinary herbs: parsley, sage, thyme, rosemary, tarragon, chives, mint, basil, dill, fennel (base choice on availability or need)
Depending on intended use, possible additions are minced garlic, ground pepper, or a squirt of lemon juice.

## Method
1. Bring the butter to room temperature in the mortar.
2. Wash and dry the fresh herbs. Finely mince by rocking the mezzaluna (a curved chopping blade) over the leaves.
3. Fold them into the butter and pound smooth with the pestle.
4. Spatula the mixture onto a piece of tin foil or wax paper.
5. Roll into a log and freeze. Include a whole branch for identification.
6. Cut off circles of butter to melt on grilled meats, roast chicken, pasta, steamed vegetables, fish.

Two Victorian authors introduced us to their favourite eaterie on our walk along the Strand. Their whiskered portraits stared at us from an attractive menu framed outside The Cock restaurant near the statue of the Griffin that marks the official entrance to the City. The décor seemed congenial and the prices suited our purse. As we enjoyed the meal, the maître de noticed my interest in the menu cover.

"Are you digesting the quote at the top of our menu?" *To each his perfect pint of stout, His proper chop to each.* "It's by one of our former clients, Alfred Lord Tennyson. He composed an entire poem set in The Cock when it was located across the street. Although the lines, *O plump head-waiter at The Cock, To which I most resort*, are not flattering, the proprietor presented him with one of our old tankards."

"Yes, we have read him. But to be truthful, I'm just as intrigued by the lobsters, hams and casks of ale that connect Tennyson to Dickens in the border around the menu cover."

"The Cock in the Strand had also been one of Charles Dickens' favourite restaurants. Please accept one of these illustrated menus with our compliments."

We still have the souvenir menu filed in the blue trunk in the attic.

# A PROPER CHOP

*When in England, chop generally refers to lamb because the countryside is dotted with sheep grazing naturally on lush green grass. To my mind, a plump, thick little chop is best grilled.*

**INGREDIENTS**
3 loin lamb chops per person or small rack of lamb chops
a non-smoking oil, such as grapeseed
rosemary or thyme
butter
salt and pepper to taste

**METHOD**
1. Bring the meat to room temperature before cooking.
2. Baste the chops lightly with oil and herbs.
3. Heat the oven broiler or a ridged cast iron grill pan. Trim off some of the fat from the chops to rub on the surface. A hot coal fire or barbeque would work well too.
4. Grill 5 or 6 minutes per side for the larger loin chops but only 4 minutes per side for the cutlets off the rack.
5. Remove to a warm platter.
6. While they rest, melt a little herb butter (see previous recipe on page 241) on each chop and season with coarse sea salt and freshly ground black pepper.

On the London streets of the 1960s, many retail firms from the eighteenth and nineteenth centuries still operated in or near their original premises. John Hatchard opened his legendary book store at 173 Piccadilly in 1797. Renowned authors continue to do book signings at the current 187 Piccadilly location. Several books that we purchased there influenced the direction of our lives - Henderson's recently published biography of William Morris, a Beatrix Potter children's book about retailing, *Ginger and Pickles*, and an 1869 *Mrs. Beeton's Household Management*. They each still offer inspiration.

Lock and Co. have been selling top hats and bowlers to gentlemen, whose heads were measured in a metal clamp to guarantee a perfect fit, from their small Regency premise at 6 St. James's Street since 1764. At Lobb's, the shoemaker, they kept your size on record by making a wooden model of your feet. The streets of central London were lined with small shops catering to specialty needs right through Victoria's reign until the arrival of the department stores curtailed much of their trade. In spite of radical economic changes, shops such as Lock's and Trumper's of Curzon Street, catering to gentlemen's personal needs, still exist to supply you with a badger hair shaving brush. David was able to buy a bottle of wine from the firm that had supplied the poet Byron (probably shipping cartloads at a time over to his flat in Albany).

A time-traveller from 1850 could stroll into James Smith and Sons Umbrellas (founded 1830) with a broken spoke and get it repaired, just as we did in 1968. He would feel at home among the handsome wooden fixtures, the continuity of stock and the respectful tone which bolsters staff morale and soothes the customers. They were pleased to do a complete new cover on a handsome gold-knobbed Victorian umbrella frame and handle I had picked up at a flea market.

"We can assure you, madam, you won't be ashamed to carry it when we have done the work." To shop in these nostalgic premises is to make a journey back to a time when retail combined elegance with service. Their secret lies in specialization.

One morning in December 1968, we were coming out of Hatchard's bookstore when a horse-drawn carriage pulled up a little further along Piccadilly and two be-wigged gents in eighteenth century costume stepped out and entered Fortnum and Mason's. This daily ceremony was to remind Londoners that Mr. Fortnum and Mr. Mason still sent wines, hampers and quality goods around the globe, as had been their custom since 1707, when William Fortnum, one of Queen Anne's footmen, opened the store.

The Old Curiosity Shop, Little Nell's place of business in Dickens' novel, claims to be London's oldest shop, built 1567. We walked round to see if it was still operating on its original site, Portsmouth Street near Lincoln's Inn Fields. It is. Literary fame can boost retail longevity.

The elegant glassed arcades of specialty stores, connecting prime shopping streets, were built during the nineteenth century. In the Burlington Arcade, which runs between Cork Street and Piccadilly, along the side of The Royal Academy of Arts, iron lanterns hanging from a high curved ceiling, cast light on a parade of fashionable shoppers, as they did on Charles Dickens when he met his friends here 150 years ago. The Piccadilly Arcade, a 1910 extension of the Burlington, continues this covered shopping lane south to Jermyn Street, verging into St. James Palace environs and exclusive clubland. This was the area the perfumer, Floris chose when he came from Majorca to set up shop in 1730. It continues to sell scents on Jermyn Street. Versions of these elegantly proportioned street arcades are making a comeback as upmarket malls.

Tourists rush to the dining room of Ye Olde Cheshire Cheese, to get their Dr. Johnson fix. To feel more like locals, we climbed to the upper room where the Rhymers' Club, including Yeats and Oscar Wilde, used to sit around the black barrel tables. During a traditional roast beef dinner at this 1667 tavern, we thought about the staying power of the businesses we had visited the last few days. They certainly hadn't been in it for the quick kill. We wondered if public taste had become fickle to the extent that longevity was no longer a small business possibility. Samuel Johnson's black oak booth in The Cheshire Cheese was the ideal spot for these ruminations. The barmen and waiters, still served in white hose and patent shoes with buckles, as they had done under fifteen sovereigns. We wondered if the current monarchy would survive as long as this restaurant.

Queen Boadicea and Big Ben

Produce stall in Portobello Market.

## Chapter Thirteen

## LONDON'S MARKETS

*It was odd to see the White Elephant table set up over the tombs
in St. Martin's crypt, people leaning over each other,
picking through old hats and sweaters for a bargain.
Journal entry, London, November 17, 1968*

Unlike the van, the bed in the Cranley Gardens apartment accommodated our full length. We were not early risers during our time there. Too late to experience Covent Garden Market in full fig - between six a.m. and eight a.m. Actually, between three a.m. and four a.m. was the hour when most of the produce for the entire country traded hands in this enormous wholesale market. It had started as a kitchen garden supplying herbs, vegetables, fruit and flowers to the monks of Westminster Abbey as early as the twelfth century. At that time it was called Garden of the Abbey and Convent. Covent is a derivative of the Norman French, couvent. I got in touch with the Abbey and the office told me that a bouquet of herbs traditionally has been sent to Westminster through the years, in recognition of that early bond. Over the centuries a strong community spirit developed among porters, vendors, and grocers, whose families handed down their place in the market to the next generation. Markets are my weakness, especially one that swirls around an Opera House. Vendors hawk peaches to sopranos; butchers rub shoulders with ballerinas in the local pubs. A heady camaraderie crossed all social classes in this corner of the city that embraced publishing houses, theatres and cabbages. Medieval chaos and colour characterized the stalls right up until the last turnip was sold in the 1970s.

The Floral Hall is mourned as my greatest loss. I experience it only through written descriptions of oval wooden baskets lined with lacy ferns, tightly packed with dozens of pink, apricot and cream English rose buds. We didn't even make it down in the evening to spot Eliza Doolittle's descendant offering her nosegays of violets to the gents coming out of the Opera House. Today this restored building's soaring steel arches have been repainted white and now you can sip flutes of champagne at intermission under the great glass dome that once covered the daisies.

Late one morning, as a worker was sweeping up the cabbage leaves, I did catch a bit of the periphery action. He told me to go down the lane that borders the flower market. As it was a few weeks before Christmas, this side lane was fragrant with seasonal greenery - holly, ivy, mistletoe, and boughs of fir and cedar. The old lady who sold me a sprig of holly for the top of our plum pudding, said that what she liked best about the market were the special seasonal smells.

"Right now dearie, if you get around early when they're unpacking the crates, you'll get a real whiff of dates and figs, not to mention the baskets of tangerines, each wrapped in silver paper, so as it can be presented as a gift." Silvers were traditionally tucked into the toe of a stocking.

# CLEMENTINE/MANDARIN/TANGERINE SAUCE

*The substitution of clementine, mandarin or tangerine adds piquancy to the usual orange version and recalls the old vendor who looked for one wrapped in foil in the toe of her Christmas stocking.*

### INGREDIENTS
For cranberry-clementine sauce which should be prepared the day before the turkey:

12 ounces fresh cranberries
3 clementines or tangerines or 2 mandarins which tend to be larger
1 cup of sugar
1/8 teaspoon each of ground ginger and cinnamon

### METHOD
1. Wash and dry the cranberries and fruit.
2. Cut clementines, skin on, into halves and then quarters.
3. Remove seeds.
4. Whirl the cranberries and citrus fruit in the processor until very finely chopped.
5. Sprinkle on 1/2 cup of sugar and the spices. Incorporate.
6. Transfer to a covered glass bowl and refrigerate overnight.

The annual stuffing and accompaniments for our roast turkey has been influenced by London's markets. Parsley, sage, rosemary and thyme are included in the stuffing, as they were in the early kitchens of Westminster.

Between the stone columns of Inigo Jones' piazza, net sacks of onions and potatoes were stacked. Carts and carters jostled amicably with toffs in evening dress in the wee hours when everyone crowded the local pubs. In 1970, this pulsing heart would celebrate 300 years beating in the centre of London. And a few years later the entire operation would be removed to Nine Elms in the suburbs. Now café chairs and tables replace the sacks of onions stacked between the columns and street entertainment has replaced the hawkers.

Although local small provisioners met all of our needs, we couldn't resist London's street food markets that year. They instilled a passionate commitment that has prompted us to champion our local markets here in Ontario. Virginia Woolf in her diary chose the word "cheapness" to describe the Berwick market, noted for its consistently low prices, six days a week. The vendors here cleverly fill tin buckets with produce, be it bananas or onions, and set an attractive price on the lot. These brilliant stalls of oranges, eggplants and berries have the advantage of being set in front of the foreign food shops of Soho. From the open doorways, wafts the scent of garlic-stuffed olives, freshly ground espresso and pungent parmesan cheese. One of my favourite Italian delicatessens, Lina Stores Ltd., still sells freshly made pumpkin ravioli a few steps from Berwick Market.

An established Italian grocer near Berwick Market.

# HOME GROWN PUMPKIN RAVIOLI

*This recipe stands or falls on the freshness of the ingredients. The pumpkin was one of the small pie varieties grown in our community garden plot. You could substitute a dark orange variety of squash. I wanted to go in the direction of savoury rather than spicey which is too reminiscent of pie. So I turned to the herb garden rather than the spice cupboard. Italian herbs - fennel, sage, flat leaf parsley, basil - just one tablespoon each of minced fresh leaves are used. Do not try this with dried herbs. Cubes of frozen turkey stock from the Thanksgiving bird were reduced for the sauce. Other poultry stock could be substituted. No fresh sheets of pasta I have tried are as thin as Lina's; so I chose to use won ton wrappers. They hold together beautifully. Marco Polo brought pasta back to Italy from his 1293 voyage to China. They had been using it for over two thousand years.*

**INGREDIENTS**

For the filling:

2 cups of pumpkin purée

2 tablespoons chili oil or olive oil infused with a bit of dried chili

5 tablespoons of grated Parmigiano-Reggiano

1 tablespoon each fresh leaves of sage, basil, Italian parsley, fennel frond or chives all finely chopped

1 tablespoon grated lemon zest

a few scrapings of nutmeg

1/2 teaspoon salt

2 tablespoons finely ground almonds

a package of 3 inch square or round thin won ton skins
white of one egg

For the sauce:
1 cup of poultry or vegetable stock
1 shallot finely minced
6 tablespoons of butter
2 tablespoons finely chopped fresh sage
2 tablespoons Reggiano-Parmigiano grated
garlic chive blossoms if in season make a fine garnish, or use chive stalks

## Method
1. Preheat oven to 375F.
2. Line a baking tray with foil or parchment paper.
3. Cut the pumpkin into quarters. Remove seeds.
4. Brush the inside with a little oil. Olive oil infused with chili seeds punch up the blandness of the purée. Bake for 1 hour to 1-1/2 depending on size and thickness. Pumpkin should be soft.
5. Scoop flesh into a fine sieve set over a bowl. Press out moisture then let drain.
6. Whirl all of the filling ingredients in a processor or sieve together through a food mill.
7. Bring a stock pot with water to a boil. Melt some butter in a large au gratin dish.
8. Brush eight won ton skins with egg white on one side. Place a tablespoon of filling in the centre of each square. Press top sheet around the filling sliding your fingers out to the edge in all directions to make a tight seal.
9. Using a spoon/strainer lower several ravioli into gently boiling water. Lift out after 3 minutes. Strain and transfer to the dish of warm but-

ter. Brush lightly with melted butter on top. Cover with foil while you proceed to make another batch. You may continue in this manner until the filling is used up. If you do not intend to cook all of the ravioli, crimp them between 2 sheets of foil and freeze flat for another occasion.
10. Reduce oven temperature to warm only.
11. Prepare the glazing sauce by sautéing the shallot and sage in a bit of butter. Add the stock, and reduce to a syrup consistency.
12. Baste over ravioli in the pan. Re-cover and warm through for 5 minutes.
13. Serve 3 or 4 to each person sprinkled with freshly grated cheese in warmed rim soup plates.

Garnish with long chive stems.

Halibut in a fish stall on a London street.

Professional suppliers of culinary equipment wisely locate on the fringes of market areas. Leon Jaeggi is a supplier of catering equipment to neighbouring Soho restaurants, London's top hotels and Her Majesty the Queen. The place remains a treasure trove of serious Swiss copper. Graduated sizes of tall stock pots, brass-handled saucepans, fish poachers and preserving kettles were lined up along their shelves. It took me a few minutes to realize that this was not a museum exhibit. All this handsome copper was for sale. At that point, we had neither the space, knowledge or money to take advantage of their extensive stock; but the first year we were in business, I brazenly strode into this Shaftesbury Avenue premise and asked them to ship an order of Swiss catering copper to a new small kitchen shop in Canada. To my delight, they did exactly that without fuss.

Every morning we got into the habit of attending a different street market to kick start the day. We tramped through aisles of cattle hanging from hooks at Smithfield meat market, as restaurateurs and butchers loaded their square baskets with cutlets and innards wrapped in brown paper. We marvelled at the skill with which the porters at Billingsgate fish market balanced crates on flat hats that looked like someone had sat on them. This market, which had operated on the same site for over six hundred years, has outgrown its original Victorian hall and now stands on a thirteen acre lot facing the Canary Wharf Tower. The site of Leadenhall Market is reputed to have sold poultry since the fourteenth century. This lofty Victorian iron arcade has protected a food market in the heart of the financial district since the 1880s. On our most recent visit to London, businessmen in dark suits and ties, were picking up a fillet of sole or a couple of chops at the well-stocked provisioners to carry home for supper.

Fruits and vegetables have been sold on the site of the Borough Market for over one thousand years. The first vendors set up their stalls right on London Bridge, the only bridge that spanned the Thames at that time. Goods had been bartered on the banks of the Thames by farmers even before the Romans established their trading stronghold at this site. Since the nineteenth century the traders have set up shop under the railway arches of London Bridge. Near the turn of this millennium, the increasingly food-conscious Brits tarted up the market which has expanded to mythic proportions. The Euro Chunnel makes it possible for suppliers to come from the continent with their specialties. Organic farm produce from across the channel as well as from all parts of Britain, now pulls in a discerning crowd every weekend.

When my niece, was working at St. Thomas Hospital on the banks of the Thames, she sent us a report on this truly super market:

*THE BOROUGH MARKET..........what a feast for the senses.....it is ginormous. Piles of bread, any shape, size or flavour. Stacks and stacks of cheese rounds the size of transport wheels that stood probably about 12 feet high. Wild boar bacon, fully feathered pheasants hanging from their necks next to furred rabbits hanging by their feet. You have to be there, smelling, touching, tasting, like I will be every Saturday I'm in London.*

— Jennifer

*November 16, 1968*

As we were on a tight budget, street flea markets were a more sensible source of holiday fixings for our flat than Harrods. You turn history over as you rummage through the scrap heaps, especially in a city like London, one big market, recycling the flotsam of generations. At Portobello Market, one stall was piled with a brass and copper representation of the last two hundred years - Edwardian andirons, Prussian helmets, Georgian candlesticks, Victorian kettles and Art Nouveau door plates. A copper saucepan with a riveted brass handle seemed a bargain at two pounds [$5]. A notation in my journal states that it was intended for French stews, an encouraging culinary progression from my sad Windsor efforts of just a few months previous. Further up the north end of the road, carts were piled with bric-a-brac, plastic madonnas, plaster dwarves, a jumble of cultural icons that crossed all social barriers. The coup of the day was the discovery of a sixpence barrow filled with old kitchen implements,

"Your choice madame. Just a sixpence for this glass jelly mould." At that rate you could equip a kitchen for a pound or set yourself up in business for ten.

Crowds surge up Middlesex Street in the East End on Sunday mornings to experience real Cockney salesmanship at Petticoat Lane. Sets of dinnerware, nylon stockings, stuffed toys, all crammed in barrows down both sides of an already narrow street rule out freedom of movement. The energy from sheer numbers pushes you along past hucksters twirling butcher knives like jugglers as they keep up a raucous barking,

"Only ten shillings. Come on, you won't forgive yourself if you miss this chance."

The East End still showed the effects of heavy bombing. Buildings behind the market stalls were partially demolished shells. Cheap blouses were hung from corrugated tin hoardings. The imagination and gumption that could turn a wasteland into a thriving centre for business appealed to my sense of thrift. Regular shoppers at "the Lanes" usually treated themselves to a dish of jellied eels and a glass of fruit wine. Since this was our first visit, we just watched the locals gobble the eels while we sipped an unadventurous cup of tea.

Near Southwark Cathedral, the Caledonian Market just off Bermondsey Street was offering acres of antiques. Dealers had been trading amongst themselves since dawn, but we were content to find a few holiday accessories. A six-bottle crystal cruet set, with all of its stoppers, would take pride of place in its silver holder on the festive table. An odd pale pink and green china clock with art nouveau styling caught David's eye. The young stall proprietor was quick to yell out, "Yours for ten bob!" At that price he had a deal. It would sit on our mantle in Cranley Gardens surrounded by greeting cards from Canada. Underneath a wheel barrow, a large Victorian print of a little girl being pulled off her stool by a naughty small white dog lay discarded. No one objected to us tucking it under our arms. Under layers of varnish, it was dated 1886.

On a sunny Saturday before Christmas I hopped onto a #53 bus for the long ride to Greenwich on the trail of a street market a friend had told me was in Blackheath. It was difficult to locate until a young boy from a baker's shop directed me to a parking lot behind the pub. There were some fifty stalls all offering a decent selection of reasonably priced goods. I asked a young chap the price of a wooden butler's tray and folding stand. He said he thought it would be one pound but would check with his pal. Meanwhile I bought a round oriental table with bone and pearl inlay. The price on the walnut butler's tray was confirmed at one pound – so I handed over the note and figured it would make a great drinks table. Jumping onto a bus with a table tucked under each arm was a challenge amidst the Saturday before Christmas crowds. But that back platform on the double-deckers is a godsend and the conductor was helpful if slightly bemused.

Chapter Fourteen

## CHRISTMAS IN LONDON

Under the decorated tree beside the altar in St-Martin-in-the-Fields,
presents had been donated for the needy of this core parish.
One of them bore the eloquent greeting:
To a small boy at Christmas,
With Love.
Journal entry, London, December 25, 1968

London in December of 1968 was shrouded in a black Victorian cloak, the legacy of centuries of coal fires. From Big Ben to the Tower, we viewed the streets through fog-coloured glasses. Early dark nights and heavy smog made us as appreciative as the Druids of a festival to break the bleak mid-winter. A copy of "What's On in London" helped plan a week's entertainment and sent us over to the British Museum to view the Sutton Hoo burial treasures, a hoard of 8th century Anglo-Saxon artifacts, including bronze bowls, cups and cauldrons. For once our predilection for checking out the refreshment facilities was justified. As we carried a tray of warm currant scones across the museum tea room, we passed Dr. LeMire, my professor of Victorian literature from the University of Windsor. He was on sabbatical, staying in a flat in Bloomsbury with his wife and children. In the reading room of the British Mu-

The English lion in Trafalgar Square guarding the giant Norwegian fir in front of the National Art Gallery.

seum he had just completed his book on William Morris and had started two others. 1968 was a rich year for Morris fans. Henderson's handsome biography had come out; pre-Raphaelite velvet robes and long hair were in fashion; you could still buy rolls of Morris wallpapers printed from the original blocks at Sanderson's off Oxford Street. We planned to take the new Victoria Underground line to its northeast terminus of Walthamstow, the village where Morris was born and grew up.

When we came up at the end of the line, we were in a small village rather than the city. The menu in the window of the White Castle Restaurant on Hoe Street, reflected the bargain prices outside of London:

>   minestrone soup....10 pence
>   steak pie with cabbage....3 shillings 6 pence
>   sultana pudding with custard....9 pence
>   and probably the last time we had tea for....5 pence

# SULTANA PUDDING WITH CUSTARD SAUCE

*In remembrance of this excellent meal, here is my version of the pudding. I am certain William Morris would have tucked into this one. Boiled or steamed puddings have been a national dish for centuries, a sustaining dessert to suit the climate. The pudding basin can be set in a two-tier steamer or on top of an inverted smaller bowl or trivet in a large pot. Just make sure that water can be kept on a gentle boil at least 1/3 of the way up the sides of the basin.*

### INGREDIENTS

1/4 cup brown sugar
4 tablespoons golden syrup
1/2 cup unsalted butter plus some to grease bowl
2 large eggs at room temperature
1/2 teaspoon pure vanilla
3/4 cup self raising flour, sifted
1/2 cup sultanas
1/4 cup chopped citrus peel

### METHOD

1. Grease a 6 cup pudding bowl with butter. A pudding bowl is narrower and deeper than regular mixing bowls. Set the steaming water on to come to a boil.

2. Cream the butter with the sugar, by hand or by machine. Blend in the golden syrup.
3. Beat the eggs in a small bowl. Stir in the vanilla.
4. Alternate amounts of flour and egg mixture into the creamed butter and sugar. Blend well after each addition to ensure a creamy smooth batter.
5. Fold in the sultanas and peel.
6. Spoon into the prepared basin, smoothing the surface. It should be no more than 2/3 full.
7. Cut a circle of greaseproof paper to fit over the top then cover it with foil, crimped around the edges and tied on with string. A sling of folded foil placed under the basin is handy for lifting it out when hot.
8. Bring the water back to a boil, moderate the roll to gentle bubbles. Keep a kettle of water on the boil to top up the steamer about every half hour.
9. If kept on the boil with a tight lid the pudding should be cooked in about 1-1/2 hours. Lift the basin out, remove the covers. The surface should look firm and feel spongy. Investigate with the end of a small sharp knife. Run a long blunt knife around the sides of the bowl if it is ready to turn out.
10. Let the pudding sit on a trivet for at least half an hour so that it will keep its shape when cut.
11. This amount will make enough to serve eight people. Pour warm custard sauce over each slice and charge them 9 pence each.

Prepare a steamed pudding on a dismal, chilly day. The kitchen will fill with heat and fragrance.

Seasonal celebrations in London were very low profile compared to the madness that rages for several months before Christmas in North America. Commercial restraint created a pleasing pace to the season. Only Regent Street was to be decked with Christmas illuminations and we were the only spectators standing near Liberty's department store at 5:30 p.m. on the first evening in December, eager for the switch to be thrown that would light the arches of garlands strung across this main street. No one else seemed to care. The large department stores' grand concession to seasonal shopping was the announcement: "We will remain open one hour later on Thursday evenings to accommodate Christmas shoppers."

Even in London times have changed.

Freed from artificial pressures we were able to get closer to the spirit of the season than in any subsequent year. What impressed us most was the smallness of everything, a scale that was appropriate to the place. Instead of parking lots crammed with dozens of eight foot felled firs, a row of tiny healthy spruce trees, braced in crossed sawn logs, stood against the green grocer's carts at our corner. As we walked along Downing Street one frosty morning, we noticed the Public Work's truck was delivering Harold Wilson's pint-sized Christmas tree and a bunch of holly to Number Ten.

The largest tree in London is sent annually by the people of Norway to stand in Trafalgar Square, a dramatic thank-you to the British people for their wartime sacrifices. One night we joined the scarlet-robed choir from St Martin-in-the-Fields, gathered around the life-size manger scene for the blessing of the crib which had been set up under this giant fir. One of the congregation handed us a lit candle and encouraged us to sing carols with them to the spirited accompaniment of the Salvation Army Band.

An ornate Victorian poultry store with Christmas fowl on display.

Tiny Tim Christmas trees set the tone of the celebrations that year.

*December 23, 1968*

It was time to give some serious thought to the purchase of provisions and presents. A fondness for nostalgia reinforced by annual viewings of Alastair Sim in *A Christmas Carol*, had primed us for a Dickensian celebration. This special December in London, we had attended the public events and entertainments that represented a Victorian Christmas, now it was time to assemble the elements required for a proper Bob Cratchit Christmas dinner. It was amazing that so little had changed in over one hundred years. There still were traditional toy shops selling peg dolls and hobby horses. The fir trees lined up on the sidewalk were the size of Tiny Tim. Poultry still hung on hooks outside the shop window and holly could be bought from street sellers.

William Morris is said to have spent most of his income on fine books and fine wine, so I followed suit and spent a day on Piccadilly Street buying presents in Hatchard's Bookstore and Fortnum and Mason's Food Hall. Their Olde English Plum Pudding came in its own traditional white pudding bowl with the name of the firm engraved on its side.

An article by the wine writer in the Sunday Times had recommended a Bordeaux Graves 1962. We could just afford a half bottle to stand on the newly acquired drinks table. Jackson's on Piccadilly supplied the cranberry sauce and we picked up the turkey and vegetables from our local provisioners. Two pounds of cheddar cheese had been sent to us from David's sister in Canada, courtesy of the now defunct Eaton's gift catalogue. Mrs. Bacon handed us the parcel with a sniff,

"Rather like sending coals to Newcastle I would have thought."

I upheld the honour of our country's cheddar with the retort,

"This cheese is very special. The cows' diet includes maple syrup."

But we still did not have a platter for the bird. One of the officials at the Geffrye Museum had recommended a street market on Club Row where they dispense with the formality of stalls or barrows. Everything is spread out on the ground like a Middle Eastern bazaar. The bus dropped me at Bethnal Green, where the market was recognizable by the cages of cats, parrots, goldfish, and squirrels. Just off Brick Lane is the infamous area where the rag-and-bone men sell whatever they've managed to gather through the week. Most of the stalls were offering modern mass-produced junk and jars of pickles. At the bottom of the market proper was the field as described by the museum guard. It was a walled bombsite, two feet deep in mud, on which had been spread sheets of linoleum so that the old timers could set out their paltry offerings. Puppies were shivering in straw-lined boxes, eager for homes. It was late in the day,

December 24, and pickings were slim. Just as I was despairing of a dramatic presentation for our turkey, a large white oval platter appeared like a benediction from the bog. An old bloke huddled against the wall told me to help myself and pressed a box of used clothing on me which he didn't want to be bothered carting away. I refused his kind offer of a vintage wardrobe, but accepted the platter with thanks and seasonal good wishes.

Elegant decorations befit Regent Street.

Dr. LeMire had telephoned on December 23 to invite us to his apartment in Bloomsbury for a Christmas Eve drink. It turned out to be as significant an evening for us as it had been for Ebenezer Scrooge. If you exit from the Russell Square Underground Station intending to reach Dr. LeMire on Mecklenburgh Square, you cross one of the streets that Percy Bysshe Shelley lived on briefly. On the same square as my professor's apartment, Virginia and Leonard Woolf lived the last years of her life. Facing his building is Brunswick Square where almost every known Bloomsbury writer and artist lived at one time or another. A block away on Great Ormond Street, William and Jane Morris spent the first few years of their married life. To tie it all up into one big Christmas present, one side of Mecklenburgh Square runs into Doughty Street where a museum to the writer marks the house in which Charles Dickens worked on four of his novels. The location of this apartment had the correct Feng Shui for a synthesis to take place.

When we arrived, Dr. LeMire and his wife were putting a stuffed toy into each of their two small children's socks, which had been hung on the electric heater with care. Mrs. LeMire was furiously knitting a skirt to cover one doll's bare bottom. As she worked away, Dr. LeMire passed the Scotch and cheese and biscuits. They had been too immersed in research and family affairs to do the town, so we dominated the conversation with summaries of the season's plays and entertainments. Mrs. LeMire had read Jane Austen's complete works several times and was pleased to hear accounts of our visits to her homes. Their apartment house was full of overseas profs and their families. Mrs. L. mentioned receiving a bowl of Sudan salad from a neighbour and soon we were joined by a Bermudian couple who were pleased that it had begun to snow, as their small boys had never experienced a white Christmas.

Dr. L. proposed that he prepare crêpes Suzette for the company, as was his custom on this special night. The group of us from different continents gathered around the chafing dish to watch him roll the thin pancakes, which he had just made in a small cast iron pan, soak them in cognac, then briefly flame in the chafing dish. Simple ingredients with proper equipment created a festive atmosphere. As Dr. LeMire transformed flour and milk into a celebration, I realized that food preparation would be part of my future. While we ate, we discussed Morris' belief that the kitchen was the only room in the house where objects could be beautiful as well as useful. Kitchen utensils are one of the few household furnishings which have retained simplicity of design without becoming obsolete.

When Dr. LeMire noticed my interest in his cookware he made a fateful suggestion. "You are staying in South Kensington? That is quite near Elizabeth David's Kitchen Shop on Bourne Street where we bought this pan. Have a look at a few of her cookery books. She has been credited with injecting the colours of a Mediterranean ratatouille into the dun postwar British stodge and has presented Britons with their first specialty kitchenwares store just a few years ago."

Her insistence was on authentic ingredients and simple cookery, "carried out with care and skill, with due regard to the quality of the materials, but without extravagance or pretensions."

A unique brand of kitchen alchemy was at work in that small Bloomsbury apartment on Christmas Eve. Spirits from my past, present and future had been represented around the chafing dish fire to work their magic again on a snowy Christmas Eve in London, joining opposing aspects of our personalities into a coherent whole. Or in Elizabeth's words,

*Quick transformation of the simplest ingredients.*

Another ghost we were not aware of was circling Mecklenburgh Square that Christmas Eve. R.H. Tawney, a professor at The London School of Economics, had lived in four different addresses around the square until his death in 1962. A Labour government advisor, and one of the leading thinkers of the twentieth century, he is most noted for his books, one on the rise of capitalism and particularly one titled, The Acquisitive Society. He had us pegged.

# CHRISTMAS EVE CRÊPES

*The batter for dessert crêpes should be lighter and sweeter than for savoury crêpes. Once blended, the batter should be refrigerated for several hours, or ideally, overnight. This gives the flour time to dissolve completely. Use a six inch cast iron skillet with sharply slanting sides for ease of heating and turning. I prefer coating it with grapeseed oil rather than butter as it does not smoke or burn.*

**INGREDIENTS**
For the batter:
3 eggs
1 extra yolk
1-1/4 cups of sifted instant light flour
3/4 cups milk
3/4 cups water
1 tablespoon sugar
3 tablespoons orange liqueur
2 tablespoons melted butter

For the sauce:
1/4 pound of unsalted butter
3 tablespoons granulated sugar
grated zest of an orange and of a lemon
juice of these fruits

3 tablespoons Grand Marnier liqueur

3 tablespoons of cognac

**METHOD FOR BATTER**
1. Beat the eggs and yolk in a medium bowl.
2. Stir sugar into flour and water into milk.
3. Alternate whisking the dry ingredients with the wet into the eggs.
4. Add liqueur and melted butter.
5. If you prefer, all of the above can be mixed in a blender.
6. Let it rest in the refrigerator at least several hours.
7. Bring to room temperature before cooking.
8. Heat the small iron pan coated with some oil.
9. Ladle in about 1/4 cup of batter, swirling it around to cover the surface of the pan.
10. Once the batter has firmed, turn it over using a thin spatula.
11. You may store or freeze crêpes separated with pieces of wax paper.
12. If using right away, fold them over twice making small triangles.

**METHOD FOR SAUCE**
1. A copper chafing dish makes the most elegant presentation, but the finishing sauce can be prepared in a skillet at the stove and then poured over warmed crêpes on each plate.
2. Cream the sugar with the butter.
3. Zest the citrus fruits and stir into the butter.
4. Melt this flavoured butter in the copper pan or skillet.
5. Squeeze the juice from the fruits into the pan.
6. Warm the folded crêpes in this sauce.
7. Heat the liqueurs in a small warming pan and ignite using a long match.
8. Pour over the crêpes and serve immediately.

*December 25, 1968*

The bells do ring on Christmas Day in the morning, from just about every one of the city's churches. As we leaned out our window, the black-robed verger of St Paul's Church, Onslow Square, slipped into the bell tower to contribute his few peals. Pigeons took flight and the air was heavy with hymns of praise.

David had bought me a comprehensive book on Christmas traditions in other times and other countries. Inside the front page he had composed a sonnet to our special Christmas this year in London. His gift book on sports cars kept him amused while the turkey roasted, the pudding steamed and we fed shillings into the meter for the gas fireplace. The author of my book had wisely refrained from delivering a homily on the evils of commercialized Christmas and stressed instead the value of indulging in sentimentalities once a year. So we pulled out the stoppers and thoroughly wallowed in soup, turkey, brussels sprouts, mashed potatoes, gravy, sherry, nuts and Canadian cheese arriving finally at the pudding. F & M had made it thick with fruit and soaked it in rum and brandy. No concern about the quantity of flour in this one. David poured a small bottle of cognac over its hollied crown, applied a match and we clapped as a circle of blue danced around the pudding and sputtered up its sides.

Christmas dinner at our flat.
The Victorian painting and cruet set - both street market finds.

# FIGGY PUDDING

*One Christmas while out carolling, we sang "Bring us some figgy pudding" on the steps of a men's rehab home. One of the chaps yelled out "What the heck's a figgy pudding?" It was a question I had often asked myself. So I researched it to beyond the 16th century in old English books and put together a version with ingredients that appealed to me and served it to the carollers when they sang this same carol the next year in front of our house. If your market has supplied you with a box of fresh figs, they will not need to be softened.*

**INGREDIENTS**
2 cups of dried figs
1/2 cup of sherry or cider
2/3 cup chopped blanched almonds
1/2 cup sultanas
1/2 cup shredded suet
1/2 cup fine bread crumbs
1 cup self rising flour
1/2 teaspoon salt
1/2 teaspoon cinnamon
10 scrapings of nutmeg
grated peel from 1/2 lemon
2 large eggs
1 tablespoon lemon juice
1 cup of molasses

**METHOD**

1. Remove the hard stem knob from the top of the figs. Cut each fig into 16 small pieces.
2. Place in a covered bowl with the cider to sit several hours or overnight.
3. Drain the figs before mixing them with the sultanas and chopped almonds.
4. Combine the suet with the bread crumbs.
5. Sift the flour with the salt and spices. Toss it in with the suet and crumbs. Add the fig mixture.
6. Whisk the eggs. Stir in the molasses, the lemon juice and peel.
7. Stir the wet ingredients into the dry to make a sticky mass.
8. Turn the mixture into a buttered heat resistant bowl that is large enough to allow 1/3 headroom for expansion.
9. Cover the bowl with parchment paper and foil. Crimp around the edges and secure with twine.
10. Set on a trivet in a steamer of boiling water which comes 1/2 way up the side of the bowl.
11. Simmer for 2-1/2 hours.
12. Lift out the bowl and let cool to room temperature before running a knife around the sides to turn out the pudding.
13. Serve with thick cream flavoured with liqueur of choice.

# TINY TIM'S ROAST GOOSE

*It has become our tradition to roast a goose every Christmas in memory of the Cratchit family in Dickens' "A Christmas Carol". Scrooge instructs a boy to run around to the local poultry shop and buy the big one hanging outside the shop on a hook. We drive nine miles out of London Ontario to a fresh poultry farm where we buy the smallest goose.*

### INGREDIENTS

Amounts in this recipe are for an 8 pound goose.

For the stock:

This can be made the day before roasting so that you have some to moisten the stuffing.

Reserve the fresh liver to make a small pâté, and put the other innards that come with the bird (heart, giblets, neck) into a stockpot with the following:

1 stalk of celery with leaves, cut into 1 inch chunks

1 medium carrot, cut into pieces

1 medium onion, inner skin on, studded with 4 whole cloves

1 bay leaf

3 stems of fresh parsley

1 clove of smashed garlic

1 bouquet garni of parsley, sage, rosemary and thyme

5 black peppercorns

1 teaspoon salt

5 cups of water

**METHOD**

1. Bring all ingredients to a boil. Adjust heat to simmer, covered, for one and a half to two hours.
2. After it has cooled, strain liquid through a sieve into a smaller saucepan. Discard solids.
3. Taste for seasoning and boil down to intensify flavours as required.
4. Refrigerate the stock overnight.

**INGREDIENTS**

For the stuffing:
1 cup of pitted prunes
1/2 cup Calvados apple brandy
3 tablespoons sugar
2 cups of cubed multi-grain bread
2 cups of peeled apples in 1/2 inch cubes
2 tablespoons butter
1 cup of chopped onion
1 cup of chopped celery with leaves
1/4 cup of chopped parsley
2 tablespoons of fresh sage, minced
1/2 teaspoon of fresh rosemary
1/2 teaspoon of thyme
1 teaspoon salt
3/4 cup of goose stock

**METHOD**

1. Sprinkle sugar over prunes in a small saucepan. Pour Calvados over them and simmer to make a bit of a syrup. Let cool. Cover for several hours or overnight.
2. Cube about 4 slices of whole grain bread and place in a large bowl.
3. Warm butter in a skillet. Gently sauté chopped onions and celery.
4. Stir in the apple pieces.

5. Toss the prunes and their syrup into the bread cubes with the herbs and seasonings.
6. Add the contents of the skillet.
7. Pour in enough stock to barely moisten the mixture.
8. If made in advance, refrigerate until you are ready to stuff the bird.

INGREDIENTS

For roasting the goose:
8 pound goose
1/2 lemon
salt

METHOD

1. Dry the bird, and bring it to room temperature. Remove excess fat from around the neck and cavity. Rub a cut half of lemon over the skin. Pierce skin with a fork all over the surface. Sprinkle inside and out with salt to taste.
2. Preheat oven to 425F.
3. Use a large basting spoon to scoop 1 cup of stuffing into the neck opening, 3 cups into the main cavity and the remainder into a small casserole to bake separately.
4. Secure openings with small poultry skewers or sew up with a trussing needle threaded with butcher's twine. Truss legs and wings together with twine.
5. Set the goose on a low rack in a roasting pan.
6. Start in the 425F degree oven for 30 minutes. Remove to drain off fat into a jar. Reserve for frying potatoes. Set temperature down to 350F.
7. Continue roasting at this temperature for 3 hours or until juices run clear yellow when skin is pierced around the thigh. Pour off the fat periodically. Transfer the goose to a platter to do this pouring safely.
8. Remove the goose to a large platter. Cover loosely while it rests for

20 minutes before carving and you prepare the gravy.

**INGREDIENTS**

For the gravy:

drippings in the roasting pan

3 tablespoons flour

3 tablespoons sage herb butter (see page 241)

1-1/2 cups of stock

1/4 cup of port

1 teaspoon of orange zest

1 tablespoon of red currant jelly

salt and pepper to taste

**METHOD**
1. Skim any fat left in the roasting pan.
2. Set the pan over a stove burner on medium.
3. Whisk flour mixed with butter into the residue of brown bits.
4. Keep whisking as you pour in enough liquid to reach desired thickeness.
5. Add the port to deepen the flavour and enhance the colour.
6. Stir in 1 tablespoon of currant jelly and 1 teaspoon of orange zest.
7. Simmer for a few minutes.
8. Taste to adjust seasonings before serving.

Serve with par-boiled potatoes browned crispy in goose fat and red cabbage casserole with apples.

The kitchen we rented in Dedham,
where Elizabeth David's mother once prepared meals on the AGA stove.

## Chapter Fifteen

# KITCHEN AESTHETICS

*There were perhaps only two plastic-tipped spatulas in this store. All other stock was made of natural materials.*
Journal entry, Elizabeth David's Kitchen Shop, December 27, 1968

When Elizabeth David's Kitchen Shop re-opened after the holidays on December 27, we were the first customers through the plate glass door on Bourne Street. This innocent morning's shopping expedition turned into a lifetime obsession. In today's world of mass merchandising, compulsive consumption, stores the size of football fields and just about as interesting, it takes an act of faith to believe me when I say that Elizabeth David's Kitchen Shop was a poetic experience. The symmetry, colour harmony, lure of the exotic, impacted on a visceral as well as a visual level. We were about to meet a woman who had converted the lyricism of her writings on food into a concrete aesthetic business, a Keats in the kitchen.

The bold, burnished name on the large window, "Elizabeth David's Kitchen Shop Ltd.", her public statement of personal commitment, floated above a long, hefty pine table like those we had admired in old country house kitchens. Rising from the centre of this table was a soaring tower of tin charlotte moulds, ice cream bombes, rounded French wire storage baskets arched above graduated sets of metal saucepans, a symphony of wire and metal. I coveted one of the flying egg baskets.

In the mid-sixties, cookware was generally relegated to a few dusty shelves at the back of a hardware store, or piled in its original cartons in the housewares section of the department stores. There was no romance to this category of merchandise. "Definitely bottom drawer", as classified by staunch British matrons. E.D.'s bare-boned selection of her favourite equipment stripped away the extraneous wrapping and let the essential worth of simple lines and natural materials speak for themselves. You would be hard pressed to find a logo or promotional labelling in sight.

The entry room was as chaste as a temple. There were no signs, stickers or advertisements. Cast iron brackets held white marble shelves on a wall that was the faint de lavé bleu of sun-bleached French shutters. This upstairs area showcased marble cheese and pastry boards, pale buttery beige earthen terrines, ham stands and fish poachers. The cool cleanliness and simplicity of this entrance room reminded me of the white purity I had admired in the traditional dairies and pantries we had recently visited and which had been a part of Mrs. David's childhood.

Downstairs, the white brick walls were warmed by French terra cotta casseroles stacked in graduated sizes, marmites and diables with their promise of long–simmered stews. She had ferreted out traditional factories in the French countryside who could supply these sturdy brown glazed pots, ideal for braising. These earthenware casseroles represented an earlier way of cooking, a less hurried approach to food preparation. Many years later, David and I met one of these suppliers in Burgundy who remembered sending crates of his bowls and jugs across the channel to Mrs. David's store. "She knew what she wanted; she knew how to use them and she instructed others." One of those others was Chuck Williams of the vast Williams-Sonoma chain of cook shops.

Against a black brick wall, a series of industrial steel shelves displayed elongated heavy white china fish platters and nesting sets of white au gratins and ramekins. Piles of flame enamelled cast iron cookware added a splash of brilliant colour. A caned walnut bentwood chair held a nest of collapsible wire salad baskets. Beige or grey stoneware jars bristled with bouquets of wooden spoons, forks and stirrers. A small commode chest, painted electric blue, held aluminum saucepans. Every item had been personally chosen for its practicality then arranged by a curator with a critical eye for detail.

Stella Gwynne, Elizabeth's mother had dealt in antiques for many years and may have provided the pine table and small commodes that were used so effectively for display in the store. A dealer at Bermondsey antique market recalled selling pieces to Stella, daughter of the first Viscount Ridley, who would strip the varnish from pine furniture herself before it became all the rage. He said that she had the knack of zeroing in on the worthwhile pieces. Perhaps Elizabeth had inherited this knowing eye for quality. Before the war, Stella had moved into the Old Grammar School in Dedham, a place big enough for living quarters, an antique shop, storage and refinishing space. By another of those twists of fate, David and I stayed in the residential part of these premises years later, totally unaware at the time of its connection to E.D.'s family. It was in this house that we came face to face with our first Aga stove, an old one that Elizabeth may have cooked on during a visit to Dedham. I honed my game-cooking skills by bunging partridge, pheasant and venison into the always warm ovens.

At the time of her death in 1992 it was accepted that Elizabeth David, O.B.E. had single-handedly changed the eating habits of the country. Her collections of Mediterranean, French and Middle Eastern authentic recipes read more like lyrical travel memoirs than strict lists of ingredients and instructions. Because her writings are based on personal experiences from her own kitchens in Greece, Italy, France, India and Egypt, the people and the places are brought into our kitchens, cuisine du terroir. She introduced sensuous dishes made with olive oil, garlic and herbs into the austere post-war British fare. In the middle of the coldest winter Britains had known, after five years of war and rationing, she dared to write about the apricots, almonds and lemons of the South. A small shelf under the stairway of the shop held a collection of her cookbooks that converted simple recipe ingredients into sunshine. With a sense of venturing into the unknown, I bought French Country Cooking. Our early collections of recipes for convenience foods had been jettisoned with the plastic geraniums back in Windsor. This purchase represented a brave leap into the world of authentic ingredients.

The logo on E.D.'s brown paper bags was a black silhouette of a French marmite, a tallish casserole with side handles. Since all of the merchandise carried the proprietor's seal of approval, I purchased this trademark pot, confident that it would guarantee the success of the beef daub, which I had chosen to mark my maiden voyage into French cooking. A trusted piece of cookware can become the talisman that bolsters the enthusiasm of an amateur cook. No amount of confidence in the equipment however could transform the cubes of stewing beef and cooking wine I threw into that pot for several hours. I had neglected E.D.'s other dictum, "Buy only the best ingredients."

A humble collection of utensils that fetched a
large amount at the auction of Elizabeth David's effects.

# BOEUF EN DAUBE

*Many years passed before I got the daube to be edible. The search for organically raised beef is worth it for flavour and tenderness.*

*One of Elizabeth's large cast iron enamelled Dutch ovens is an alternative to the earthen pot which cannot take stove-top heat.*

**INGREDIENTS**
To serve eight:
3 lb. rump roast
a piece of pork rind or belly
1 tablespoon tomato paste
1 cup rich beef broth
1 cup mixed green and black pitted olives
3 cloves of garlic, crushed
1 teaspoon thyme
1 bay leaf
3 sprigs of fresh parsley, chopped
3 carrots
4 cups of gnocchi
parsley for garnish

For the marinade:
2 onions, chopped
2 stalks celery with leaves, chopped

2 carrots, sliced

olive oil

2 cloves of garlic, crushed

2 cups of full-bodied red wine

a bouquet garni in a muslin bag - branches of fresh thyme, parsley, 10 green peppercorns, a bay leaf

1 teaspoon salt

a strip of orange

## Method

For the marinade:
1. Sauté onions, celery, carrots until soft in the olive oil in a large Dutch oven.
2. Add garlic, herbs, seasonings, orange and wine.
3. Simmer for 20 minutes. Cool.
4. Cut beef into large 2 inch chunks.
5. Add it to the pot of marinade ingredients.
6. If beef is not covered, add more wine.
7. Cover and refrigerate overnight. Stir at least once.

## Preparation:
1. When ready to cook, heat oven to 250F.
2. Remove the beef and dry it on paper towels.
3. Strain the marinade, reserving the liquid, discard the solids.
4. Melt the pork belly enough to provide a film of fat to cover the bottom of the Dutch oven . Heat to medium. Remove pork and slice into chunks.
5. Brown the beef chunks in two batches if necessary. Remove to a plate.
6. Deglaze the pot with beef broth and any juices which have accumulated on the platter of beef.
7. Return the beef and sliced pork to the pan.

8. Add strained marinade . Top with more wine to cover if necessary.
9. Bring to a simmer on top of the stove.
10. Put into a low oven for three hours, tightly covered. A piece of foil laid over the mixture and held in place by the lid keeps moisture in during the long cooking process.
11. At this point you could cool several hours or overnight, skim off the fat and reheat for the finishing steps of this dish.

### Finishing the Sauce
1. Bring pot back to a simmer.
2. Stir in the tomato paste.
3. Peel and slice 3 carrots.
4. Cook gently with the sauce and beef.
5. Stir in the olives.
6. Season with salt and ground pepper.
7. Serve with boiled gnocchi and a garnish of parsley.

During our remaining weeks in London, I was drawn back to this store several times to buy a natural bristle pastry brush, a set of brass weights for the old scale we had found, Scandinavian birch twigs for whisking lumps out of sauces and a small catalogue to pore over while we were travelling in the van across Europe. But the real reason for these return visits was my need to satisfy a yearning for what it all represented - order, beauty, creativity, respect for the basics of cooking.

On one of these occasions, I was thrilled to be served by the presiding spirit herself. There was no mistaking the tall, elegant lady, whose self-confidence signified her upbringing. Stylish but comfortable in black slacks and top with a wide low-slung leather belt, grey hair pulled into a low chignon. After a friendly chat about our common mistrust of electical devices, she sold me the complete boxed set of her cookbooks. The introductory chapter on batterie de cuisine justified my previously incomprehensible urges to buy old bits of kitchenwares. You could read these books as though they were literature. I put aside George Eliot and turned my attention to poulet aux herbes. A domestic heroine had replaced the literary ones.

In February of 1994 David and I were staying at a cottage in England where the morning paper announced that Phillips of Bayswater would be auctioning the contents of E.D.'s kitchen. The items would be on view for five days leading up to the sale. I arrived at the auction house on a quiet afternoon two days before the sale. The clerk gave me a catalogue with the logo of the marmite I had bought on its cover. One hundred and seventy-seven items were listed in catagories that included ceramics, books, metalware, furniture. In the oblong showroom the nineteenth century pine farmhouse dresser and several other open hutches lined the walls as they had done in E.D.'s own kitchen, their shelves filled with the pleasing but unassuming arrangement of simple domestic objects. Turkish coffee pots, ceramic cannisters, enamel bread bins, now all waiting to fall under the auctioneer's gavel. The selection was so personal, so well-used, that this felt more like a leave-taking than an auction.

When this collection had furnished her unorthodox kitchen in Halsey Street, the pine table with ladder-back chairs around it, had sat at the centre of her universe. Surrounded by open hutches crammed with utensils and still lives of fruit in handsome serving dishes, she had researched old culinary techniques, experimented with recipes, written her manuscripts then shoved all of the paperwork to one end of the table to entertain friends. The clerk in charge of the preview allowed me to photograph this table which now held a deep brown stoneware crock full of wooden spoons.

Everything went for triple the expected prices. On the day of the sale I inched up the stairway along with a record one thousand bidders, to crowd into a room intended to hold four hundred. Devotees were sitting on the floor in the yogi position at the front of the dias. I perched on top of a stool near the door to observe this ultimate justification for embracing a career in kitchenwares. Wooden spoons assumed the status of crown jewels. The most basic utensils became valuable collectors' prizes simply through their association with E.D. Even the auctioneers were amazed at the incredibly high price bid for chipped saucepans and worn chopping boards. It was a rather austere collection. She had resisted the glamour of modern appliances and denounced the synthetic in housewares as earnestly as she had avoided it in her recipe ingredients.

Signed copies of the cookbooks I had originally bought at her store fetched $2,000. They were not purchased by a collector, but by an admirer who said she would don white gloves each time she used them. The bidders were after relics that they trusted would work culinary miracles. The man who paid $1,000 for five wooden spoons said he hoped that some of the magic would rub off. The writer who had gently scolded us in her books for grumbling about having to purée food through a sieve, was vindicated posthumously by the bidder who paid over $300 for a few of her wire sieves. Prue Leith, a contempory food writer and restaurant owner, was thrilled to get Elizabeth's pine kitchen table on which she had written her books longhand and rolled her pastry dough. When some flat graters fetched three times the price of an electric food processor, the revolution she had begun in our kitchens had indeed come full turn.

One item which her four surviving nephews held back from the auction for personal use was Aunt Liz's orange enameled crêpe/omelet pan – exactly like the one in which Dr. LeMire had made those fateful Christmas Eve crêpes and the one item that would have tempted me to enter the bidding stakes. Just as well it wasn't available.

At least I had witnessed the gavel fall on the end of an era. That threshold we had crossed in 1968 had been the prototype for all the specialized cookware departments, now proliferating in drugstores, specialty stores and supermarkets. And it was the model on which we had based our business. E.D. had supplied us with more than inspiration. When we returned to England from our tour of Europe in late May 1969, with the impulsiveness of the ingenue, I telephoned Mrs. David to ask for her sources of supply, completely unaware of professional confidentiality that protects the exclusivity of product lines. She responded with kindness and generosity, providing me with the names and addresses of British manufacturers of specialty bakeware and woodware with whom we subsequently dealt for over thirty years. When I pressed her for a few French suppliers, she hesitated and said that we'd have to learn French and scour the countryside before we'd be able to negotiate in that country for the specialized types of products she carried. We worked on that challenge over the duration of our career.

One of E.D.'s dictums was that a civilized lunch should always be accompanied by a glass of wine. Since I had not been able to honour her memory with a purchase from her estate, I headed straight to Justerini and Brooks wine store for a bottle of our favourite Chianti. That night we toasted a gracious mentor in a manner which would have met with her approval.

In front of Hampton Court Palace, New Year's Day, 1969.

## Chapter Sixteen

## A BRAVE NEW YEAR

*Log fires flamed in the centre of the hall,
boars were carried in from the roasting kitchens,
as Elizabeth I watched Shakespeare perform in a new masque
Journal entry, Hampton Court Palace, January 1, 1969*

A visit to Hampton Court Palace on New Year's Day got 1969 off to a royal start. The train from Waterloo Station took only thirty minutes to deposit us at the end of a bridge facing Henry VIII's famous court. A summer sail down the Thames would have been ideal, but there was compensation for arriving here in winter. The red brick palace stood starkly bare in a grey landscape. No other day-trippers encroached on our sense of a private viewing. I raced down the long stone corridors past fifteen hundred rooms, pretending to be Anne Boleyn pursued by Henry, in search of the nucleus of fifty rooms that made up the great Tudor Kitchens of Cardinal Wolsey. As minister to Henry VIII, he was the previous owner of this palace and his kitchen complex here outdid the one we had seen at Christ Church in Oxford. Thomas Wolsey, Archbishop of York, Cardinal and Chancellor, failed to deliver Henry's divorce papers, but left England with some impressive kitchens.

A pleasant palace guide from my father's birthplace, Airdrie in

Scotland, explained that the kitchens did exist, but were not at this point completely restored. He gave us a tantalizing tour of the main wine cellar and massive kitchen, telling us that fourteen other food storage and preparation areas led off this central hub. On this New Year's Day, 1969 I made two resolutions: to return for a tour of the refurbished Great Tudor Kitchens and to design one like it for our own use.

In 1997, I made good on the first resolution. While visiting a friend who lived a few miles up the Thames from Hampton Court, she suggested that we walk down the river path to see the spring gardens and the newly restored Tudor Kitchens. A colourful brochure directed us to Henry's wine cellars, constructed in 1536. Three hundred aged black wooden hooped barrels were resting peacefully between white stone pillars in a room as serene as a vault. Further instructions led through a series of butteries, serving hatches, baking rooms, and a wonderfully fragrant spice storage room. In the game larders, we noticed the hooks from which deer hung until they were well and truly high. There were separate rooms for poultry and fish preparations. Finally we reached The Great Tudor Kitchen of Cardinal Wolsey. Here was a space for serious food preparation on a grand scale. Henry's massive roasting spits turned enough boars and deer to feed 1,200 people in the winter court. When Elizabeth became Queen, massive banquets prepared by a staff of 200 would have been brought to the Great Hall above where Shakespeare was presenting his latest masque. The huge whitewashed stone arches, slate floors and vaulted ceiling made a room noble in its simplicity. No knick-knacks dotted the wide expanse of white brick. Its severe plainness was honest and functional. I have yet to see a modern dream kitchen in any designer magazine as impressive as Cardinal Wolsey's 1500s masterpiece.

We made good on the second New Year's resolution when we converted a high-ceilinged Massey-Harris tractor warehouse at our Talbot Street store into our version of a Tudor kitchen, to be used for cooking classes. We had the brick walls whitewashed, the stone floor painted, and a tiled work surface laid over a series of brick arches that formed a work counter. As in the Hampton Court kitchen, large earthenware pots, giant porcelain mortar and pestle, glazed stoneware jugs and cast iron cauldron stood on the wall-mounted plank shelving. An AGA stove replaced the wall of flames.

A rose garden lay beyond the arched glass doors.

The kitchen of our Talbot Street Store,
a renovated repair shed for Massey Harris tractors.

A Winter Stew Festival, with celebrity chefs, champion ice skaters, and politicians in the store kitchen that was inspired by Cardinal Wolsey's Tudor Kitchen in Hampton Court Palace.

# WINTER STEW FESTIVAL

*Cooking demonstrations took place in this space on a daily basis. As its potential was realized, it hosted Callebaut chocolate making classes, political rallies, local heritage conferences, and the opening of a winter stew festival by Canadian ice skaters, cultural equivalents of Elizabethan masques. Our greatest satisfaction came from customers who gazed at this space and said,*
    "*I could live in here.*"
    *King Henry VIII wooed Anne Boleyn with a gift of venison, the meat of kings. This is a stew you can serve to local royalty.*

### INGREDIENTS

For marinating 1 pound of cubed venison meat:
1 teaspoon juniper berries
1 teaspoon green peppercorns
1 teaspoon thyme
1 tablespoon fresh parsley
1 branch of rosemary, about 3 inches
1 bay leaf
1/4 cup of brandy or cognac
1 cup of red wine (Merlot or Shiraz)
1/4 cup of balsamic or red wine vinegar

**FOR THE COOKING PROCESS:**

1 pound of venison meat serves four
1 cup of coarsely chopped onions
2 whole garlic cloves, crushed
2 tablespoons olive oil
1 cup of beef broth
1/2 cup of cubed carrots
1 cup of cubed turnip
1/2 cup of cubed parsnips

**FOR FINISHING:**

1 cup of small cremini mushrooms, quartered
1/2 cup of fresh whole cranberries
2 tablespoons of red currant jelly or Cumberland sauce
a parsley garnish

**METHOD**

For the marinade to be done the evening before cooking:
1. Mix all of the marinade ingredients together in a stainless steel bowl.
2. Add the cubed venison. Cover and allow to steep refrigerated for at least 4 hours, preferably overnight.
3. Stir when possible.

**FOR THE COOKING:**

1. Preheat oven to 350F.
2. Heat the oil in a cast iron enamelled dutch oven.
3. Drain the meat, reserving the marinade.
4. Brown meat in batches, removing to a warm bowl when browned.
5. Quickly turn the onions and garlic in the same pot, scraping up any residue to coat them.
6. Return meat to this pan. Pour on 1/2 cup of the marinade. It is not necessary to remove all of the herbs and seasonings. Bring to a boil

for a minute.
7. Add 1 cup of beef broth. Return to the boil.
8. Cover with a large piece of foil that will reach down close to the surface of the stew and fold a bit over the sides of the pot. Hold it in place with the lid. This conserves the heat and prevents evaporation of the liquids.
9. Set in the lower half of the oven for half an hour or simmer carefully on stove top.
10. Stir in the cubed root vegetables. Allow another half hour slow cooking.

**FOR FINISHING THE STEW:**
1. Stir in the quartered cremini mushrooms and the cranberries.
2. Simmer for 15 minutes.
3. Stir in 2 tablespoons of red currant or other berry jelly. Since orange and spice flavours compliment venison, Cumberland sauce is a possibility if on hand.
4. Sprinkle with parsley.

Serve with small boiled potatoes or a wide egg noodle. Brussels sprouts are a good vegetable.

Before we could sail for the continent, we had to get the flotsam we had accumulated removed from Mrs. Bacon's apartment and stored somewhere in London until late spring. She made it clear that she did not run a left luggage depository. The street markets of London had enticed us to become the owners of a serious collection of old kitchenwares. Impossibe to trek around Europe with that lot in the van.

Just as we despaired of finding a storage spot, a friend from Windsor wrote a timely note urging us to visit her aunt and uncle in Blackheath. When I called, Mrs. Charman graciously invited us to Sunday lunch. They lived in a lower flat near Greenwich facing the heath where anti-aircraft guns had been set up during the Second World War to deter German bombers on their way into London. In one of the side tragedies of war, the back of their house was demolished. As enemy aircraft didn't like returning loaded with ammunition, they would drop it around Blackheath.

Lt. Colonel Charman was in his eighties when we visited but he was still teaching at a boys' school after having put in full terms of duty in two World Wars in India, Mesopotamia and other corners of the Empire. He and Mrs. Charman had met in India, where she had grown up in the hills, a true colonial daughter. They were engaged when she was only sixteen and she could not remember a time when she had not been married. She was a practising artist, still attending classes in pottery, collage and metal enameling, on a daily bases.  Two of her oils had been hung in the Royal Academy.  She caught David's interest with her account of meeting a grandson of Joseph Severn, a close friend of the poet John Keats, who had done a drawing of the poet on his deathbed.

After a delicious roast lamb lunch we had coffee, then only a short while later preparations were underway for tea. Mrs. C. rolled a trolley into the sittingroom, all three levels filled with mince and jam tarts, thin slices of brown and white bread and butter, sponge cakes and muffins. She was an excellent cook and hostess who shared our interest in collecting unusual culinary accessories. Six months after our return home, she sent me a recipe for Highland Flummery, a Scottish version of syllabub which she found pasted onto the bottom of an antique pewter Flummery bowl she had found in Blackheath market. Her accompanying sketch shows a circle of spoons hanging from little hooks around the rim of the bowl for dipping and sipping.

# HIGHLAND FLUMMERY

*An original eighteenth century highland 'receipt', mailed to me with others in Mrs. Charman's handwriting, for four servings. I have cut it down to make two tall thin glasses or four half glasses served with fresh fruit, as it is so rich. In Scotland it is often served at the turn of the year. Thus for us it celebrates the time we met the Charmans.*

### Ingredients
1/2 cup of whipping cream
2 tablespoons of heather honey
2 tablespoons single malt whisky
1/2 teaspoon lemon juice
toasted finely ground almonds (or oatmeal)
1 cup of fresh strawberries, raspberries, blueberries or blackberries

### Method
1. Warm the honey just to melt until runny.
2. Whip the cream until stiff.
3. Gradually stir the honey, liquor and lemon juice into the cream.
4. Fill the bottom half of each glass with fresh fruit.
5. Spoon the cream mixture on top.
6. Sprinkle on the lightly toasted garnish.
7. Serve with a spoon and a wafer biscuit or shortbread.

Grand Marnier or Amaretto are equally delicious if you are celebrating at a different time of year.

Their offer to store our trunks while we were in Europe was very generous, considering their limited space. Now we just had to find a trunk and cram everything into it.

A block down from us on Old Brompton Road was an auction house where I spent a couple of hours in hopes that a trunk would be offered. Sets of Limoges, Spode and Wedgewood went for a fraction of the prices charged at the retail china store I had worked in as a student. Serving pieces and decorative items sold in job lots for a few pounds. One item in the pile might be worth double this investment. The auction house offered free first-hand experience in assessing values and product demand. But it did not turn up a trunk.

We scoured some street markets, like Leather Lane near the Holborn Viaduct, but ended up in the impressive Silver Galleries under the arches. Not trunk territory. Finally took the plunge and bought a new aluminum one, whose purchase I justified by imagining it back in Canada at the foot of a brass bed with a fur rug slung over it.

An evening was spent wrapping up bits and pieces that were scattered around the flat, and packing the trunk with twice as much as it could safely hold. This was to be a trial run, as we could never haul it filled down four flights of stairs. The plan was to unpack it, cart everything to Blackheath in the van, and repack the trunk at the Charman's apartment.

*January 11, 1969*

Up at eight a.m., out by nine, at Mrs.C's by ten, with all our boxes and bags ready to reload into the empty trunk, which was safely locked with the key left miles back in Cranley Gardens. We resisted blaming each other for forgetting it on the table. Resigned to the fact that the trip would have to be made again the next day, we set off to explore Greenwich. After a tour of the village we cut through the park where the first Queen Elizabeth romped, passed the church in which Henry VIII was christened, and clambered over all three decks of the Cutty Sark. Nearby is Sir Francis Chichester's Gypsy Moth IV, the small craft which carried him solo around the globe. I don't imagine he was laden down by trunks.

The following day when I returned with the key to pack the trunk, Mrs. C. let me chose one of her paintings of flowers to place on top of our things as a memento. There was no reason for their excessive kindness to us other than the generosity of their personalities.

*January 15, 1969*

The next morning we managed to pull away from the shelter of Angela Bacon's roof by ten o'clock and follow her suggested route out along the Cromwell Road to Southampton. We arrived at the dock simultaneously with the *Patricia*, the car ferry that would carry the van and us to Spain. She was five hours late due to force nine gales in the Bay of Biscay and a spot of engine trouble. None of this news was encouraging.

The Q.E.2 was sitting innocently at the Cunard berth, unaware of the furor created by her incompleteness and mechanical faults. It was permissible to mount the visitors viewing platform and walk the length of this beauty within touching distance of the railings. We could spot the unmistakable swagger of the Glaswegian shipbuilders, still buzzing around their crowning glory, getting her ready for the first voyage. It had been built in John Brown's shipyard, across the street from my birthplace. Now we were both ready to sail from the UK.

The Q.E.2 being outfitted in Southampton prior to going into service.

*January 16, 1969*

Our cabin on the Patricia was commodious, usually occupied by four people, panelled in natural wood with blue upholstery and long blue curtains on fat wooden rings to draw across the bed. If previous sea voyages were any indication I'd be pulling them closed soon. The continuous buffet in the dining room would not be visited.

For the next twenty-four hours we were barely out of the blue bunk. The sea drew us in and threw us out relentlessly. On the second day, as the Patricia slipped around the coast of France, I optimistically struggled to the reading lounge with my journal to review and assess our personal progress over the last six months.

Britain had been an immersion course in unique commercial architecture and imaginative retailing. In spite of our admiration for these concepts, we were still intending to be academics on our return to Canada; blind to sign posts that were now pointing in a different direction. PhD applications were to be forwarded to American Express offices along our route. In spite of this tenuous string of forms, the bookish world was loosening its hold. On the continent another sea change would take effect. The urge to create would be quickened as the Mediterranean sun brought physical senses to life. The logistics of heading in a completely different direction still lay outside our grasp. To be frank, we were enjoying ourselves too much to think seriously. Like everything else on this trip, the wherewithal would appear when we least expected it - on a Spanish beach.

# Chapter Seventeen

# SOL Y SOMBRA

> The roads between cities gave us glimpses of an ageless country: clusters of adobe huts, hard packed mud from door to door; women drawing water from village wells in huge clay jars or washing their clothes by a small stream.
> Journal entry, between Madrid and Toledo, January 23, 1969

Time to put aside the books and join the Spanish olive pickers. The van was developing an interior layer of green mould to match the moss clinging to us. Prime Minister Trudeau had motor biked around Spain with a Spanish copy of Cervantes in his back pack. The least we could do was forget Jane Austen and English gentility for a while. Goodbye tea rooms, pubs, antiquarian bookstores, museums, the cosseting world of the mother country. Embrace a country whose character is in crowded back lanes and markets; immerse in the smells, tastes, and warm sun. It would be too much to expect that we'd learn how to cook in a month, but we could hope to come to terms with raw ingredients. On the continent, we would find out what to do with kitchenwares we had collected in Britain.

*January 17, 1969*

As we polished off our last English breakfast in The Patricia's Ascot Restaurant, the black mountains of Spain loomed off starboard. Their silhouette was more rugged and formidable than the friendly hills of the St. Lawrence or the Clyde. The port of Bilbao seemed darker and more foreboding than the familiar English villages of Mr. Badger. Basque men wore black berets as they walked with heavy-set women draped in perpetual mourning. No lights shone from the secretive cave-like entrances to the small stores. We had entered a foreign territory whose first impressions were sombra rather than sol.

The pass up through the mountains was a sharp gradient requiring four or five hairpin turns to bring us to the top of the plateau. Over a virtually empty highway, a relentless rain was hammering this plain in Spain. Tottering brick huts with red tiled roofs huddled around the bell tower of a mission, waiting for John Huston to stride on to this set and start directing.

We booked into a hotel in Burgos and took a tour of the cathedral. The height, the scale, the chiselled stone, impressed with a cold grandeur. Even God seemed more austere here.

Breakfast the next morning sweetened the scene. Warm, soft rolls, dusted with icing sugar, served with cups of very rich chocolate, so thick we spooned it up like pudding. The French poet, Gide, caught the experience perfectly:

*To drink a cup of Spanish chocolate was to hold all Spain in one's mouth.* Ingredients on this side of the channel had an integrity, an intense, essential flavour.

A huge sow was rooting at the side of the road leading out of Burgos to Madrid. Old steam engines halted traffic as they pulled their loads nineteenth-century style. Stunted scrub growth dotted undulating plains. We climbed a range of black snow-capped mountains to a height of 4,000 feet, until Madrid became visible on its mile-high Castilian plateau twenty miles away.

*January 18, 1969*

The Hotel Carlos V was hidden down a maze of narrow back streets, crowded with unfamiliar smells, noises, and faces, but well-worth the search. This being January, the Spanish felt comfortable with hot, steamy rooms, full of large, imposing pieces of walnut furniture, tiled interior courtyards and shuttered windows with balconies. Within forty-eight hours, we became continental converts, assuming that bedrooms would come with balconies and bidets from now on.

A simple evening stroll became an immediate immersion into Spanish culture. At six p.m. on a Saturday evening, you do not amble; you wedge into a moving throng and are carried by a tide of Madrilenos taking their evening passagerio through the streets of their city. This wave of activity continues until after nine p.m. Rest stops were permissable at cafés and tapas bars - two novel institutions for us, but eagerly adopted as stop gaps since dinner was not available until after ten p.m. The Latin tempo was such that we could never out-sit the neighbouring tables at a café. With one cup of espresso, they could claim a seat for hours. Our internal clocks needed to be re-set.

It was easier to linger in the many tapas bars that lined the streets near Plaza Santa Ana. In one of the prettiest, we nibbled surrounded by tile tableaus of Andalusia, eyes on the marble counters watching the barman bring out an endless variety of little plates.

Tapas means covers, a reference to slices of bread or ham once used as covers for wine glasses, to keep out flies as patrons lingered around a bar. Now it refers to the numerous dishes offered as appetizers. Partnered with sherry, a sampling of these tempting snacks can make a meal. And the bars offered a dizzying selection. Long curved black marble counters were lined with over thirty shallow round earthenware dishes containing marinated mushroms, shrimp in garlic oil, salt cod in sauce, small meatballs with peas, black olives, red pepper strips, snails, baby eels, marinated mussels, small squid in their ink, sausages with broad beans. According to the barman at Cerveceria Aleman, Hemingway loaded his plate and his glass as frequently as legend would have us believe. Standard pub fare had been usurped. We piled samples onto little white oval platters and stood amazed as dormant taste buds were finally aroused by hot chillis, pickled capers, oregano, olive oil and garlic. The routine of three squares a day was replaced by taste samplings of Latin culture.

# CHORIZOS WITH GREEN PEPPERS

*We adapted many of the tapas into meals by adding a dish of rice or a crusty loaf. Their simplicity and skillet preparation made them perfect for camping stove meals. This amount should make a tasty tapas for four or a side dish with pasta or potatoes for two.*

### INGREDIENTS
1/2 pound of uncooked or cooked chorizo sausage (hot garlic will work)
3 tablespoons olive oil
1/3 cup of chopped Spanish onion
1/3 cup of sweet green pepper, deveined, seeded and chopped
2 teaspoons of jalapeno pepper, seeds removed and finely chopped (wear plastic gloves!)
8 black Spanish olives, pitted and halved
1/3 cup of red wine
1 tablespoon Dijon mustard

### METHOD
1. Poach the sausage (if uncooked) in water, left whole in its casing for 30 minutes, turning three or four times. Drain and slice into 3/4 inch pieces.
2. In the same skillet, brown the pieces in 1 tablespoon of oil, about 10 minutes.
3. Remove sausage and set aside. Add more oil to sauté the vegetables.

Add the olives and wine.
4. Simmer almost to the point of evaporation.
5. Return the sausage to the pan and stir to coat in the sauce.
6. Stir in the Dijon mustard. Do not expect a liquid. You need a coating that can be picked up on a toothpick if necessary.

Our hotel restaurant introduced us to paella. The fame of this national speciality had not reached Ontario in the 1960s, so the half hour preparation time piqued our curiosity. A carafe of white wine and a basket of soft rolls helped until the paella was placed in the centre of the table. Black mussel shells, a red langosta claw and curled pink shrimp peeked out from a bed of yellow saffron rice. Fresh peas and strips of red peppers added dots and dashes of colour to the composition. Lemon wedges gripped the edges of the dish. We were still sucking grains of rice out of clam shells at eleven p.m.

There are as many variations of the ingredients for this national dish as there are Spaniards. In Valencia, where we saw two men carrying a five-foot diameter pan of paella through the streets, they tend to be purists and not mix land and sea ingredients. Other regions include pieces of chicken, discs of spicy chorizo sausage and bits of rabbit. The rice absorbs all of the flavours and the saffron sharpens the blend. Traditionally, Spaniards prefer to cook this dish out-of-doors, over an open fire.

On a subsequent trip, we had the good fortune to experience the preparation of a gigantic paella over a wood fire on the sands of the Mediterranean by an ex-marathon runner named Ayo. His athletic prowess was put to use as he scampered along the beach collecting wood and ingredients for his production. The theatre involved in the preparation was heightened by the suspense of the serving logistics. Although this flat iron pan spanned more than five feet, a loyal clientele of fifty strong were waiting to dig in. It was tantalizing to watch this tall, athletic Spaniard in swim trunks, kindle the firewood, toss the rice in oil, add the freshly caught shellfish, pour on the broth, quicken the flames, deftly dance around the perimeter, without having any assurance that a portion would be left for us at the end of it all. Anxious diners sat at tables bordering the sea, swilling Sangre de Torre, devouring baskets of crusty bread, while trying to catch Ayo's eye. The regulars, who came every Sunday after mass, were served first; the Virgin and her heavenly host made sure that the plates of the faithful got filled. Saintless, we could only rely on chance. The level in the pan was dangerously low. But magically he scraped up enough clams and saffron rice to make two Canadian Presbyterians happy.

A recent television travel programme on Spain featured Ayo, forty years later, still making paella at his now extensive beachside restaurant and making a hundred or more diners very happy.

Back home, we've served massive paellas under a grape arbour for a birthday dinner, and stirred one intended to feed two hundred wedding guests in a field during a rainstorm. The preparations never seem to be without drama. Considering the current charges of obesity-causing ingredients being levelled at the fast food industry, I am amazed that some enterprising restauranteur has not set up a string of Paella Party Parlours. Pizza dough would be replaced by healthful rice, and the ingredient range from vegetarian to seafood to chicken offers a broad taste spectrum. The only possible objection could be that you have to sit down and eat with a fork. But this has long been considered an aid to digestion.

The traditional outdoor method of preparing paella over a wood fire.

# VAN PAELLA PARTY

*We began to research the specialty equipment necessary to make paella in the van. It boiled down to procuring the proper size paellera. These flat iron pans with looped side handles hung arched over the entrance to hardware stores in sizes ranging from frisbee to satellite dish. Our gas camping stove could accommodate one up to twelve inches in diameter. A recipe was pasted on to the pan, but we tended to rely on market availability of ingredients as we travelled along the coast.*

### Ingredients
Ample for 4 servings:
2 chorizo sausages
leg and breast of chicken
1/2 cup of olive oil
2 cloves of garlic
1 large local, fresh tomato or preserved tomato if they are out of season
1-1/2 cups short grain rice
3 cups stock - chicken or seafood or vegetarian
1 teaspoon pure saffron
ground pepper and salt
1 cup of fresh peas
1/4 pound of whole, long green beans
1 sweet red pepper
1 kilo mussels
1/2 pound of large shrimp
1 lemon

## Method

1. Poach the whole sausages in hot water gently for 5 minutes to firm. Cut into 1 inch thick pieces.
2. With a sharp boning knife, remove meat from the chicken pieces. Cut into chunks, season with salt and pepper and set aside with the sausage pieces. Cover the bones with water and simmer for a light stock.
3. Steam whole green beans to crunchy tender. Rinse in cold water and drain.
4. Roast and peel the red pepper to cut into strips or use pimento strips from a jar.
5. Soak mussels in cold water. Scrub and beard them. Discard any broken or open mussels.
6. Heat oil in paella pan or skillet at least 14 inches in diameter.
7. Brown the pieces of sausage and chicken.
8. Crush the garlic cloves and add to the pan.
9. Stir in the chopped tomato.
10. Sprinkle rice evenly over the ingredients.
11. Pour 1-1/2 cups of stock into the pan. Bring to a simmer. Add the saffron.
12. When liquid is absorbed, add more of the stock.
13. Sprinkle the fresh peas over the surface.
14. Place mussels evenly over the paella.
15. Add the shrimps.
16. Cover loosely with foil to steam open. Add stock or water if more liquid is needed.
17. When all of the mussels are open and the shrimp are pink, turn off the heat.
18. Garnish with alternating strips of red pepper and green beans.
19. Cut lemons to grip the edges of the pan.

A jug of Sangria is a fine beverage to serve with paella.

We also began a search for the low earthenware bowls, called tripe dishes, in which the bars displayed their tapas. Gallerias Preciosos, Madrid's department store, seemed a likely stockist. A range of sizes was on display in the second floor kitchenwares department. Before the saleslady would sell them to us, she called up an interpreter to explain that these dishes were not ovenproof. The interpreter in turn passed on the message to the saleslady that we did not have an oven. Satisfied that the dishes would be safe with us, the saleslady sold us two. It was an impressive example of personal service. On the way back down to the main floor, the escalator stopped midway. Everything shut down at noon sharp for the four hour lunch-siesta break. We ran the rest of the way down and exited just in time, clutching our tripe bowls. On the streets, all shutters were drawn against the sun.

Enjoy paella out of doors if possible.

# MARINATED MUSHROOMS

*We christened our new tapas dishes with one of the simpler appetizers that did not require an oven. Firm, fresh, white button mushrooms work best for this dish. This amount makes an hors d'oeuvre for four.*

### Ingredients
1/2 pound of small button mushrooms
2 tablespoons olive oil
2 cloves of garlic, minced
1/4 cup of finely chopped onion
1 tablespoon white wine or lemon juice
1/4 teaspoon of celery seed
2 sprigs of lemon thyme
1 bay leaf
4 peppercorns
5 coriander seeds
1 tablespoon of cold pressed oil for dressing
1 tablespoon chopped parsley
salt to taste

### Method
1. Trim the ends of the mushrooms. Rinse them quickly in cold water, brushing off any particles of soil. Toss dry in a clean towel.
2. Heat the 2 tablespoons of oil in a skillet. Soften the chopped onion

and minced garlic in the warm oil.
3. Toss the mushroom caps in the pan.
4. Add all the herbs except the parsley. Sprinkle with wine or lemon juice.
5. Cover and set on low heat to sweat for five or six minutes.
6. Remove the cover, turn up the heat a bit, and shake the pan to evaporate some of the excess liquid that may have accumulated.
7. Transfer mushrooms and seasonings to a small round shallow dish. Pour a fresh tablespoon of olive oil over and sprinkle with chopped parsley.
8. Let marinate for several hours.

Spanish hardware stores of the 1960s were showcases of merchandising technique. The darkened entrance to those treasure caves was more alluring than any flashing neon signs. As soon as a customer entered, the store owner turned on the electricity. Admirable thrift turned into a warm welcome. Instead of the assault created by a crazy jumble of stock, order and harmony reigned. Shiny metal funnels were turned into towering sculptures, the largest at the base and the smallest as a finial on the top. Iron pans hung in graduated rows. Coffee pots stood ranked like soldiers on the shelf, spouts saluting. The stock resembled the objects displayed in the museums we had visited in Britain. Those A-shaped coffee pots with straight black wooden handles projecting midway down their sides, were exact replicas of their silver Georgian ancestors in the Victoria and Albert Museum. The clay water jugs looked like Greek amphoras. Surely those olive jars had recently been unearthed on an archaeological dig? We were gazing at pre-industrial goods being offered for pesetas to fill mundane household needs. Everything was both handsome and utilitarian. These timeless utensils had obviously influenced the merchandising of both Terence Conran and Elizabeth David. In our later business years, whenever a salesman tempted us with fripperies, the recollection of this classic, basic stock would help to preserve the purity of our purchasing.

A more far-reaching economic principle lurked on these shelves. Practically every item was stamped Made in Spain. Local factories using local raw materials helped to control pricing. Throughout our career, we lamented the dearth of small houseware items made in Canada. We bought whatever we could of the domestic product, but more and more imports flooded the utensil market every year. The situation hasn't changed. Christmas 2005, I bought some glass bottles at a store near our home in Ontario to do up gifts of homemade salad dressing. They were stamped Made in Spain.

Traffic-free Sunday was the best time to walk the city. Plaza Mayor, a beautifully proportioned historic square, was having its surface rebricked after the construction of an underground garage. Beneath its arched arcades, men were selling stamps and colourful cigar bands to ardent collectors. In past years, the buildings surrounding this square had looked down on a very different activity. Autos-da-fe (public burning of heretics) had taken place here during the Spanish Inquisition.

At the Rastro, a sprawling outdoor flea market, there were more stalls selling football cards. Perhaps it was the Spanish equivalent to scrap collecting. The market winds uphill and down over a very large area, offering old and new to throngs of buyers. Piles of brass hinges, doorknobs, lamps, copper pans and ladles, were seductive, but ignorance of the language was definitely a drawback since bargaining looked like a necessary art here.

This antique market outing introduced us to two popular local snack foods. Tortilla de patata is not related to the Mexican flour tortilla. Rather, it is egg-based, like a thick, more substantial omelette. Usually it is served cold, cut into wedges from a round plate on the bar. Since olive oil rather than butter is the cooking medium, it is not as rich as a French omelette and is firm enough to be eaten as finger food. Variations can be made with herbs and other vegetables such as asparagus.

A proud Spanish beauty.

# TORTILLA DE PATATA

*These amounts make enough to slice onto an appetizer platter with olives for eight or a luncheon serving of a quarter wedge each with salad for four. Variations with peas or peppers or ham make this an easy and filling skillet supper to prepare on a camping gas stove. You will need a 12 inch non-stick skillet with rounded sides for the tortilla to slide out. Don't be surprised by the amount of oil - it is not all consumed, but it is needed in the preparation. The vegetables fry covered in oil as opposed to the more usual sautéing in a few tablespoons.*

**INGREDIENTS**
1 cup of olive oil
4 medium potatoes peeled and thinly sliced
1 cup of Spanish onion chopped
4 eggs
10 strands of saffron
1 tablespoon chopped parsley
1/4 teaspoon paprika
salt and pepper
2 tablespoons of red pimento strips in small dice

**METHOD**
1. Heat all of the oil in the skillet over medium heat until it is hot enough to fry.

2. Add the potato slices a few at a time so that they are floating free.
3. Use a wooden or steel spatula to keep them from sticking to each other as they fry in the oil for about 8 minutes.
4. Add the chopped onions and stir the mixture for another 8 minutes.
5. Meanwhile, whisk the eggs in a large bowl with salt and pepper, saffron, parsley, paprika, pimentos.
6. Remove the potatoes and onions using a slotted spoon into a sieve which has been placed over a bowl to drain. Sprinkle them with salt.
7. Reserve most of the oil in a storage container. It is nicely flavoured for future use.
8. Add the potatoes and onions to the whisked eggs.
9. Heat 2 tablespoons of the reserved oil in the same skillet. Pour in the egg mixture.
10. Cook over med-high heat until the edges appear firm and the centre is almost done.
11. Now for the tricky part. You need to turn the whole thing over by placing a round platter, slightly larger than the pan over the top. Flip the tortilla on to it. Slide it back into the skillet uncooked side down.
12. Cook for less than 5 minutes, just to set the other side.

We serve it with a chunky tomato salsa. Accompaniments could be spicey sausage slices or cubes of smoked ham.

Another addiction we formed that day was for churros, a deep-fried crinkly cruller, hawked on the streets by cart vendors who press long ribbons of dough into portable vats of hot oil. They use a special steel tube with a star-cut metal disc on the end and force the thick dough through with a wooden pestle, similar to a heavier version of a cookie press. A Portuguese importer in London, Ontario used to supply our shop with this item. Icing sugar is sprinkled on the warm drained churros. It is advisable to have a cup of hot chocolate on hand for dunking. One morning, not so long ago, while strolling a Paris street market, we noticed a Spaniard had set up a churros stand and was doing a brisk business. Versions have appeared in local doughnut shops.

Following a concert in the Royal Opera House, we booked a table for dinner at Antigua Casa Sobrino de Botin, the restaurant made famous in the last scene of Hemingway's *The Sun Also Rises*. Since Papa had been an aficionado of authentic food, we expected a real dining experience. This restaurant, that claims to be the oldest in the world (1725), is tucked off the Plaza Mayor, exiting the Cuchilleros Arch in the original quarter of the city where the sun rarely penetrates. The novelist, Graham Greene had found his way there, so we persevered in our search. From the secretive front entrance, you can glimpse into the blue-tiled kitchen hung with copper pots, ropes of garlic and red peppers. We were led up a dark wooden staircase hung with green velvet draperies to a plank table in a niche lined with a tiled tableaux and traditional pottery wine and olive jars.

The menu was entirely in Spanish, so our choices were limited to words we could understand. Lunches in British tearooms had not prepared us to decipher a Spanish menu. Although our conservative meal of consommé, shrimp in oil, steak with mushrooms and chocolate mousse was well-prepared, it paled in comparison to the food being brought in a steady stream to the tables of more knowledgeable diners. The waiters were passing us with roast suckling pigs, their skins crisp and succulent, surrounded by roast potatoes and whole cloves of garlic on the paddle boards that had been used to slip them out of the wood-fired ovens. Steaming black cauldrons of quarter-hour soup - a seafood concoction with intriguing large shells - wafted tantalizing aromas from a fragrant broth as it passed our table. Our waiter comforted us with the promise that their sister restaurant in Toledo, L'Hostal del Cardenal, served these same specialties. We would be more menu-wise when we hit Toledo.

That was our first encounter with a whole, roasted baby pig, but it would not be our last. At least one vendor in every Italian market brought a large roasted adult pig, stuffed with sage and garlic, from which he sliced succulent servings to make panini. As he handed you this tasty sandwich he asked, Piqante? If the answer was Si, he sprinkled on more coarse salt and pepper and roasted garlic slices.

A generous friend in Canada gave me a small booklet, an original edition of Canada's first cookbook. Here is the recipe for roast pig, backwoods, 1831 style.

> Boil the innards tender, mince fine, add half loaf bread, half pound butter, four eggs, salt, pepper, sweet marjoram, sage, summer savory, thyme, mix the whole well together; stuff and sew up; if the pig be large let it be doing two and a half hours; baste with salt and water.

Our neighbourhood hosted roast pig parties in the local school yard. Coals glowed in a metal trough over which the pig was turned on a spit. We lined up, crusty Portuguese rolls in hand, waiting for a slice with crackling attached. Inspired by these experiences, we installed rotisserie hardware on the front of our kitchen fireplace and invited friends over to watch the fat crackling in the flames.

Botin Restaurant, a Hemingway haunt in Madrid.

# PIG PARTY

*A local Portuguese butcher promised to procure a suckling (very young) pig, scalded, soaked in brine and ready for roasting. A large mature pig was delivered to us the day of our party. So David cut him into two pieces (head and tail) and we spit-roasted one piece at a time. He was re-assembled on a wooden board and the seam was camouflaged with parsley.*

### Ingredients
1 small piglet - 10 to 12 pounds, anything larger will be too big, too tough and not a baby
a bottle olive oil
2 lemons
salt and black pepper
12 cloves of garlic
a bunch of fresh sage
a bunch of thyme
White wine or sherry
a red apple

### Method
1. Prepare a bed of glowing wood embers if using a live fire or set the oven to 450F. Make sure the pig's roasting pan will fit in your oven.
2. Mix the juice from the lemons with 1 cup of the olive oil and at least 2 tablespoons of coarse salt and 6 turns of the pepper mill.
3. Chop the fresh sage (about 1/2 cup). Add to above mix.
4. Peel and chop the garlic cloves. Stir into the other seasonings.

5. If baking in the oven, cut the pig all the way along the stomach to flatten so that it spreads out in one layer in the pan. Pour in enough wine to moisten the bottom of the dish. If cooking on a rotisserie, cover the ears and nose with foil to prevent scorching.
6. Rub both inside and outside with the aromatic blend. If your piglet is too big, prepare more mix.
7. Roast in the hot oven (450F) for the first hour, basting every 15 minutes using the thyme branches as a brush. Reduce heat to 350F and continue cooking for 2 more hours depending on size. Pierce fatty bubbles as they form on the skin. Brush on more oil, and seasoned wine drippings twice during baking and once at the end when it comes out.
8. Since we were doing it on the fireplace, David sewed the pig's belly together with butchers' twine, pushed the steel rod through the middle, set the ends in the rotisserie brackets and gave volunteer turners a glass of Chianti while they tended the spit.
9. Check for doneness with an instant read thermometer or by piercing with a knife to see if juices run clear.

Serve on a wooden board with a rosy apple in the pig's mouth. Yes, you cook with the head intact.

Vegetarian readers will be heartened to know that in later years I followed a strict macrobiotic regime.

A pig roasting in our
kitchen in London, Ontario.

*January 23, 1969*

Our Robarts' forms for the fall term at university had arrived at the American Express office in Madrid. Their relevance didn't live up to the moment, so we stuffed them into our bags and left the city, wrapped in mist, by way of the Toledo Bridge. Soon we were at the source of the heavy shroud that had draped Madrid on the drive out. The sun was warming the wet clay in the surrounding fields, giving the city and its environs a steam bath that slowed the driving down enough for us to absorb a landscape calculated to put us in touch with the basics. Frequent clear sunny breaks allowed glimpses into a Spain thousands of years old: clusters of adobe huts surrounded by hard packed mud; women drawing water from the village wells in large clay jars or washing their clothes by a small stream.

Only forty miles separates Toledo from Madrid, and if it had been a clear day, we would have seen this imposing former capital from a distance, sitting on its austere rocky crook in the arm of the River Tagus. As it was, we knew we had reached this fabled city when we passed the factory for Damascene work, the gold and steel industry, active here since the time of the Arabs. For centuries, Castilian, Jewish and Moorish cultures had co-existed within the stone walls of the city. We drove in through one of the historic gates, up through the tortuous winding roads to the highest point, the Alcazar Fortress, which once boasted of being the world's largest stable, capable of holding two thousand horses in its subterranean halls. It now provided a safe parking space for the van.

This was a special holy day in honour of the city's patron saint, bringing all Toledans out onto the Plaza de Zocodover in their Sunday finery. An Arab market, or zoco, had taken place centuries ago on this square. Tapestries from India, spices from Malaya, silks from Damascus, had changed hands here. A traffic policeman directed us to Les Tres Carabelas, a new hotel retaining the traditional details: tiled pictures of the Virgin and child, iron chandeliers swagged over studded red velvet chairs in the lounge. Our room held a brass bed with a separate bathroom complete with bidet. The long shuttered windows of both rooms opened onto balconies that hung over a narrow street, brilliant with hanging flower boxes. For four dollars a night, accommodation in small city hotels exposed us to an urban Spanish way of life, different from the one we would later experience in campsites.

The welcoming warmth of noon hour lured us out to bask in the curative rays of the sun, soothed by the patter of a fountain in the plaza fronting the cathedral. Restaurant Rio was near enough to our hotel to become a habit, especially as it had a congenial waiter anxious to try out his English. He happily led us through their five course service: an hors d'oeuvres platter of cold meats, creamed potato salad, olives; a small serving of clam and chicken paella; roast lamb chops and endive salad; fruit, bread and a large bottle of local wine. Hard to believe, but my journal records that we paid $1.50 each for this meal. Two elderly ladies, sharing a green litre bottle over a companionable meal at a neighbouring table, inspired us to order the large bottle of wine. Our months in England had introduced us to timid experimental tastings of a few half bottles recommended by The Sunday Times wine writer. Our occasional glass seemed faint-hearted compared to the obvious abandon of the ladies at the next table. These two healthy, happy temptresses recalibrated our wine intake. From this point on, straw-covered flasks dangled from the ceiling crossbars of the van. In the campsites, we practised squirting wine from a skin bottle through the air in an arc to our mouths.

# CREAMED POTATO SALAD

*Salads similar to this one, appear on the bars as one of the many tapas served before serious eating begins. Or in this case, as an appetizer at the start of a meal.*

**INGREDIENTS**
6 medium potatoes
salt
2 tablespoons 10% cream mixed with 2 tablespoons mayonnaise
1 tablespoon of Dijon mustard
1 scallion (green onion) thinly sliced
1 tablespoon of chopped chives
2 teaspoons of capers
2 or 3 large radishes, halved and sliced
2 garlic dill pickles, chopped

**METHOD**
1. Scrub or peel the potatoes. Boil in salted water. Drain and cool.
2. Whisk together the mustard, cream and mayo in a small bowl.
3. Stir in the scallions, chives and capers.
4. Toss the radish, pickles and potatoes together in a glass serving bowl.
5. Coat the vegetables with the sauce.

Great with steaks or burgers.

Guide books strongly recommend the panoranic view of Toledo from the terrace of the hermitage of the Virgin of the Valley, reached by the Carretera de Circunvalacion, a road which encircles the entire city following the Tagus River. On this afternoon of brilliant sun, after lunching like locals, we joined the parade snaking up the side of the hill to enjoy the scene that had inspired El Greco's *View of Toledo* now hanging in the Metropolitan Museum of Art in New York. From every prospect on the trail the city appears, perched dramatically amidst harsh brown hills framed by distant blue mountains. Ochre houses rising in tiers, crowned by the Gothic stone cathedral, loomed like a visionary island suspended between the Tagus River and the azure sky.

The road follows the river around on the other side of the gorge to re-enter the city at the Bridge of St. Martin. Approaching from an unfamiliar direction, it was easy for us to become disoriented in the labyrinth of streets as dusk closed in on the city. It was the hour when the Toledans began to crowd the streets, streaming towards the cathedral. We let ourselves be carried by them safely home to the sanctuary of Les Tres Carabelas.

A chilly January morning grew warm as we sat in the courtyard of El Greco's 1577 house. To provide shade, a row of simple white columns covered with ivy support a second-storey terrace. The rooms are furnished with heavy, studded leather and carved wooden stools that epitomize old Spain. The painter's portrait of Saint Peter leaned against a large easel in the studio. El Greco must have enjoyed his kitchen just off the courtyard. If this one was any indication, European kitchens would stand in contrast to those I had admired in stately British homes. As opposed to being "downstairs", they were more open to the outside and filled with air and light. These cooks wanted to be able to step out into their herb gardens or peel tomatoes in the sun. Food preparation was not banished to the cold nether regions; it was a more integral part of the life of the household. Meals were a natural celebration of life rather than a grudging routine. In this kitchen they had been prepared in a room covered with russet tiles which formed the background for a design of deep green and blue diamond-shapes. The open hearth in the centre of the room was flanked by long brick benches. Niches set in the walls held mortars and pestles and pottery vessels similar to those currently for sale in Toledo stores. Although the housewares and furnishings had been chosen to reflect the sixteenth century, these classic appointments could still be found in homes, hotels and reataurants that we visited.

A store specializing in pottery jars, plates and tiles, caught our attention on the walk back to the hotel. An impressive wall of blue and white sangria jugs covered its front. We bought one to add to the growing stock of a basic Spanish cucina in the van.

We followed the directions given to us by the waiter in Casa Botin in Madrid to its sister restaurant, Hostal del Cardenal, built into the original fortified walls of Toledo. Two large square glass lanterns swinging from the massive stone gates welcome visitors to this former Cardinal's Palace. The sunken garden contained a small pool in which the wine for our meal was cooling in three wooden casks. The flames from a log fire reflected off the tiled diningroom walls. To call the roof beamed would be an understatement. Intricate carving covered every inch of its rosewood surface. We had plenty of time to stare at it. As usual, we were the first diners, so that we enjoyed the full attention of the waiters. First they brought an earthen jug of cool wine, drawn from the cask in the pond, to sip during the quarter hour required to prepare the soup. Out of the steam from a silver tureen emerged pieces of white fillet, clams, shrimp, egg slices, vegetables, all simmered in a tomato-fish broth. This was followed by the black clay dish containing the roast suckling pig. We were a universe away from fish and chips. Coffee was served in armchairs in front of the fireplace under crossed swords and brass candlesticks. On the way out, we glimpsed the red coal ovens where the three week-old piglet had been roasted. The kitchen staff were just starting to stoke it up for a busy night.

Brilliant stars lit the black sky over the main gate, emblazoned with the double-headed eagle of Charles V. We passed between the pyramidal spires of the Puerta Nueva Bisagra to enter the dark maze of the city's winding lanes.

The restaurant, L'Hostal del Cardenal, is on the other side of the massive wall that surrounds Toledo.

# SOPA AL CUARTO DE HORA
# QUARTER HOUR SOUP

*It takes about two hours to prepare authentic quarter hour soup. There are clams to be cleaned and steamed and strained. Shrimp to shell. Other fish (if including) to cut. Tomatoes to blanch, peel, seed and chop. Ham to cube. And the all important sofrito to prepare.*

*The 15 minutes refers to the amount of time it takes to cook the rice in the resulting broth. Therefore, I will give you the essential steps in preparing the broth, and you can add whatever seafood, takes your fancy.*

### Ingredients
1/4 cup of dry white wine
10 strands of saffron
2 tablespoons of olive oil
1 medium onion finely chopped
2 cloves of garlic
1 bay leaf
1 teaspoon paprika
1 teaspoon coarse sea salt
1/4 cup of cubed smoked ham
2 medium tomatoes, blanched, peeled, seeded and chopped
1/4 cup chopped flat-leaf parsley
1-1/2 cups of water
3/4 cup of clam juice (bottled, tinned or procured by natural means)
1/4 cup of medium grain rice

## Method

1. Spanish and Italian cooks rely on a basic sauce or sofrito to give flavour to their dishes. This one provides the cooking medium for the fish which are added later.
2. Before you start, soak the saffron leaves in the wine.
3. Sautée the chopped onions and minced garlic gently in the olive oil.
4. Add the herbs and seasonings, stirring over low heat for a few minutes.
5. Stir in the ham, parsley and tomatoes. Allow to simmer.
6. Pour in the clam juice and water. Bring close to a boil before adding the rice.
7. Cover and simmer for fifteen minutes, or until the rice is cooked.

This is a super, fragrant soup base. Now for the interesting part. You can introduce some steamed clams (one source of natural clam juice). Steamed mussels are possible. Shrimps definitely. They will turn pink in the soup immediately. Flesh of white fish could work.

*January 25, 1969*

Our departure from Toledo was fraught with concern over those bothersome forms for Robarts' grants. David used all three copies forwarded to us by his parents, before he filled one in correctly; and I posted mine filled with errors. These fleeting concerns for our future were dispelled by the blazing sun as the van rolled across the plains that stretched south towards Cordoba. All sights on the horizon were reduced to black silhouettes against a vivid blue sky. Gradually the landscape was covered with olive groves emerging from tilled russet soil in endless rows. Gnarled trunks split off into two main branches that sprouted wands of willow-shaped silvery green leaves. David tasted one of the olives - red inside and rather bitter. It must have been time to harvest; green cloths spread under the trees caught the olives that fell when the workers beat the branches with wooden sticks. The van skirted donkeys carrying sacks brimming with shiny black olives along the highway.

As we passed through La Mancha, white windmills on the hilltops affirmed that this was the land of Don Quixote. Black wire statues of Don and Sancho stood guard at restaurant doorways. A final push up and over a steep mountain range and we descended into lotus land. Now came the wonder of experiencing tropical vegetation for the first time in our lives: oranges nestled amidst dark green boughs free of any Product of Florida stickers; rows of palm trees from a film set; swaying pampas grass; formidable cacti hedges; cotton fields filled with bent pickers. It was hard to believe that just a year ago, this was the landscape of our grade four social studies lessons to classrooms of inattentive students.

The road passes under a thick stone archway into Cordoba, a city that can feel like Las Vegas if you get lost among its large modern buildings; or it can transport you back centuries if you wander into the old corner that surrounds the Great Mosque in the quarter near the river. This greatest monument to Islamic culture in Spain was designed to be open, allowing light to flow freely through a forest of marble columns.

The cathedral marooned in its centre by the reconquering Christians, challenges the tranquility of the original structure.

The scene from The Wizard of Oz where Dorothy and friends dance along a road winding across softly rolling green hills, could easily have been shot on the road from Cordoba to Seville. It had the same sense of enchantment. Pigs, goats, donkeys, kids, all romped happily on the hard clay between the open well and the black straw huts. Settlements were protected by a cacti hedge, so thick that El Cid would have had trouble chopping through. We parked the van in an olive grove, slid open the side door, and exposed everything to the healing rays of the sun. An elemental picnic of bread, cheese, meat and wine was eaten beside the Spanish workers. A pot of soup simmered on our gas camping stove. Born and raised in northern climates, we enthusiastically embraced the sights, smells and tastes of the fabled land of Andalusia. To be finally seated among the olive pickers was a milestone.

Simone de Beauvoir and Jean Paul Sartre stayed at the Hotel Simon in Seville forty years before we arrived, but their creative spirits lingered in the interior arched courtyard. My journal entry records that this skylit terrace was most conducive for writing. In a country where the heat can be oppressive, cool courtyards are a welcome oasis. Here a central stone fountain was surrounded by pots of broad-leafed greenery and comfortable bamboo armchairs on rush mats. Through one of the columned arches that led off from this patio, our room was a haven of cool serenity. Yellow and green tiles covered the lower half of the walls, blue and white ones continued to the ceiling, green rattan blinds covered the tall windows.

We left the sombre gloom of the cathedral to walk the white laneways of the Santa Cruz district. Black-robed nuns fluttered like ravens between white walls covered with jasmine vines. Lanes bowered with bougainvillea, carried us in a perfumed haze to a park where fountains played in palm groves and romantic alcoves holding tiled benches encouraged lingering. By seven in the evening, we had moved with the rest of Seville to the hundred or more tapas bars that dot the streets of the city. We had developed a fondness for these little gastronomic tidbits and viewed them as a necessary antidote to the powerful glasses of manzanilla, the preferred tipple of the region. At the first one, we sampled garbanzo beans in a tomato sauce. Further along we were treated to a special cured ham (jabugo). Calamari were offered at the third stop. By this point, we felt relaxed enough to attempt to out-sit the natives at a sidewalk cafe. We took up position and watched the parade of life go by for half an hour, an hour, an hour and a half . . . . . the tables on either side of us won. In spite of the city still throbbing all around us, we never found it difficult to doze off.

The first warm picnic in an olive grove outside of Seville.

# GARBANZO BEANS IN A TOMATO SAUCE

*These are offered at the bars on little oval platters with small forks. No reason why you should not treat them as a side dish with a meal.*

### INGREDIENTS
1 cup of dry chickpeas (garbanzo)
1/2 cup of chopped Spanish onion
2 cloves of garlic, sliced
2 tablespoons olive oil
1/2 teaspoon of whole cumin seed
1/2 teaspoon whole coriander seed
1 teaspoon of coarse salt
black pepper to taste, coarsely ground
1/4 teaspoon of paprika
1/4 teaspoon of curry
1 tablespoon of fresh ginger root, peeled and grated
3 plum tomatoes, peeled, seeded and chopped
3 tablespoons tomato sauce
a handful of blanched green beans
freshly chopped coriander leaves

### METHOD
1. Sort through the beans to remove any dark or irregular ones
2. Soak them overnight covered by several inches of water above their

surface.
3. Drain off water. Add fresh and bring to a boil.
4. Skim foam from surface. Reduce heat to simmer for an hour or more until beans are soft.
5. Heat the chopped onion and garlic in warm oil in a large skillet.
6. Grind the whole spices in a mortar, adding the powdered paprika, salt, pepper, grated ginger and curry.
7. Stir into the skillet with the onion mixture.
8. Add the tomatoes and sauce.
9. Drain the chick peas, reserving the liquid in a separate bowl.
10. Add 1/4 cup of the drained liquid to the tomato sauce.
11. Stir the drained garbanzos into the spicey sauce. Simmer about 30 minutes, adding more liquid if required.
12. Garnish with finely chopped fresh coriander.

This makes a fine vegetarian meal when served with steamed cauliflower or grilled patty pan squash.

# Chapter Eighteen

# CAMPING ON SPANISH BEACHES

*The half-bare fishermen stood on the rainy pebbled beach,
staring with disappointment at the few fish in their net.
Six families would share the few pesetas.
Journal entry, beach at Almeria, February 7. 1969*

At British seaside resorts we had re-lived our past; on the beaches of Spain, we mapped out our future. From the Costa de la Luz, along the Costa del Sol to the Costa Blanca the sea fed us; pulled us down to its beaches every night to lull us to sleep; and taught us humility. Although endless rows of hotels make it tempting now to label that whole strip the Costa del Concrete, forty years ago there was still more of nature than of man edging the water. Fresh sea breezes opened us up to be more receptive to new concepts, including the one that turned our lives around on the beach at Alicante.

*January 27, 1969*

Living up to the name bestowed on it by Byron, Cadiz, Siren of the Sea, lured us with its white sandy coast and unique claim to be Europe's oldest city (1100 B.C.). We pulled up parallel to an intensely blue Atlantic Ocean, slid open the side door of the van, and breathed deeply before getting down to some serious picnicking.

The condition of the roads grew worse the further we travelled from Madrid. Now that we had reached the southern extremity of Iberia, the paved highway dissolved into a series of potholes, so we bumped and jiggled our way to Tarifa, receiving a splinter in the windshield from a piece of flying pavement. The Arabs arrived in this southernmost city of Europe in the eighth century and constructed a castle on a finger of land that juts towards Africa, only eight miles away across the Strait of Gibraltar. Almost on the exact spot, a new campsite was receiving the last trowel of cement on its plaque: ENERO (JANUARY) 1969. We were the first guests in this pristine camp and had the whole magnificent natural setting to ourselves. From the old tower on our hill, the mountains of Africa looked close enough to climb. Further up the terraced ramps, workmen had set a stone bench into the wall of the cliff and planted brilliant pink flowering cacti and red-tongued plants along the sites. Pottery urns holding bouquets of pampas grass, flanked the doorway to the as-yet-unused washrooms. From the topmost clearing we saw that our bar of land separated the calm, blue Mediterranean sea from the Atlantic breakers. We were at the crux of two worlds and could feel the stimulation of the one we were about to enter replacing the security of the one we had just left.

The spectacle of that evening's sunset has yet to be equalled. From our high crest of land overlooking another continent, the brilliant orange sun sank through flamingo pink clouds then crossed a stretch of very pale lime green sky near the horizon, to disappear behind the black mountains of Africa.

*January 28, 1969*

At the top of the last mountain pass before Algeciras, we stopped to look down on Gibraltar, connected to the mainland by a very thin strip of land (Linea de Concepción) that soon Spain would close to both motor and pedestrian traffic. We headed directly to the docks to pick up a sailing schedule for Gibraltar and Tangiers. The port has the flavour of international adventure with cars from all over Europe and North America waiting to board The Virgin of Africa. In the waiting room, tourists from Florida in T-shirts and shorts, sat beside turbanned shieks from Morocco. On the other side of the dock, fishermen had spread out their nets to stitch up any loopholes. The results of their labours were everywhere on the streets of Algeciras - wicker baskets filled with silvery fish or pink shelled crayfish. For the rest of this trip, we never had to stare into the eyes of a fish to determine whether or not it was fresh. They were still quivering. Most evenings from now on, we would be making dinner with produce picked that morning within a few miles of the campsite.

At the local market, we bought shrimp and whitefish for supper, as well as fruit, cheese, and a primitive pottery water jug that we kept filled with drinking water the rest of the trip. David pointed out a perfect still-life: a wicker basket brimming with cauliflower, long red radishes, huge plump oranges. The markets in this part of the world fed our hungry hearts. They captured the essence of the country and magnified it. A campsite, complete with a bar, hot showers and a grocery store, topped our expectations.

# SHRIMP AND WHITEFISH

*This dish can be prepared with cod, sole or other whitefish. We first prepared it on the camper stove, but at home I prefer it in the oven.*

### Ingredients
1 fillet of sole per person
6 small or 4 medium shrimp per fillet
2 tablespoons of butter for the pan
1 tablespoon butter for the sauce
1 tablespoon of flour
1/2 cup light fish or vegetable stock
1/4 teaspoon salt and white pepper
1 tablespoon lemon juice
2 tablespoons white wine
1/3 cup 10% cream
chopped parsley garnish

### Method
1. Preheat oven to 350F.
2. Melt 2 tablespoons butter in an oval au gratin dish that is stove-to-oven.
3. Lightly sauté the fillets turning once for a total of no longer than 5 minutes. Thicker fish could take longer. Remove from heat.
4. If using raw shrimp, boil it for 5 minutes in fish stock or water. Peel.

5. To make a sauce for three fillets, whisk the flour into the melted butter in a small pan. Off the heat, whisk in the stock. (make sure it is not too strong or it will overpower the fish)
6. Add the white wine and lemon juice.
7. Stir in the cream. Taste before seasoning with salt and pepper.
8. Distribute the shrimp over the fillets then cover with the sauce.
9. Warm the dish through in the oven. It should need only 5 minutes. Garnish with parsley.

We were the first visitors to this spectacular
new campsite at Tarifa, facing Africa.

Our second visit to the market in Algeciras was more adventurous. When I asked for a fresh chicken, the vendor plucked one from its cage and wrang its neck. I did not need it that fresh. David met me carrying a string bag of just-caught clams. After a brief consultation with fellow campers, he felt confident enough to try his own version of steamed clams à la Lindsay. He'd made a culinary leap from his mastery of packaged pizza mixes in Windsor.

Sketching propped up by Rafael.

# STEAMED CLAMS

*Our Portuguese fish monger in London Ontario sells littleneck or round, hard-shell clams which are not little - they are one of the larger members of the clam family. He also sells our preferred "pasta" clams, tiny ones, which Italians term vongole. This recipe is for clams with spaghetti for two. Use the smaller clams which are sweeter and more tender.*

### Ingredients
24 small clams, well scrubbed in a basin of cold water
1/2 cup chopped onion
2 large cloves of garlic chopped
1/4 cup chopped parsley plus extra for garnish
1 bay leaf
1/8 teaspoon chilli pepper flakes
1/4 cup white wine
2 tablespoons of butter
salt and pepper
2 ounces of thin spaghetti per person
a crusty baguette to dip into the broth.

### Method
1. Soak clams in a basin of cold water for several hours, changing the water twice. Scrub them clean under running water discarding any that are open.

2. In a large lidded pot, bring the onions, butter, garlic, herbs and seasonings to a simmer in the white wine. Stir until the onions are soft. Set the pasta water on to boil in another large pot.
3. Add the clams to the wine broth, cover tightly and allow them to steam open on a gentle flame for almost 10 minutes. Cook the spaghetti at the same time.
4. Discard any clams that do not open during cooking. Let your nose be your guide when cooking shellfish.
5. Serve spaghetti in a flat pasta plate with the clams and sauce spooned over. Top with additional chopped fresh parsley.

After our feast, we joined the rest of the townsfolk in the central square, where pottery frogs sat around the edge of a fountain. Benches tiled with scenes from Don Quixote were arranged under orange trees facing the baroque cathedral. At a small marble table, we sipped dos cafés con leches as paseo, the evening walk, began.

*February 1, 1969*

The next day, as we headed up the Costa del Sol toward Malaga, we noticed more of an international presence in the small towns and cafés. Long hair and sandals were not typical in the staid Spain of Franco. The campsite was filled with vans from France, the Netherlands and Germany; but the largest representation came from Australia and Canada. Either our incomes encouraged travel, or we were more bored than the rest of the world. Up until now, we had considered our adventure to be unique; but it seemed that half of Canada had got here first. Down at the docks, a tug was bringing in the Christoforo Columbo, a large Italian cruise ship packed with holiday makers from the continent he had discovered.

It was easy to see why this town was a popular tourist destination. Cafés on long wide avenues of palm trees serve cold drinks and plates of boiled shrimp. Dim, meandering back streets, bustling with shoppers at small, well-stocked stalls, suddenly burst open onto sunlit squares, where nature's arc lamp highlights a small shrine or chapel. The ladies with baskets over their arms, lead you to the mercado, a large stone structure with built-in marble counters, scrubbed clean for each day's produce. The selection of seafood from Mediterranean waters intrigues most northerners: squid, eel, anchovies, octopus, prawns, sole, swordfish. We made a point of buying a different kind each day to cook in the campsite, and sampled as much seafood as was offered at the small cafés. The produce side of the market was always a painter's delight with its straight rows of lemons in brilliant contrast beside the tomatoes; royal purple eggplants; bouquets of lettuce with small snails clinging to the wet leaves; coils of garlic and red peppers. The act of buying and preparing ingredients that still have some of the land and the sea clinging to them, connects the traveller with the country on a survival level.

# CALAMARI IN A SPICEY TOMATO SAUCE

*We learned the simple procedure for cleaning calamari from the other campers at the communal sink. Separate the main fin and tail section from the head and tentacles. Remove the ink sac from inside the tail. Cut the tentacles off just above the eyes. Discard the eyes and the transparent cartilage skeleton from inside the tail. Run the remaining fleshy bits under cold water, releasing as much of the reddish membrane as possible. Slice the tail across into 1/2 inch rings. Halve the tentacles. Throw the innards down to the waiting cats.*

*This recipe fed two of us with rice and bread as a supper dish. You could include it in an open shallow baker with other tapas for a party.*

INGREDIENTS
1 tablespoon olive oil
1 tablespoon chopped shallots
2 cloves of garlic
1/2 teaspoon of sea salt
3 good grinds of black pepper
a decent pinch of red chilli flakes
3/4 cup of plum tomato sauce (just the tomatoes peeled, seeded and puréed, no additional seasonings)
1/4 cup of red wine
1/2 pound of calamari, prepared as above or you can use already cut frozen rings

1 lemon
several sprigs of lemon thyme
1 tablespoon chopped parsley

## Method

1. Heat the oil in a straight-sided 10 inch skillet which can be covered later.
2. Gently warm the chopped shallots and garlic, being careful not to brown.
3. Add the tomato sauce. Stir, then season with chillis, salt and pepper.
4. Pour in the wine.
5. Stir and simmer gently for about 10 minutes.
6. Add the squid rings and other pieces you might chose to use.
7. Cover and simmer very gently for about 15 to 20 minutes. There are several schools of thought on the length of cooking time for squid. Much of it depends on the cooking medium, the temperature and the freshness of the squid. It can become rubbery if subjected to high heat sautéing for too long.
8. In the last minutes of cooking, squeeze in 1 tablespoon of lemon juice, chopped parsley and some crumbled thyme (we grow a lemon variety which is perfect in seafood dishes).
9. Serve with cut lemon wedges, rice and/or crusty bread to sop up the delicious sauce.

All roads hugging the Mediterranean present a challenge to the driver.

The van nestled between two arms of rock near Almeria.

As we followed the Mediterranean up toward the Costa Blanca, the road wound around rocky promontories that plunged down into a sea the colour of blueberries. On a walk into the upper, isolated reaches, beyond the pink and white almond blossoms that lined the slopes, a civil guard, rifle poised, admonished us for holding hands. It was an indication that life for the locals might not be the dream we had coveted.

Stands of cedars gave off a refreshing, pleasant aroma, mingled with the scent of wild herbs. Picnics under their branches were accompanied by birdsong. The highway wound in and out along small coves and bays which harboured gem-like campsites. On our travels up this coast, we'd tuck the van between two walls of rock where waves lapped a quiet beach, prepare one of our infinite varieties of paella, toss some rocks into the waves, and hold hands, as another MGM production filled the sky with a flaming sun crashing into a wine-dark sea.

Our kitchen skills were on fast track now since most Spanish restaurants and bars obligingly keep the cucina open to view. In one small bar, a talented waiter prepared several little servings of mushrooms, fish, shrimp and sausage using only the top of a burner plate and some saucepan lids. He flipped the cap off a beer bottle onto the ceiling, and caught it while sliding the bottle to us down the bar. His sense of fun was infectious and he had a healthy irreverence toward food preparation.

# SHRIMP IN GARLIC AND OIL

*Round earthenware dishes of this classic tapas appear on marble bars or beach tables. My favourite memory is of watching a lady, seated alone at an outdoor table on a beautiful tiled promenade, enjoying a plate of these shrimp with a glass of cold coke.*

### Ingredients
6 whole large shrimp per person with shells on
4 tablespoons olive oil for each 1/2 pound of shrimp
3 cloves of garlic peeled and chopped
1 tablespoon chopped shallot
1 tablespoon Spanish brandy or fino (dry) sherry
a generous pinch of dried red chilli flakes - use a spoon rather than your hands to prevent burning
coarse sea salt
2 lemons
chopped parsley
a crusty loaf

### Method
1. Peel the shrimp if you prefer. I usually leave on the tails. Remove the black vein.
2. Sprinkle salt on the shrimp while you heat the olive oil in a large skillet.

3. Do not let the oil smoke before adding the garlic, shallots and chilli flakes.
4. Stir with a wooden spatula until oil is flavoured but nothing has browned or crisped.
5. Toss the shrimp, peeled or not, in the hot oil until they turn pink and slightly curl. A few minutes.
6. Splash on the brandy and squeeze in some lemon. Heat another minute before serving.
7. Cut wedges of lemon to put around the serving platter or shallow bowl.
8. Sprinkle chopped parsley sparingly on top.

Another informal cooking lesson took place in a restaurant near one of the campsites run by an English lady who had married a Spaniard. As we sat around her open-sided fireplace, she shared many tips on preparing classic Spanish dishes, such as gazpacho soup and custard flan.

A road stop at a small bar whose counter was lined with dozens of oval white platters, each offering a different variety of seafood, gave us a chance to sample dishes we would wait a long time to see again. David tried some octopus, while I started with small slices of herring marinated in vinegar and green onions. We shared a plate of tiny silver fish, breaded and fried whole; you eat the head, eyes, insides . . .the lot. And very good it all is too.

Al fresco and loving it in Malaga.

# HERRING IN VINEGAR AND ONIONS

*We had developed a taste for herrings while touring Scotland. These silver fish were golden for centuries to British fishermen who built villages and towns around herring ports. In the Highlands, we had enjoyed kippered herrings in sandwiches and eaten fillets coated in fine oatmeal. Here in Spain, chunks were served marinated in vinegar and onions.*

*In Canada, you can buy four whole frozen herring for about $2 and get all of your omega 3 fatty acids while enjoying a fish dinner. Here are two ways of serving these inexpensive and nutritious silver treasures.*

**INGREDIENTS**
2 whole herring
salt
1 cup water
1 cup cider vinegar
2 bay leaves
6 black pepper corns
1 teaspoon pickling spice
6 allspice berries
4 or 5 gratings of nutmeg
4 whole cloves
2 teaspoons brown sugar
1 teaspoon Kosher salt
2 teaspoons of grainy mustard (Dijon makes one)
1 mild white onion
3 or 4 small potatoes per person
1/4 cup of sour cream
1 tablespoon finely chopped green onions
parsley to garnish the fish

## Method

1. Preheat oven to 300F.
2. Gut, clean and remove heads and tails from the fish.
3. Debone and cut into 4 fillets.
4. Soak in salted water for a few hours, changing the water at least once.
5. Bring the next group of ingredients to a boil for a poaching liquid.
6. Lay the fillets, skin side down, in one layer in an ovenproof au gratin dish or rectangular shallow baker.
7. Paint the fleshy side of the fillets with 1/2 teaspoon each of the granular mustard.
8. Cover with thin slices of the peeled onion.
9. Pour the marinade over to cover the ingredients.
10. Cover the dish with foil.
11. Place in the low temperature oven to keep the liquid at a poaching level for 20 minutes if fillets are thin or 30 minutes if you have rolled them up to bake as "rollmops".
12. Lift fillets out with a slotted spatula.
13. Strain a little of the sauce over the fish and top with a slice or two of onion and chopped parsley.
14. Serve with boiled potatoes tossed in sour cream and chopped green onions.

Served as Tapas:

Cut the herring into large chunks or roll-ups as opposed to fillets. Bake as above. Drain and cool. Toss in a bowl sour cream, granular mustard, diced onions and capers to taste. Carefully spoon over the herring. Cubes of boiled potato or crisp green apple may be added. Serve with a basket of rye bread.

Soused herring, intended as an appetizer, is left to marinate in jars in the cider-spice mixture for a few days. If you wish to try this method, consult a recipe by someone who has prepared raw fish with confidence.

*February 7, 1969*

Heavy rain pounding the van roof woke us early this morning. Just as we were feeling sorry for ourselves, David spotted a small rowboat struggling into our bay with six or seven men, dressed only in bathing trunks and sweaters this cold, wet morning. We watched from the comfort of the van as they put out a net to sweep the bay for fish. One man stayed out in the boat, the others clambered ashore and began to hoist in the net, rotating their way down the seemingly endless coil, tramping barefoot up the slope of the pebbled beach with the rope slung over their backs. As the net closed in, David and a few of the other campers, went down to watch them land the catch. Their disappointment at a meagre catch after so much effort was evident. The few pesetas they received for them from a camper had to be divided among many heads. As we retired to hot coffee and eggs in the van, these half-bare men huddled in a cave until the rain stopped. These realities of earning a living on Spanish beaches had not been in the geography books.

*February 8, 1969*

Foul weather chased us up to Alicante, a town with a beautiful natural harbour facing out towards Ibiza. I sat on the Esplanada de Espana, a palm-lined promenade, whose brown, yellow and white tiles are laid in a zebra pattern, zig-zagging along beside the sea. David had taken a measure of the weather and decided to buy a supply of magazines and newspapers on the Rambla, Alicante's bustling main street, to buffer what could be a boring stay at the campsite across the bay. We bumped down muddy ruts, parked near an angry sea, then followed a path through the grounds to a trio of campers, sitting out in front of an English caravan, absorbed in making marmalade. The gentlemen rose to greet me as I approached.

"This is the month for Seville oranges", the tall frail one explained.

"We go through jars of it over the rest of the season. Been here since before Christmas and don't intend to return to England until Easter."

He resumed his seat in the canvas chair next to an elderly lady who was passing curls of peel from the mountain of huge oranges in front of her to the two gents, so that they could cut it into proper size slivers for the jam. A large copper preserving pan bubbled on the camping gas stove, sending out waves of a sweet syrupy citrus fragrance. I sat patiently on a stool in front of them to receive instructions on the fine art of preserving.

On the way back to the van, we stopped to talk, or rather listen, to another senior, who was not quite as comfortable as the marmalade makers.

"I'm well over seventy, got arthritis bad. That makes sleeping in this tent a bit of a trial. But my two cats keep me warm. This green tent and I have gone across continents. Even slept one night in the cave Jesus slept in. Content now just to eke out my pension on the beach."

This trio of encounters with independent diehards living on their own resources, put us in a receptive mood for the concept that floated to the surface the next day.

*February 9, 1969, Journal Entry*

> *I am all sympathy today for that old fellow up in his tent. It has been raining steadily since morning, and it's cold as well. We've managed to survive with rounds of hot ovaltine, coffee, soup, tea and brandy. A good job David bought the reading matter yesterday. The women's magazines helped to pass the hours as well as giving inspiration. I've thought of opening an antique-kitchenwares shop, but never felt adequate. After reading about a successful trio of housewives who opened a craft store called, Whichcraft, I decided my time had come.*

That was it. There was not the slightest doubt or ambivalence with this decision. Nothing nasty and irrelevant, like business projections, clouded my optimism. There were no apprehensions about facing a bank manager across his desk as he quizzed me:

"What business courses did you take?"

"I skimmed through a copy of Women's Weekly on the beach at Alicante."

I simply knew that it would all work out if we followed the instuctions of the ladies in the article. You buy three of every item: one for stock, one for display, and one to sell. Canada in 1969 did not need another craft store. But one specializing in kitchenwares would be novel, since most people still didn't know their ashets from their bombes. At least it would lend logic to my mad impulses to amass cookware. The colossal naiveté of this simplistic procedure did not strike me at the time. On the contrary, these basic instructions were significant because they brought a career within anyone's grasp. I actually adopted their plan as a modus operandi. In retrospect, I can see that we suceeded because of the preparation Britain had given us in all manner of retail. This magic magazine article was a tiny seed dropped into a fertilized bed at the rainy period. And if you believe in auguries, the Romans called Alicante, Lucentum, the city of light. I had finally seen it.

This career decision did not alter our itinerary one millimeter. The epiphanic moment was absorbed, as though it were as natural as breathing. In my mind, retailing was every bit as creative as literature. Our studies had not been a false start, but a grounding in understanding the complexities of human relationships. They had also introduced us to the writers who had travelled this path before us, connecting their inner dreams with the outer world of commercial reality. We had just joined a fine company.

Market shopping did assume a different focus. The stalls of kitchen utensils became potential sources of supply. Before we left Alicante, I picked up three wooden spoons at five pesetas each (merely pennies). David suggested that it might be expeditious to stretch a point and buy three times three, as we wouldn't likely be running back here for more stock once the store opened. This additional purchase did not pose a problem for the granny calculator who sat behind the stall totting up the total with a stub of pencil on a scrap of paper, three times faster than any computerized cash register. No future enterprise could have had a humbler beginning.

*February 11, 1969*

The rain dogged us out of Alicante, all through the hour's drive up to Benidorm. Other campers had praised this place as though it were a mecca for travellers. But it didn't look promising under grey skies as we bumped along muddy trenches in a trailer park fringed with dispiriting bungalows.

We were awakened by arrows of sun piercing the brown checkered curtains on the back window of the van. Blue skies smiled at us above an impressive range of ochre mountains that protected this favoured haven from northern winds. The tallest had a chunk out of its crest. A Benidorm legend claims that Roland, an angry giant, kicked the missing piece out into the bay. Sail boats bob down at the dock, ready to take you out to Calpe, this rocky island. We walked that morning along a golden beach that curves for three miles on both sides of the town, skirting the spume from the waves rolling gently onto fine, hard-packed sand. It was one of those poster perfect beaches, swept clean daily by the municipality. Before you book your flight, let me remind you that I am describing 1969 Costa Blanca, when development was rearing its head from the sands, but was still in its infancy. Today it is the Miami of Europe, with blood pressure stations set along a beach that is backed by a solid phalanx of hotels. I suppose you could say that the town has kept tempo with the changing times, as we all have.

These graceful wings of sand, called the Playa Levante and Playa Poniente (Sunrise and Sunset), are separated by a promentary on which the original village stands. At its foot, we came to the little harbour of Van Gogh fishing boats and net menders, a reminder that this town was a fishing village before its many natural attractions transformed it into a holiday resort. From a pristine white platform, perched on the outermost tip of the rocky headland, we felt marooned amidst the sparkling blue of the sea, with the old town comfortably nestled at our backs. Two white-washed dovecotes stood at the bottom of a narrow street, broken on its fall to the sea by white stone arches garlanded with hot pink bougainvillea. On our way up to the commercial centre, Casco Antiguo, we passed white houses with curved tile roofs, their black iron balconies restraining cascades of scarlet geraniums. Street names are helpfully pictorial; Gato street, indicated by a cat on the tile affixed to a house wall.

Our first glimpse of the town's amenities, convinced us that God had indeed made Benidorm for tourists. Besides all of this charm, history and natural beauty, there were English bookshops and newspaper stalls; open squares with flowers, benches and agreeable townsfolk; bread and pastry shops; gift boutiques, and a well-stocked market with produce arranged appealingly on immaculate white tiles. In this biblical landscape of terraced olive and orange groves, we thought there surely must be an Eden where we could settle in for the duration.

Within walking distance of the Playa Levante, we found Los Olivos, every camper's dream. Hot showers and spotless sinks in a well-heated North American style bathroom; tree-lined sites for each tent or van; a supermercado across the way for necessities; and wonderfully friendly cats and campers. On the first day, the couple beside us from the Netherlands were moved by the pitiful sight of us perched on the ivory suitcases beside the van.

"Please accept these canvas deck chairs." The next morning they returned with an electic lamp. "We noticed you trying to read by the light of that oil lamp last night. It is no problem to hook this up to the outlet in our caravan."

We were becoming dangerously civilized. A couple of just-married young Canadians, Ted and Pam, were parked on our other side. She seemed anxious to return to Canada and start nesting. I wanted to tell her to go slowly and enjoy her moment in the sun. Behind our site, a teacher from Windsor, Ontario had been encamped since October. Her husband was a former employee of Chrysler's automotive factory where my father had worked. We asked them how they were putting in their days.

"Now that we're free agents, I'm taking a writing course by correspondence. Lots of raw material for potential stories drifting through the camp on a regular basis. My husband is turning out some decent oil paintings." These aptitudes only floated to the surface after they had crossed an ocean.

At a long, communal zinc sink, we'd all catch up on the international news while gutting the calamari purchased at the fish market. A colony of camp cats sat behind us to catch the innards. The favoured local recipe for squid instructed us to sauté it with onions, almonds and oregano. Our reputation as camp gourmands was the result of our improvised version of Mediterranean fish stew: clams, whitefish, squid, giant shrimp, simmered in a tomato-wine sauce with the correct herbs. The availability of bountiful fresh seafood made this a natural favourite.

Ann completely relaxed in a Benidorm campsite.

# MEDITERRANEAN SEAFOOD STEW

*Do not confuse this simple stew with the more complex bouillabaisse, even if it does contain the same basic ingredients used all along the coast. We made many variations of this stew depending on what bits and pieces we could pick up at the fish market. Do not despair if you are land bound. Supermarket freezers now keep bags of frozen mixed Mediteranean seafood - probably the best way to buy it here.*

**INGREDIENTS**
Cooking base for preparing 4 servings:
4 tablespoons of olive oil
1/2 cup of chopped onion
2 cloves of garlic finely minced
1/2 cup of diced green or red sweet pepper
1-1/2 cups of tomatoes, peeled, seeded and chopped
1 teaspoon of salt
about 4 grinds of pepper
1 bay leaf
1/2 teaspoon fennel seeds or dill seeds
1 pinch of hot chilli flakes (that means half of an eighth of a teaspoon)
1 cup of dry white wine

**SEAFOOD:**
 The bag of frozen shellfish comes with them peeled, shelled and cut.

You miss all the fun at the sink, but it provides a selection in small amounts otherwise not usually available. Chunks of whitefish are also included. Use 3 to 4 cups of frozen fish depending on your numbers and appetites. Thaw it covered in the refrigerator. Do not let it sit out at any time.

If you are rounding up fresh from a fishmonger, try to get this total amount with a variety of octopus, small shrimp, squid and mussels. The whitefish can be 1 inch pieces of cod, hake, pollock, or haddock.

Chopped parsley for garnish.

## Method
1. Choose a skillet which has a lid large enough to hold all of the ingredients.
2. Warm the onions, garlic and pepper in the oil until soft but still translucent.
3. Stir in the tomatoes, seasonings and herbs. Simmer for 5 minutes.
4. Add the wine. Simmer for 10 minutes on low heat.
5. Add the seafood mixture and simmer covered for 20 minutes.
6. If you are using shellfish in their shells, start with the clams or mussels first, steaming covered to make sure they all open. Discard any which do not open. Add the chunks of whitefish next for the final 10 minutes. You might want to sprinkle more salt on the fish.

## Garlic Crostinis
1. Heat 1 tablespoon of oil in a skillet.
2. Peel 4 cloves of garlic. Cut in half lengthwise. Warm 4 of the halves in the oil.
3. Cut 8 rounds of the closest bread to a baguette you can get.
4. Rub the bread slices with the other pieces of garlic.
5. Fry until crisp.
6. Serve the stew in a rim soup bowl with the crusty bread stuck in it. Sprinkle with parsley.

The herb stall offers a selection to cure gout, fever, and impotence, in addition to the more usual bouquets for soups and stews.

*February 13, 1969, Benidorm*

*This is the first day of our trip that I can truly say I feel marvellous, as though nowhere else in the world existed except this spot of sun in our Benidorm campsite.*

This blissful ease with the moment was no doubt induced by the recent awareness that I would be spending the rest of my life doing what I enjoyed. In fact, that morning had been spent in happy reverie, as I sat in the sun poring over the scrap collection picked up in England, figuring out how they could be used to make greeting cards, menu and place-cards, gift wraps. The Spanish children's counting cards from the flea market in Madrid inspired me to compose possible birthday greetings that would make them commercially viable. When I re-read these attempts recently, I felt a rush of protectiveness for my naive younger self:

| | |
|---|---|
| In uniforms gay, | Games for your play, |
| Toy soldiers bold, | Toys by the score, |
| Salute you today, | Are all yours today, |
| Proud three-year old. | Now that you're four. |

Pathetic, when you think of it.

I started merchandising idea lists based on the concepts we had most admired in the British retail stores and set up fictional "departments" based on the meagre hoard of finds left in the trunk with Mrs. Charman. Outdoor markets spread mountains of locally made wooden, pottery and tin implements on blankets under striped awnings. With a real sense of accomplishment, I purchased three olive wood egg cups and three matching napkin rings, which just proves that once I adopt an idea, no matter how illogical, it sticks. David took a photo of me playing store by the side of the van with my sad little cache of stock.

A full week passed without a journal entry because we were doing nothing and loving it, true lotus eaters in lotus land. We had become regulars of a small café set on the sands near the harbour where the fishermen repaired their nets. They would serve large white cups of chocolate or a small dark espresso every morning. You could let the fine sand run between your toes as you sipped and read monstrous Trollope novels, chosen for their sheer bulk. Or in the evening, as the sun set, work through a piece of meat or grilled mullet with a litro of wine, no other entertainment necessary.

David completely relaxed on a Benidorm beach.

# RED SNAPPER WITH FENNEL

*In London, Ontario we have several Portuguese fish stores which bring fresh seafood in from Toronto twice a week. Usually David can bring home a red snapper, mullet or small bass to prepare any one of several ways. Grill, pan fry, bake - for the first part of this recipe you can choose - with just a portable gas stove, our only option was a skillet. But you can step up the presentation with the accompanying Spanish vegetable and herbal flavours.*

INGREDIENTS

a whole 12 ounce fish serves two
1 fennel bulb with fronds
1/4 cup white wine
1 cup of fish stock
1 bay leaf
1 tablespoon olive oil
1/2 teaspoon salt
5 sliced black olives
3 medium potatoes

1/4 cup chopped parsley
2 tablespoons lemon juice
2 cloves minced garlic
3 tablespoons olive oil - 2 for the fish rub; 1 for the pan
1/8 teaspoon saffron
1 teaspoon coarse salt
several grinds of black pepper

## Method

1. Preheat oven to 375F.
2. Trim the thick base off the fennel. Slice the bulb vertically. Remove half of the fine top leaves. Chop and reserve.
3. Warm the fish stock, white wine, bay leaf, salt and oil in an iron oval gratin dish that is ovenproof. Poach the fennel in this stock while preparing the fish.
4. Peel 3 medium potatoes and put on to boil whole.
5. In a small bowl, combine the minced parsley, fennel tops, garlic, lemon juice, saffron, salt, pepper and olive oil.
6. Rinse the fish and pat dry. Leave head and tail on. Rub the mixture both inside and out.
7. Heat olive oil in another skillet. Sear the fish for 3 minutes per side until the herbal rub forms a crust.
8. Spread the slices of olive over the poached fennel. Lay the fish on top. Bake for 6 minutes.
9. Check with a small sharp knife just behind the gills to see if the flesh flakes and juices run white. The rule is 10 minutes per inch measured by thickness, not length of the fish.
10. Slice the cooked potatoes. Arrange them along one side of the platter.
11. Using a large spatula with holes, carefully lift the fish onto a separate plate.
12. With a large slotted spoon, drain the fennel and olive slices out of the liquid and spread them down the platter. Lay the fish on top of the braised fennel.
13. Spoon on a dribble of the poaching liquid and a sprinkle of finely minced fennel leaves.

No commercial equipment needed for this barbeque.

The fishermen struggle for a living even though the sea is bountiful.

*February 23, 1969*

We had decided that February would be spent in Spain, March in France and Italy, leaving the more northern countries for April and May when it would be warmer. With just a week left in February, we reluctantly returned lights and chairs to our neighbours, and left for Valencia. On our first drive through the city, we noticed that it lived up to its reputation as paella capital of Spain. Against the walls of every house, round iron paelleras were drying in the sun after lunch. Two men were carrying a six foot diameter paella, the saffron rice decorated with pimento strips and black clams, through the streets to a family gathering.

That night in the van, our simple version was made with chicken and artichoke hearts. We had learned how to peel and trim the artichokes by watching one of the market vendors patiently prepare a basket of them while sitting at her stall. Beside her was a large basin of acidulated water in which slices of lemons floated. With a stubby carbon steel knife she cut off the top inch and the stem of each artichoke. The tough dark outer layers were peeled back to reveal pale inner leaves. Most were left whole bobbing in her basin. Others were cut in halves and even quarters so that the hairy choke in the centre could be removed if the customer requested it. They were rubbed with a half of a lemon.

# RICE, CHICKEN AND ARTICHOKES

*Since there are only three main ingredients in this simple camping stove casserole, the emphasis is on quality of the products. The authentic paella rice from Valencia is called "Bomba". It is a round, medium short-grained rice that absorbs three times its volume of cooking broth. The grains do not stick together. The chicken should be farm-fresh and flavourful. Prepare this dish in early spring when artichokes come into our stores.*

**INGREDIENTS**
For 6 to 8 servings:
a 6 pound chicken
2 tablespoons olive oil
1 shallot, chopped
1 medium onion, chopped
3 cloves of garlic, finely minced
1 cup of paella rice
salt and pepper
1/2 cup of white wine
1 to 2 cups of chicken stock
several strands of saffron
4 large artichokes or 8 small
2 lemons
1 cup of green peas - fresh or frozen

## Method

1. Preheat oven to 350F.
2. Cut chicken into individual serving pieces. Put the carcass and odd bits into a stock pot with carrot, celery, parsley and onion. Cover with water and simmer to make a stock.
3. Put the saffron into the wine to infuse.
4. Heat the oil in a large shallow round ovenproof pan with a lid.
5. Sauté the pieces of chicken until they lose their flesh tone and become opaque
6. Remove them to a warm platter.
7. Sauté the shallot, onion and garlic until soft, stirring often to scrape up the crusty pieces.
8. Stir in the rice to coat thoroughly in oil.
9. Return the chicken to the pan. Sprinkle with salt and pepper.
10. Pour on the wine. Simmer a minute before adding the broth.
11. Prepare the artichokes as described in the above passage. Cut into quarters and rub with one of the lemons.
12. Place the artichoke pieces around the top of the rice. Cover.
13. Cooking may be continued on a moderate stove burner for 20 minutes or in the preheated oven if preferred.
14. Check the moisture level every five minutes or so adding ladles of stock as needed.
15. Sprinkle on a cup of peas during the final 5 minutes of cooking.
16. When chicken is cooked, and the rice is soft, squeeze lemon juice on top.

This simple meal was eaten at an empty park full of tall pine trees in the harbour of Grao. A full fleet of fishing boats sat in the port alongside the classic bare bones of a ship under construction and the sad disembowling of a vessel in the rusty graveyard. The men lined along the wharf with poles dangling in the water told David that the fishing fleet would bring in their catch at six a.m. We got dressed early and were on the beach at six, staring out to sea, waiting for our breakfast of fresh sardines to arrive, when someone else told us that they go out at six and return hours later. Caught again.

*February 24, 1969*

The trip along the Costa Dorada to Barcelona is tortuous, so it was with a sigh of relief that we pulled into The Merry Whale, a site near the sea, carpeted with fragrant pine needles, to hear, "What kept you guys? Coffee's been on for hours."

It was Ted and Pam, our neighbours from Benidorm already set up, the only other campers in the huge park. Seemed as though we would be travelling en caravan Canadien from now on. After mutual congratulations on surviving the last stretch of highway, the four of us piled into a local bus for the half hour ride into Barcelona which took fifteen minutes because the driver kept the accelerator on the floor. This city had a more lively tempo than Madrid. Streets were broader, shadier, and Barcelonans were swinging to a hotter Latin beat. All four of us enjoyed the Rambla, a long, wide promenade lined with cages of chirping, bright orange birds and baskets spilling marigolds, tulips, apple blossoms and violets.

From the street, the Mercat Boqueria shows no hint of the explosion of colour that lies beyond the large iron archway. This central market is constructed like a Victorian railway station, with permanent vendors' stalls replacing the rows of railway carriages. Shoppers with wicker baskets make their selections from the hooks of dangling cured meats, crates of courgettes, pyramids of citrus fruits. It remains one of the chief reasons for returning to Barcelona. The other is to check the progress of Antonio Gaudi's architectural wonder, the cathedral La Sagrada Familia.

A bumper crop of mail was waiting for us at the American Express office. The news was welcome - we had both been accepted at the University of Western Ontario's Graduate School in London, a new city for us. The plan was for David to begin his doctorate while helping me to open a business. I would continue to take courses in Victorian literature for personal satisfaction. Other letters contained reports of new homes, new babies and other achievements. I felt satisfied with our choice rather than envious of these other options. Retail would be a creative adventure that would keep us spontaneous. Like artists in a garret, we planned to live in a flat above a shop, dedicated, poor and unencumbered. It is difficult to shake off a youthful romantic strain.

Voyages connect you with people and places, but I now realized that the important connecting link was interior; experiences that join the self with its delight. We continued through France, Italy, Austria, Germany, Holland and Denmark. By the time we sailed into Copenhagen (Merchants' Harbour in Danish) we were as qualified as business school grads to toss aside our teaching fellowships and enter the food business. We sailed back to Montreal on the Empress of England in May 1969 with $500 left in our pockets to open one of Canada's first kitchen shops in August of that year. For the first two years, we lived in a flat above the store. As the business prospered, we purchased four buildings (two commercial and two residential) and had them all designated as heritage properties. The smorgasbord of culinary information that we had absorbed that year on the road, supported us until our retirement in 2002.

A skilled proof-reader, Helen Luckman, returned the fifth draft of this book, bristling with over one hundred pink correction slips. She still had the grace to suggest:

"Don't leave us here at the border of France."

The next volume will follow the van along the coasts of France and Italy, sharing with you the food markets, recipes and rich history of the Mediterranean coast.

# RECIPE INDEX

## APPETIZERS AND CONDIMENTS

chorizos with green peppers, 313
clementine/mandarin/tangerine sauce, 251
creamed potato salad, 335
creamed salmon sandwiches, 193
Cumberland sauce, 127
garbanzo beans in a tomato sauce, 344
green tomato chutney, 140
herbed butters, 241
marinated mushrooms, 321
poached trout on brown, 227
smoked kipper kedgeree sandwich, 97
tortilla de patata, 325
venison pâté, 199

## BREAD AND BAKED GOODS

Bath sweet bread, 191
Devon cream tea, 173
Dundee cake, 94
gingerbread picnic in York, 143
good luck white fruit cake, 11
Grandpa Grant's shortbread, 113
hefty brown loaf, 179
maids of honour, 168
Miss Flora oatcakes, 130
potato pancakes, 60
toasted tea cakes, 87
Queen of Hearts' tarts, 209
versatile pie pastry, 211

## DESSERTS

Christmas Eve crêpes, 272
figgy pudding, 276
Grandma Annie's clootie dumpling, 39
highland flummery, 314
Jack Horner's plum cake, 25
rich chocolate cake, 72
sultana pudding with custard sauce, 264
Victoria sandwich, 103

## MEAT MAIN DISHES

a proper chop, 243
boeuf en daube, 288
herbed pork pies, 146
mince and tatties, 37
Norman roast of pork, 157
old English spiced beef loaf, 153
pig party, 330

rabbit hot pot, 45
sauté of veal Marengo, 29
shepherd's pie, 99
winter stew festival, 299

## POULTRY
citrus cornish hens, 15
country house pheasant pie, 107
rice, chicken and artichokes, 381
spiced citrus duck, 204
Tiny Tim's roast goose, 278
Wiltshire chicken braised in white wine, 223

## SEAFOOD MAIN DISHES
calamari in a spicey tomato sauce, 356
fish casserole, 118
herring in vinegar and onions, 363
mediterranean seafood stew, 372
mussels in a creamy sauce, 82
oyster casserole, 164
red snapper with fennel, 377
Roman baked trout, 188
salmon in its native waters, 49
shrimp in garlic and oil, 360
shrimp and whitefish, 350
skate poached with capers, 161
sole in cream sauce, 215
steamed clams, 353
van paella party, 318

## SOUPS
celery soup, 238
compost soup, 122
curried carrot, orange, ginger soup, 69
Dunoon tomato soup, 53

Mary Queen of Scots soup of bitter greens, 90
quarter hour soup, 339
Scotch broth, 63

## VEGETARIAN
cheddar cheese fondue with ale, 185
home grown pumpkin ravioli, 254

www.ingramcontent.com/pod-product-compliance
Lightning Source LLC
Chambersburg PA
CBHW050248170426
43202CB00011B/1597